Edexcel Advanced

DRAMA & THEATRE STUDIES

For my father, John Vergette (1923–2007), with love and gratitude

Philip Allan Updates, an imprint of Hodder Education, part of Hachette Livre UK, Market Place, Deddington, Oxfordshire OX15 0SE

Orders

Bookpoint Ltd, 130 Milton Park, Abingdon, Oxfordshire OX14 4SB
tel: 01235 827720
fax: 01235 400454
e-mail: uk.orders@bookpoint.co.uk

Lines are open 9.00 a.m.–5.00 p.m., Monday to Saturday, with a 24-hour message answering service. You can also order through the Philip Allan Updates website: www.philipallan.co.uk

© Philip Allan Updates 2008
ISBN 978-1-84489-446-8

Impression number   5   4   3   2   1
Year   2012   2011   2010   2009   2008

The front cover photograph shows Jude Law as Faustus in *Doctor Faustus*, Young Vic Theatre, 2002, and is reproduced by permission of Donald Cooper at www.photostage.co.uk

Printed in Italy

Hachette Livre UK's policy is to use papers that are natural, renewable and recyclable products and made from wood grown in sustainable forests. The logging and manufacturing processes are expected to conform to the environmental regulations of the country of origin.

Contents

Section C

Preface

This building is an example of abandoned magnificence. At one time, not so long ago, it was part of the city's pride, its towering pillars boasting its pre-eminence in both architectural achievement and in the artistic wonders it once housed. Now it stands like an obstinate and embarrassed ghost of another era, a monument to a gaudy and indulgent past. On the wall, a poster peeling and faded that no one thought to remove still hangs limply, advertising a display of ballroom gyrations from more than a year ago. If you manage to break in through the heavy wooden doors you will find a world of decaying splendour, where the dust hangs heavier than the memories of bygone triumphs and the smell of neglect is palpable. This is a building that has outlasted its usefulness — forgotten but not gone. It is an uneconomic anachronism in a world of streamlined efficiency — too large and too expensive to maintain, and far too impractical.

Through the thick walls and shuttered windows, you can still hear the sound of the capital city's gridlocked traffic imposing the noise of the present on the remainders of the past. Can it be that less than a century ago the greatest actor in the world, the first actor to receive the honour of a knighthood, displayed his virtuoso skills to the enthralled multitudes in this same building? A man who in 1870 — the same year he joined the management of the theatre in which you are standing — created such a sensation with his performance of Mathias in Leopold Lewis's *The Bells* that he was declared London's most celebrated actor overnight? Can it be that for all the triumph of past times, this once famous shrine to dramatic art became a Mecca Ballroom in 1950 and is now an abandoned shell?

You are standing in the foyer of the Lyceum Theatre in The Strand in 1986. During the late nineteenth century, this theatre was managed by the legendary Sir Henry Irving, the first world-famous actor and the man credited with revitalising a cynical public's interest in the works of William Shakespeare. And yet a mere 80 years after his death, his spiritual home does not even provide a reminder of those glory days. Less than 50 years after his death, as film and television proceeded with their inexorable rise, it became a ballroom. Only the pub of the same name, next door, carries a plaque dedicated to the great man's life and achievements. Even in the heart of London's West End, it seems there can be no purpose for a place like this. The Lyceum Theatre in 1986 is dead, and its continued existence is an uncomfortable reminder of a prevailing feature in our society: theatre is a spent force.

By 1982, 85% of theatres that were in service in 1914 had been demolished. Of the ones that remained, many were 'dark' (unused). While some were replaced with more modern theatres, many more were not. Going to the theatre as a cultural pastime declined throughout the twentieth century as television audiences increased. Even cinema audiences, which had declined during the 1970s, started to enjoy a renaissance during the 1980s as multi-screens replaced the old Art Deco picture houses of the 1930s. The president of the Frank Matcham Society — a society founded to celebrate one of the most prolific theatre architects of all time — bemoaned the statistic that of the estimated 150 theatres built by his hero between 1880 and 1915, only 28 remained, and only 25 of them as working theatres.

Surely these statistics indicate that theatre has had its day — that whatever it may have been in our society, as a social or cultural force it is now dead? Even the crudest and most basic of surveys reveal that most people do not go to the theatre — at least, not on a regular basis. And even where it thrives — in parts of London's West End, for example — it does so on adaptations from movies and on revivals of old plays. We have to face an unpalatable but unrelenting fact: theatre has had its heyday and we citizens of the twenty-first century are witnessing its inevitable wind down to extinction. In a few years it will be no more.

The A-level course on which you are embarking will be synonymous with the study of antiques: looking at where we have come from in mild curiosity, and perhaps with some bewilderment, that we, as a species, were ever tempted to leave the warmth of our homes and sit in draughty temples like the Lyceum, gazing at other living people on a stage like a set of collective Peeping Toms. There will be no live drama because there will be no need for it. Our dramatic entertainment will be piped to our small and large screens via computer-generated sets and performed by beautiful actors (some of whom, presumably, will also be computer generated). This is the inevitable future of theatre. Isn't it?

The mood of the crowd is angry — teetering on the brink of violence. These people have been protesting outside the theatre for several days, and with each passing day the crowd's impatience grows along with its numbers. At the start of the week, it made the local news, but now the event is much more high profile and well-known reporters are on hand to carry the story. Community leaders have held talks with theatre directors but have not secured the changes to the play they sought. The directors claim that talks with the Sikh community were held out of courtesy and that changing the work of a playwright was never on the agenda. As the mood of the crowd turns uglier, missiles are thrown and the theatre's plate-glass windows are shattered. Four hundred protestors attempt to storm the building as 85 police officers — 30 of them in riot gear — struggle to contain them. Leaders of the community are quick to disassociate themselves from any violent action, attributing it to the hot-headed behaviour of some of their more militant supporters. The police, attempting to avoid any further outbreaks of violence, persuade Birmingham Repertory Theatre to close the production of *Behzti*. The playwright Gurpreet Kaur Bhatti goes into hiding as she becomes the subject of threats of violence. Her play, which depicts rape and murder in a Sikh temple, has enraged the local Sikh community. In her programme note, she praises Sikhism but then adds the following statement:

> Clearly the fallibility of human nature means that the simple Sikh principles of equality, compassion and modesty are sometimes discarded in favour of outward appearance, wealth and the quest for power. I believe that drama should be provocative and relevant. I wrote *Behzti* because I passionately oppose injustice and hypocrisy.

The play's performance on 18 December is called off and further performances are suspended. Since then, the play has never been revived and Bhatti has so far not permitted any other theatre to stage it.

If theatre is dead, if it is truly a thing of the past — an extinct art form that has made way for the more advanced technology and mass appeal of film and television — how could a play arouse such passionate feelings in Birmingham as recently as December 2004? Why would members of a community mobilise, besiege a theatre and force a play to close if theatre is without potency or influence? Dominic Dromgoole, Artistic Director of the Oxford Stage Company, writing in the *Guardian* 2 days after the closure of *Behzti*, observed of the incident that it was something:

> …to shut the pundits up. Every tired old ageing punk who drones on at self-defeating length about the death of theatre — its marginalisation and irrelevance to the modern world — can put this in their pipe and smoke it.

Rather provocatively, he adds later in the article that: 'Theatre asks for this trouble. It has to. Nonconformity is as natural to theatre as conformity is to religion.' He passionately expresses the view that theatre must rigorously challenge the 'various blind yeses' that are part of religious fundamentalism. He sees in theatre the most potent of all media in dealing with and challenging the issues of our time. If Dromgoole is right, not only is theatre not dead, it is more alive than ever before, and possibly more alive than its rivals of television and cinema. What took place outside the Birmingham Repertory Theatre towards the end of 2004 was a remarkable event in the modern era of theatre but by no means unique.

In 1996, a performance of Mark Ravenhill's play *Shopping and Fucking* was interrupted by a group of Christians who, 10 minutes into the first act, stood up in the stalls and started singing hymns as a protest at the play's graphic and, as they perceived it, blasphemous content. Urged on perhaps by the success of members of the Sikh community in cancelling *Behzti*, the BBC was beset by thousands of protestors objecting to the screening of the National Theatre's triumphant production of *Jerry Springer: The Opera*. The protestors gathered outside Broadcasting House, burning their television licences in anger. Although they were objecting to a proposed television event, it was a televising of a theatrical production that was at the root of their complaint.

Although the violent events in Birmingham are hardly cause for celebration, they prove that theatre — as Dromgoole says — is not an 'irrelevance to the modern world'. Birmingham Repertory Theatre has continued to promote plays that raise the profile of black and Asian issues. Ayab Khan-Din's *East is East* is perhaps the most famous example, given its premiere in 1996 and later made into a highly successful film. During 2005, it staged Jess Walter's *Low Dat* about sexual relationships among young black teenagers. The play was toured in schools before enjoying a successful run in the Birmingham Repertory Theatre's studio, 'The Door'. If the experience of *Behzti* has made the theatre directors wary of controversial material, they are doing little to show it.

However, it would be wrong to assume that there is a universally shared set of aims in theatre. The aims of Birmingham Repertory Theatre — reflected by Dromgoole's statement quoted earlier — need not necessarily be those of other practitioners. Just because theatre *can* cause controversy, does not mean that it always does or always should. Gurpreet Kaur Bhatti's aims in writing *Behzti* are different, say, from Ben Elton's aims in creating the 'Queen' tribute show, *We Will Rock You*. It is inevitable that theatre containing technical wizardry, seductive songs and breathtaking scenery, and which unashamedly promotes the 'feel-good factor', is going to be more commercially successful than theatre that aims to challenge and even disturb its audience. Many people view theatre as the means by which they can escape issues of controversy and, as they might see it, heartrending misery — and it is not the purpose of this book to say that they should not.

However, a serious study of the theatre must involve students examining work which has in some way changed the world, or at least made a serious analysis of it, rather than merely celebrated it. Nonetheless, even if some elements of theatre are groundbreaking, controversial and hard hitting, if they are only experienced by a tiny minority can theatre truly be said to be relevant? After all, whatever storms of protest and counter-protest may have occurred outside a theatre in Birmingham just before Christmas 2004, the truth, surely, is that most of the population of this country will remain unaffected by them. In fact, those events will have repercussions for all who make or watch entertainment. Producers of theatre and television will always consider the likely response to pieces of work by an audience before commissioning it, basing the prediction of that response on previous experiences. Will the BBC shy away from aggravating the anger of religious groups in the future by choosing less controversial work to screen than *Jerry Springer: The Opera*? Only time will tell.

Although it is true that there are far fewer theatres than there once were, that is an inevitable consequence of the expansion of entertainment media. The power of theatre is not determined by the number of theatres to be found but by the significance of the events that take place in them and our ability to be stirred by such events. Theatres thrived to the extent they did during the early part of the twentieth century because there was no equivalent entertainment medium to compete with them. It would not be unusual, therefore, for a small town to have four or five theatres in the early part of the last century. Although that is no longer the case, it does not mean that theatre has ceased to be important. A happy epilogue to the gloomy description of the disused Lyceum Theatre of 1986 is that it is now thriving once again, has been completely refitted and for the last few years has been home to one of the biggest hits of the West End, *The Lion King*. In January 2005, a joint submission by the Society of London Theatre and the Theatrical Management Association reported an attendance in London theatres of around 12 million in 2004 — 'one of the best years on record'. And as for Frank Matcham's legacy, his supporters may glory in the knowledge that all save one of his surviving theatres are listed buildings, the vast majority of them full-time working theatres. Theatre in the first decade of the twenty-first century, whether controversial or not, seems to be enjoying greater popularity than for some time.

Richard Vergette

Introduction

Notes for the teacher

As we move towards the second decade of the twenty-first century, the curriculum is, yet again, subject to substantial revision. Increasingly, the knowledge-dominated National Curriculum introduced 20 years ago is a thing of the past, and a greater emphasis is being placed on skills. This is made evident in the 14–19 initiatives and, in particular, the government's aims for the newly created diplomas. There is an expectation that learning will equip students with the transferable skills needed to adapt to a changing and challenging world, dictated by the vagaries of a global economy. Whatever the vices or virtues of such a society, issues of how our young people learn and how they develop their curiosities about the world have never been more important.

The new specification for Edexcel Drama and Theatre Studies in many respects mirrors the changing expectations of education. There is a greater emphasis on the student as an independent learner, gathering evidence and undertaking research about plays and playwrights. Students then need to explore how that information is presented in theatre work — even if it is work written centuries ago — so that it reflects and challenges the society in which the student is living and working now. However, there is also an emphasis on the student's ability to work as part of a team — either leading the decision-making process, or supporting or challenging it as the case may be. While Drama and Theatre Studies is not, in itself, an applied or vocational qualification, this course cannot be delivered successfully without the student developing an understanding and appreciation of the working, functioning modern theatre.

The Drama and Theatre Studies specification enables the teacher to decide the texts to be studied — particularly at AS. Creating a textbook for such a course inevitably involves citing examples that may well not be used by the teacher. However, in choosing the quoted plays, playwrights and practitioners, I would offer them as good examples to those of you requiring direction in what best to study. These examples present enormous scope for research and exploration for you and your students, although the specification is deliberate in its trust of teachers in choosing the work that is most appropriate for their groups.

This book should be seen as a companion piece to the specification, offering insights into the various areas of study without the specificity of a study guide.

Specification coverage

- Section A is essential reading for Unit 1. Chapters 7 and 8 are particularly useful for those students studying *Doctor Faustus* for Unit 4.
- The information in Section B also relates to the specification requirements for Unit 1. Chapter 14 is especially relevant for those students studying *Woyzeck* for Unit 4. Chapters 15 and 16 are key reading for the completion of Unit 3.
- Section C covers the relevant areas for Unit 4, although Chapter 20 is also applicable to Unit 1.
- The chapters on language and characterisation in Section A and on practitioners in Section B are useful for the practical assessment in Unit 2.

Notes for the student

As a student of drama and theatre studies, you are part of a growing population. The number of students taking the subject at A-level has been rising steadily over the last 5 years, reflecting a nationally increased interest in the power of live theatre both to challenge and to entertain its audience.

The first aim of the Edexcel Drama and Theatre Studies course is 'to promote an enjoyment of and interest in drama and theatre both as a participant and as an informed member of an audience'. It is important that you are able to define the purpose of theatre *for you*. In attempting to define that purpose, you might consider the following questions:

- Should theatre change the world or celebrate it?
- Is your interest in theatre as a performer, a member of an audience, a writer or a designer?
- Would you rather charm members of an audience with your performance than shock them, or do you think it is possible to achieve both effects?

As you ask yourself what the purpose of theatre is and what your purpose is in studying it, you should realise that your responses to these questions may well change over the 2 years of the course as your knowledge and experience develop. You are about to undertake a course of study that will make considerable demands on your ability to research and organise information and to express your opinions clearly and persuasively, both on and off stage.

The structure of this book

Section A

The focus for the first section of this book is the world and language of the play-wright. Every play that has ever been written was done so to achieve an aim and composed within a certain social, cultural and historical context.

Plays can, of course, emerge from improvisation and devising, without a word having been written down. However, the relationship between the written script and the actor's interpretation is an important element in a great deal of drama. In addition to context, therefore, this section examines the language and structure of a play from the point of view of performance. The processes of creating theatre are central to your studies, distinguishing this course from one where you would explore plays purely as pieces of literature.

Section B

The second section of this book focuses on the work of the people who deliver the play to the audience, taking the words of the playwright and interpreting them for the stage: directors and devisors. It looks at the work of influential practitioners who have helped to shape — and in some cases continue to shape — the work we see on stage today.

This section provides insight into how you might approach performances of plays with which you will be involved and how you might then evaluate your performance and make positive and analytical criticisms of it. Notes on the process of devising are included here.

Section C

The third section of this book considers the responses to live theatre that you are required to make. It explores the nature of a theatre audience, focusing especially on how the audience has changed throughout theatre history and how it changes depending on the theme or style of production being watched. This background knowledge is important when you are reflecting on audience response, both to what you are watching and what you are performing.

Section A

The craft of the playwright

Using context and language

Global, national and personal events inevitably combine to influence how playwrights perceive the world and how they express their feelings about it. The work of playwrights is linked to observations or criticisms of the world in which they find themselves. For example, Willy Russell's television play *Our Day Out* (1977), about a riotous school outing from a tough Liverpool comprehensive in the 1970s, could not have been written if the playwright had not had some knowledge and experience of the life of teachers and school children in that environment. If Russell had been born in a different era or a different part of the world, it is highly unlikely that such themes would have preoccupied him.

It is important that when we try to understand the work of a playwright, we do so by exploring his or her background and the circumstances that may have influenced him or her at the time the play was written.

Sometimes playwrights break trends and work in a bold and experimental way. While the trends they break are part of the influences upon them, their experiments become in turn a lasting source of influence on other playwrights. All the playwrights discussed in this section have had a powerful effect on the world of theatre.

Whatever plays have been chosen for you to study, perform or watch, it is important that you explore the lives of, and influences upon, the playwrights concerned, particularly in terms of social, political, historical and cultural contexts. Such information is essential if you are to come to an informed appreciation and understanding of the plays they have written.

Chapter 1

Understanding social context

In the next four chapters, we will examine the work of a number of prominent playwrights, but with a particular focus on the social, political, historical and cultural contexts of the plays of Arthur Miller. We will explore the ways in which Miller's personal experiences and political attitudes were both powerful and sustained sources of influence on his play writing.

TopFoto

Arthur Miller

Arthur Miller (1915–2005)

Arthur Miller, the pre-eminent American twentieth-century dramatist, was representative of his times in both his life and in his writings. He was the second son of an illiterate but highly successful clothing manufacturer, Isidore Miller, a Polish-Jewish immigrant, and his wife Augusta, the New-York-born daughter of German-Jewish immigrants. Arthur's prosperous childhood came to a dramatic close with the Wall Street Crash of 1929, as his father struggled to save his company.

Miller's career, which spanned more than six decades, was notable for the early successes *All My Sons* (1947) and *Death of a Salesman* (1949). *The Crucible* (1953) used the real-life Salem witch-hunt trials as an allegory for the McCarthy trials in the USA dedicated to routing out Communists.

Perhaps equally famous for his colourful but brief marriage to Marilyn Monroe, Miller was popularly regarded as one of the finest playwrights of his generation. He won many awards, including the Pulitzer Prize for Drama.

'Panic deep in the spirit'

Arthur Miller's father, who was from a well-to-do Jewish family, arrived in New York as a refugee from Poland at the beginning of the twentieth century, as did so many of his generation. He initially established a thriving business but then suffered sudden bankruptcy during the collapse of the stock market in 1929 (the 'Wall Street Crash'). The Miller family were foreced to move from their fashionable Central Park apartment to a tiny house in Brooklyn, which they shared with a number of relatives. As a boy, therefore, Miller observed the effects of catastrophic financial failure, not only on his own family but also on many other families: the collapse of the stock market led to a high rate of suicide, especially among financiers and brokers.

In his autobiography, *Timebends* (1987), Miller says:

> When the market collapsed practically overnight…a panic deep in the spirit made questionable any and all belief in everything official.

(p. 85)

This painful, forced questioning of a belief in systems and accepted ways of life is a significant element in Miller's plays. This is evident in *The Crucible* (1953), Miller's account of the true story of witch hunts in Massachusetts in 1692. The citizens of the community of Salem are convinced that the devil is among them, bewitching the young girls of the village. As the girls begin to accuse various people in the village of witchcraft, a growing realisation spreads among some members of the Salem community, particularly John Proctor, that the girls — led by Abigail Williams, who is in love with John — are using accusations of witchcraft as a vehicle for achieving personal revenge.

As the play unfolds, we see the whole system of faith upon which the community of Salem, and indeed the whole civilisation of the New World, is based opened up to question and doubt. Even a devoutly religious man, the Reverend Hale, who initially assists in the arrests and interrogations of suspects, has by the end of the play ceased to believe in the previously unshakeable certainties of his faith. As he says in the final act of the play:

> **Hale:** …the very crowns of holy law I brought, and what I touched with my bright confidence, it died; and where I turned the eye of my great faith, blood flowed up…cleave to no faith when faith brings blood…life is God's most precious gift.

(IV.4)

The American Dream

Miller began to write plays while he was at university in Michigan. Winning a number of monetary prizes and earning $22.77 a week on the Federal Theatre Project, he was able to support himself as he wrote. His earliest work did not attract large audiences, and his first attempt at conquering Broadway — the capital of America's theatre — ended in failure, with his play *The Man Who Had All the Luck* (1940). Undaunted, Miller continued to work and in 1947, at the age of 31, his play *All My Sons* was produced on Broadway, affording him his first success and earning him the New York Drama Critics' Circle award for best play of the season.

However, it was his next major play, *Death of a Salesman* (1949), which was to secure Miller's reputation as one of the world's leading playwrights of the twentieth century. The central character, Willy Loman, is a man who believes passionately in the truth of the 'American Dream'.

Loman tries relentlessly to be a successful salesman, to fulfil for himself and his family the American Dream. His attempts ultimately fail. Despite his own failure, he tries to motivate his sons to aspire to the dream; however, his efforts lead only to despair, conflict and finally tragedy as Willy commits suicide.

Death of a Salesman was inspired not only by the struggles of Miller's own father and many like him, but also by an encounter Miller had with his uncle at a performance of *All My Sons*, 2 years earlier. Miller recounts this story in *Timebends* (pp. 130–131). His uncle, Manny, had two sons, both of whom had proved a disappointment to him. One of these sons was called Buddy. As Miller, a newly successful playwright winning praise and fame, greeted his uncle, Manny said to him in an almost defiant manner, without greeting or handshake, 'Buddy is doing very well'.

It was seeing his uncle's agony over his nephew's success compared with the failure of his sons that set Miller thinking about the desires and aspirations of ordinary people — not only about how difficult they were to achieve, but also about the often shallow nature of the dreams to which they aspired.

The American Dream

The 'American Dream' is the ideal that any American, no matter how humble his or her origins, can aspire, through hard work and dedication, to achieve any position in society that his or her abilities merit, even becoming president of the USA itself. A number of Americans have fulfilled the dream. Abraham Lincoln came from an impoverished family in Illinois and rose to be the sixteenth president of the USA in 1861. More recently, William Jefferson Clinton, brought up in a one-parent family in Little Rock, Arkansas, managed the same feat, becoming forty-second president in 1993. Even Miller's father, Isidore Miller, a Polish immigrant, rose to a position of power and prominence in financial circles before the Wall Street Crash.

Relationship with Marilyn Monroe

Even those unfamiliar with Miller's plays often know about his colourful personal life, in particular his marriage to the 'screen goddess' Marilyn Monroe, his second wife. Although Miller had married Mary Grace Slattery in 1940, fathering two children, by the early 1950s he had met and fallen in love with Monroe.

Miller's feelings of confusion and guilt as his first marriage collapsed and his relationship with Monroe intensified undoubtedly influenced his depiction of the relationships in *The Crucible* between John Proctor, his wife Elizabeth and Abigail Williams, a young girl with whom Proctor has had a brief but passionate affair. At the beginning of Act II, the silence and suspicion which dominate the atmosphere as Proctor arrives home late are palpable. At length, he can stand the atmosphere no more:

Proctor: You forget nothin' and forgive nothin'. Learn charity, woman. I have gone tiptoe in this house all seven month since she is gone. I have not moved from there to there without I think to please you, and still an everlasting funeral marches round your heart.

In the same way that Proctor becomes more and more infuriated with his world of order, obedience and religious fundamentalism, so Miller must have felt increasingly stifled by the circumstances of his personal life and the society in which he lived. He wrote in *Timebends*:

> Respectable conformity was the killer of the dream; I was sick of being afraid, of life and of myself. (*Timebends*, p. 313)

Miller's marriage to Marilyn Monroe in 1956, perhaps predictably, did not last. By 1961 the marriage had foundered, and Monroe died of a drugs overdose the following year aged just 36. At the time, Miller was accused in some quarters of being cold hearted, as he made it clear that he felt her death was inevitable. When asked if he would attend her funeral, he was reported to have responded 'Why, will she be there?' In fact, his response was inaccurately reported and he had said 'She won't be there' (*Timebends*, p. 531). Miller's autobiography makes it clear that he felt great affection for Monroe, as well as having respect for her talent. He wrote the part of Roslyn Taber in the film *The Misfits* (1961) for her — one of her few serious roles and one of her best.

Some critics have commented that after his marriage to Monroe, Miller's pre-eminence as a playwright declined. While this is a rather harsh judgement, it is the case that much of his most celebrated work was completed before their marriage.

Arthur Miller with Marilyn Monroe in 1956

After Monroe died, Miller produced his most autobiographical play *After the Fall* (1964). Although he consistently denied that the character of Maggie was based on Monroe, the parallels between the two are apparent — especially as Maggie dies of an overdose shortly before the end of the play.

Miller's last completed play was *Finishing the Picture*, performed in Chicago in the autumn of 2004. In this semi-autobiographical piece he depicts an ailing drug-addict film star being hectored by acting coaches and directors to complete a film. It is clearly the story of Monroe's heroic struggle to complete her work in *The Misfits* and Miller's own desperate attempts to help her. It seems that the most turbulent yet most high-profile moments of his personal life form the basis of his final work.

Individual responsibility

A consistent theme in Miller's work is the importance of an individual taking responsibility for his or her actions but demonstrating an understanding for how those actions can affect society as a whole.

In *All My Sons*, Joe Keller — an apparently pleasant and loving family man — supplies faulty machine parts to fighter planes during the Second World War.

All the pilots die in action. When his actions are revealed at the end of the play, he claims that he only acted as he did to keep his business alive, in order to pass it on to his son. However, when he discovers that his younger son, Larry — also a fighter pilot — deliberately got himself killed out of disgust at his father's actions, Joe finally acknowledges that the airmen were 'all my sons'.

Similarly in *The Crucible*, it is not enough for Proctor simply to save the life of his wife, who has been accused of witchcraft by his former lover, Abigail. He has to pursue his case against the court for the sake of all the falsely accused citizens of Salem and in the process is accused himself. In Act IV, when faced with the option of having his life spared if he will consent to having his written confession to witchcraft being posted on the church door, he tears up the confession with the anguished cry:

Proctor: I have three children — how may I teach them to walk like men in the world, and I sold my friends?

In some of his later work — most notably *Incident at Vichy* (1964), the film *Playing for Time* (1980) and *Broken Glass* (1994) — Miller explores the horrors of the Holocaust, a theme close to his heart because of his Jewish background. However, it is in the actions of the central characters — in the choices they make — that Miller's concern that individuals understand the weight of influence of their actions can be demonstrated.

Responsibility and public involvement

Many aspects of Miller's own life reflect his sense of public as well as private responsibility.

In 1965, he was elected president of International PEN, an international literary organisation. In 1967, he visited Moscow in his capacity as president to persuade Soviet writers to join. In 1969, again as president of PEN, he appealed to President Gowon of Nigeria to spare the life of the dissident playwright Wole Soyinka, who was due to be executed for treason. Miller recounts on p. 597 of *Timebends* how Gowon asked an aide with some incredulity whether the appeal had come from the former husband of Marilyn Monroe, and on receiving assurances that it had, ordered Soyinka's immediate release.

Not only was Miller involved with PEN during the 1960s, he was also one of a number of party activists who attempted to persuade the US Democratic Party to oppose the war in Vietnam — unsuccessfully as it turned out.

As we see on pp.14–18, however, his most prominent action of protest was his refusal to cooperate with the House Un-American Activities Committee.

In 1962, Miller married the Austrian-born photographer Inge Morath. Although they both travelled extensively, Miller never stopped work as a playwright and often involved himself in the productions of revivals of his plays. In 1983, he directed a celebrated Chinese production of *Death of a Salesman* and subsequently wrote a fascinating account of the experience entitled *'Salesman' in Beijing*. He and his wife were invited to meet Fidel Castro, the president of Cuba, in 2000, and although his greatest work was perhaps long behind him, he continued to write new work for the theatre almost to his dying day.

Summary

When considering the context of a play, there may well be aspects of a playwright's personal life that are relevant to how the play came into being. However, not all the elements of a playwright's personal life will be relevant and you need to choose carefully. For example, if you are writing notes on *The Crucible*, you do not need to mention that Miller directed a production of *Death of a Salesman* in Beijing in 1983. However, discussion of the importance of other elements of his life — his divorce from his first wife and his interest in human rights — could make more persuasive reading.

Discussion questions

1 Identify two elements of Miller's personal life that influenced his career as a playwright.
2 Explain how Miller's personal life influenced aspects of *The Crucible*.

Hints

- Ensure you confine your notes to the relevant sections of the playwright's life when considering its impact on his work.
- Avoid lapsing into a 'story telling' of the playwright's life.
- Use quotations from plays when discussing how they have been shaped or developed by aspects of the playwright's life.

Chapter 2

Understanding political context

Arthur Miller was passionately interested in politics — he was politically active for much of his life — and his plays generally focus on the ways in which politics influence ordinary people's lives. Miller was most active as a playwright before, during and the two decades after the Second World War, an event which profoundly influenced the social circumstances and outlook of the citizens of both the USA and Europe.

Historical backdrop to Miller's activities

Roosevelt and the New Deal

Following the Wall Street Crash in 1929 in the USA, and the inability of the US Republican President Herbert Hoover to stem the tide of the Depression or to restore confidence in the US economy, the Democrat Franklin Delano Roosevelt was elected in 1932. Through a process of investment, planning and a massive legislative programme, Roosevelt established the New Deal, the means by which America effected an economic turnaround. This scheme was an intervention by government to create more opportunities for work rather than allowing market forces to dictate levels of employment; it was seen as an action bordering on socialism.

Stalin and the Five Year Plans

American agricultural economist Rexford Tugwell made comparisons at the time between Roosevelt's New Deal and Soviet dictator Josef Stalin's Five Year Plans for economic and industrial recovery in the USSR. However, each of these leaders had a different motivation: Roosevelt was motivated by the desire to improve the welfare of ordinary Americans; Stalin was motivated by the need to modernise the USSR, even if it meant the loss of millions of lives — which, in relation to his agricultural policy and the resultant starvation of farmers, it did.

Although broadly successful, the American New Deal made its impact on some impoverished families more effectively than on others. Many people in America were therefore left disillusioned by an economic system that promised so much to the 'little man' but in fact led many honest, hardworking citizens to bankruptcy, homelessness and even starvation. Many such people looked with fascination at the example of the Soviet Union. That the starvation of millions was a calculated part of Stalin's plans for economic success in the Soviet Union was a fact known to only a few in the West. As far as many ordinary Americans (and indeed onlookers from all over the world) were concerned, Russia had rebelled against its autocratic and fabulously wealthy and powerful royal family and replaced it with a Communist system to benefit all the citizens of the USSR equally — and it seemed that communism was working.

The Second World War

In June 1941, Germany tore up the terms of the 1939 non-aggression pact that it had signed with the Soviet Union and invaded it with a force of 3 million troops. This was the largest invasion in written history. At the end of the same year, the bombing of Pearl Harbor — America's principal naval base — by the Japanese empire forced Great Britain and the USA into an unlikely alliance with the Soviet Union (they were known as 'the allies'). Consequently, the two largest countries in the world, with systems of government ideologically opposed to each other, found themselves working together to defeat Nazism.

A new world order?

Some Americans — particularly those opposed to the war — were concerned about the closer relationship between the USA and the Soviet Union, however necessary. President Roosevelt appeared to have developed a close personal rapport with Stalin, even addressing him as 'Uncle Joe' at the Yalta Conference in 1945. At that same conference, however, an ailing Roosevelt was unable to stop Stalin laying territorial claims to much of eastern Europe. A sense began to grow in America that the Roosevelt administration, and the Truman one which succeeded it in 1945, were somehow too 'soft' on communism. Although many ordinary Americans had regarded communism as highly successful after seeing the apparent benefits brought about by the Soviet Union's Five Year Plans, the establishment's fear of communism was intensified by the revolution in China.

In 1949, China — the country with the world's highest population — became a Communist state, after a long and bloody revolution. This fuelled fears that the same revolution could all too easily befall the USA. By the middle of the twentieth century, therefore, the world had witnessed the Communist revolution in China, the rise and fall of fascism in Europe, the entire state of Germany wiped out by the ravages of Nazism and the destruction of most royal families in Europe and Russia. It is hardly surprising that some feared that the new world order, with communism in the ascendancy, should maintain what appeared to be its relentless march. What was so unique about America that it should avoid the same fate?

The House Un-American Activities

In 1940, the Alien Registration Act had made it illegal for anyone in the USA 'to advocate, abet or teach' the desirability of overthrowing the government. This Act was used in order to weed out and undermine radical left-wing organisations, such as the American Communist Party or similar organisations sympathetic to them.

The House Un-American Activities Committee (HUAC) was established to investigate people suspected of unpatriotic behaviour, using the Alien Registration Act to justify and further its investigations. By 1950, the HUAC had become a strong and influential force in American politics, and its chairman, Joseph McCarthy, became one of the most feared political figures in the land.

The HUAC became interested in the activities of Hollywood directors, writers and performers. If the committee summoned you, you had to confess or deny that you were a member of the Communist Party. In addition, you were expected to 'name names' — to reveal to the HUAC the names of any individuals you knew to be members of the Communist Party or to sympathise with its cause.

Miller knew many individuals who worked in the film as well as the theatre industry. Moreover, Miller's two successful plays in the 1940s, *All My Sons* and *Death of a Salesman*, were clearly critical of the principles of the capitalist system. Joe Keller in *All My Sons* is a success of the system but is morally (and fatally) compromised in wanting to maintain his success — using his son's welfare as an excuse for his crimes. Willy Loman, conversely, is a failure of the system and damages both his relationship with his family and his moral integrity trying to 'be a success'. Both these plays lean in their philosophies towards a more egalitarian socialist ideal, suggesting strongly that life is not (or should not be) a competition and that our fellow human beings are precisely that, not our economic rivals. In such a volatile political climate as the one in which Miller was working, such messages would have been enough to attract the attention of the HUAC. However, by the time he started work on *The Crucible*, Miller had still not been summoned to appear before it.

Confessions to the HUAC

The original director of *Death of a Salesman*, Elia Kazan, had been a member of the Communist Party in his youth during the 1930s, when working for the Group Theatre. At the time, the Group Theatre included several people with Communist, or at least left-wing, sympathies. A committed socialist, Kazan nonetheless came to feel betrayed by Stalin's atrocities and the rigid ideologies of communism, and he objected when Party officials tried to interfere in the artistic decisions of his theatre.

When he was summoned before the HUAC, Kazan therefore agreed to testify and readily admitted his former membership of the Communist Party. However, he refused to name others who had been members. As a result, Kazan suffered increasing pressure from Hollywood studio management to cooperate with the HUAC. He did eventually comply with the demands and provided the committee with the names of former Communist Party members, or those connected with Party activities, in order to preserve his career.

A delegation of film stars, led by Lauren Bacall and Humphrey Bogart, marches to the Capitol for the morning session of the HUAC's hearing on communism, 27 October 1947

Miller met Kazan around this time and expressed his anger, not so much at what Kazan had done, but at the HUAC itself:

> He [Kazan] was trying, I thought, to appear relieved in his mind, to present the issue as settled, even happily so.   (*Timebends*, p. 333)

Miller felt that Kazan's confession and the confessions of others had been brought about by:

> ...a governmental decree of *moral* guilt that could easily be made to disappear by ritual speech: intoning names of fellow sinners and recanting former beliefs.   (*Timebends*, p. 331)

Witches and Communists

On the same day that he visited Kazan and heard his excuses, Miller journeyed to Salem to research the witch-hunt trials of 1692. Kazan's wife, when she knew of Miller's intentions, remarked that there might not be witches but there certainly were Communists.

(*Timebends*, p. 339).

Miller compared the ritual speech required of the accused with the kind of speech associated with religious confession and ceremony: confess with a sombre enough tone and be prepared to point the finger at a few other well-known liberals and you could not only go free but also enjoy the exoneration of your fellow patriotic countrymen.

Miller's own fate at the hands of the HUAC is interesting. He was not summoned until 1956, after *The Crucible* had been staged. By then, the power of the committee was on the wane. Miller claimed that he had only been summoned because of his high-profile engagement to Marilyn Monroe and that if he had allowed the chairman of the committee, Francis E. Walter, to meet her and be photographed with her, Miller would have been released. As it was, he was given a suspended sentence and a minimal fine.

Other people working in the film industry who refused to testify fared much worse; a large number of talented directors, writers, actors and producers were found guilty by the committee and put on the 'Hollywood blacklist', ruining their careers and, in some cases, their lives.

Summary

It is impossible to divorce Miller's political awareness and experiences from a study of his plays. Undoubtedly, the turmoil he witnessed in the aftermath of the Wall Street Crash, the bloodshed and Holocaust of the Second World War and the hysteria of the McCarthy Communist witch hunts were all contributory factors to his work. Therefore, in approaching any of his compositions, it is important to investigate the political context of the time and Miller's attitude towards it. Certainly, his plays often become sagas of the struggle of the 'little man', or the antihero, to deal with social forces beyond his comprehension or control.

Discussion questions

1 Do you think that plays that reflect social or political issues (for example *The Crucible*) are less entertaining than more spectacular forms of theatre (such as the West End musical)?

2 Explain the features of the McCarthy witch-hunt trials that were reminiscent of the Salem witch hunts.

Hint

Ensure the points you research regarding the McCarthy hearings are relevant to a discussion of the play and the dramatist's quest. Do not just provide a history lesson about communism in the USA.

Chapter 3

Understanding historical context

Why did Arthur Miller want to write a play, *The Crucible*, about a bizarre series of events that had occurred in Massachusetts more than 250 years previously?

The Crucible is set in 1692, when America was still a 'new' country. Settlers had arrived from Britain only a generation earlier in order to establish a Puritan state — a state founded on uncompromising, pure Christian principles. Their society adopted the articles of Christianity as the laws of the land. For instance, it was held that adultery was not solely a contravention of one of the Ten Commandments, it was also punishable by law. Such a society is known as a theocracy — a society for which the presence of Satan is not an idea, it is a fact.

For the citizens of seventeenth-century Salem, therefore, the presence of witches was fact. Heaven and hell were believed in without question, and everyone's first concern was to maintain a chaste, virtuous lifestyle. At the centre of their society was the church. Regular attendance at church was expected and an irregularity in an attendance record, such as John Proctor's, would invite suspicion and disapproval.

'Naming names'

At the opening of *The Crucible*, a group of girls, including the minister's niece and daughter, are caught dancing naked in the forest. The minister's daughter subsequently falls into a trance induced by hysteria. Witchcraft is suspected and a local expert — Reverend Hale — is summoned. The girls confess that they have been cajoled into the worship of Satan by the minister's maid, who in turn confesses to being bewitched by Satan. The girls start to 'name names', identifying members of the community they claim to have seen with the devil, and of course they are believed. All of a sudden a group of girls, in trouble for illicit naked dancing, find themselves in a position of considerable authority. The deputy governor (Danforth) is called from Boston to sit in judgement as the witch trials proceed.

As the play progresses and the accusations of witchcraft become more widespread, Reverend Hale begins to cast doubt on the assumptions of guilt being made. The doctrine determining the outcome of the trials is made clear to the audience as Danforth explains his reasoning to Hale in Act III:

Danforth: ...In an ordinary crime, how does one defend the accused? One calls up witnesses to prove his innocence. But witchcraft is *ipso facto,* on its face and by its nature, an invisible crime, is it not? Therefore, who may possibly be witness to it? The witch and the victim. None other. Now we cannot hope the witch will accuse herself; granted? Therefore, we must rely upon her victims — and they do testify, the children certainly do testify.

The Salem witch trials

The Salem witch trials were a series of court hearings and County Court trials to prosecute people accused of witchcraft in the counties of Essex, Suffolk and Middlesex in Massachusetts. Between February 1692 and May 1693, over 150 people were arrested, and many more were accused. Eventually two Superior Courts of Judicature, sitting in 1693, convicted 29 people of witchcraft. This was considered to be a 'capital felony' — a crime punishable by death. Nineteen people were hanged (14 women and 5 men). One man died under torture having refused to admit to witchcraft, and at least 5 more of the accused appear to have died in prison.

The Salem witch trials were not the first or only witch hunt to take place in New England or Europe, but they seem to have captured the imaginations of Americans.

The girls identify members of the Salem community they claim to have seen with the devil

In this speech, Miller shows Danforth assuming that if an accusation of witchcraft is made it must be legitimate. What possible motivation can the girls have for making their accusations other than to rid the world of witches, in a society that fears the presence of the devil and witches above anything else?

'Crying out' against the neighbours

Miller explores the way that members of the outwardly simple Salem community start to use the trials for their own ends. Thomas Putnam — a wealthy landowner — is overheard persuading his daughter to 'cry out' against his neighbours. Those accused and convicted of witchcraft had their lands confiscated, and Putnam — a friend of the local minister — is in a position to profit personally from the misfortune of others. Miller's play reveals the way in which individuals can exploit the fears and vulnerabilities of society to exact personal revenge. It also demonstrates how the obsessive anxiety of a society to rid itself of what it sees as dangerous and undermining elements can paradoxically lead to its own destruction.

Witch trial or Communist trial?

In *The Crucible*, the most damaging features of Salem society are the instruments of justice it uses to protect itself against possible danger. This is where the historical context of the play can be seen to correspond to significant questions of Miller's own era. While McCarthy's aims were ostensibly to rid America of undesirable elements through the activities of the HUAC, it soon became clear that it was the HUAC itself, under his chairmanship, that was the actual source of fear and cause of social disintegration, not the people with a Communist past.

Summary

The historical context of a play is vital to understanding the themes and issues that the playwright is presenting. *The Crucible* has a specific historical and political context, which is used as a deliberate allegory for the context in which the playwright is writing. The destruction of the society of Salem demonstrates the danger of a system that attempts to impose beliefs on its citizenry. The links with 1950s America are unmistakable.

Discussion questions

1 Identify the principal historical features that influenced Arthur Miller in writing *The Crucible*.

2 Explain how *The Crucible* reflects historical features of the seventeenth century while still being relevant to the modern day.

Essay questions

1 Explain the use of the historical allegory in linking issues concerning the events of 1692 in Salem with the events surrounding the activities of the House of Un-American Activities Committee.

2 Justify Miller's use of dramatic licence in altering events from history when writing *The Crucible*.

Hint

Remember you are discussing a piece of drama and not a historical document. As a student of drama and theatre studies, your research and responses to questions should always reflect an appreciation of the play as a piece of live performance.

Chapter 4

Understanding cultural context

In exploring the cultural context of the work of Arthur Miller, it is necessary to consider two important factors:

- What was the nature of the cultural influences on Miller and how are these made evident in *The Crucible* and some of his other major works?
- What was happening in the worlds of theatre and other artistic media in the United States in the early 1950s?

Ancient Greek tragedy

Arthur Miller's plays are often described as tragedies. 'Tragedy' in the context of plays defines a specific type of dramatic event. In its modern everyday usage, tragedy is often used in association with sudden loss of life: for instance, we refer to the 'Hillsborough tragedy' (when 96 football fans were crushed to death at an FA-Cup semi-final match in 1989). However, while the events of a tragedy may, and indeed often do, involve loss of life, that is not the only distinguishing feature of dramatic tragedy.

The term 'tragedy' has its roots in the earliest forms of surviving theatre — Greek tragedy. The oldest trilogy of tragedy plays in existence, still frequently performed, is the *Oresteia* (Aeschylus *c.* 458 BC). Perhaps the most famous of all Greek tragedies, however, is *Oedipus Rex* (Sophocles *c.* 430 BC). *Oedipus Rex* provides us with a useful model for tragedy, and its influence can be seen in the later tragedies of Shakespeare and, significantly for us, in the works of Arthur Miller.

Oedipus Rex

This play tells the story of a man who, it is predicted, will murder his father and marry his mother.

At the opening of the play, Oedipus, a king, has already (unknowingly) fulfilled his destiny. Because of his crimes, the gods have visited an appalling plague on his city, Thebes, and its suffering citizens appeal to their king to find the solution. In the early stages of the play, we see Oedipus proudly declare that he will take it upon himself to seek out the cause of the plague and prosecute whatever justice is deemed necessary by the gods. He is then confronted by a soothsayer, Tiresias, who tells him that Oedipus is the cause of the plague and that it is he who has offended the gods. Oedipus angrily refutes the soothsayer's claims, denouncing him as a fraud. Thereafter, the more strenuous Oedipus's efforts to determine the truth of events, the more inevitably he seals his own fate; the more he tries to assert himself over the events of the play, the more we realise how much he is at the mercy of forces far stronger than himself.

Aeschylus (c. 525–456 BC)

Aeschylus holds the distinction of being the earliest playwright whose plays — or at least some of them — still survive. He is often referred to as the 'father of tragedy'. Born in Eleusis in 525 BC, he was 26 when he wrote his first tragedy, although his early life was punctuated more by his military service than by his work as a dramatist.

Aeschylus was responsible for the development of drama by introducing the idea of the second actor, taking some of the emphasis off the chorus and enhancing the notion of character. The *Oresteia* trilogy is probably his most famous work, chronicling the story of the House of Atreus, the murder of the Greek king Agamemnon by his wife, Clytemnaestra, and the revenge of his children against their mother. Although his works are perhaps not as renowned as those of Euripides or Sophocles, there is no doubt that Aeschylus's influence on the shape and development of drama was pivotal.

Sophocles (c. 496–406 BC)

If Aeschylus's influence was assured by the addition of the second actor, Sophocles's place was assured by the addition of the third. Sophocles won first prize the first time he entered the Festival of Dionysus — beating the father of tragedy himself, Aeschylus.
Oedipus Rex is generally regarded as his finest play, although the third play in the Theban trilogy, *Antigone*, is also seen as a masterpiece. The addition of the third actor enhanced the notion of characterisation and made for complex three-way arguments, for example when Jocasta impatiently interjects during the argument between Oedipus and Creon.

While Aeschylus wrote trilogies, Sophocles wrote single tragedies that were complete in themselves and, therefore, dramatically more intense.

By the end of the play, Oedipus has grown in knowledge and wisdom but cannot avoid his terrible ultimate fate. He does not die at the end of the play but blinds himself at the moment when he realises the true nature of his own terrible actions.

Blindness in Classical drama

Blindness is often used in a dramatically ironic way in Classical drama. In *Oedipus Rex*, Tiresias the soothsayer is blind yet has the gift of insight. Later dramatists used the same image. For example, the Earl of Gloucester in Shakespeare's *King Lear* suffers the torture of having his eyes pulled out seconds before realising that he has been duped by his treacherous son, Edmund. In John Milton's tragic poem in blank verse, *Samson Agonistes*, Samson only realises the truth of Delilah's treachery at the moment of his blinding.

The tragic hero

At the centre of the action in a tragedy is the tragic hero. The Greek philosopher Aristotle identified the main qualities of the tragic hero in the *Poetics*:

> …a man who is not eminently good and just, yet whose misfortune is brought about not by vice or depravity, but by some error or frailty.

> (Section 13, trans. S. H. Butler)

Aristotle (384–322 BC)

Aristotle's writings have influenced many aspects of modern life, from religion to science and natural history, from politics to philosophy. Although some of his work has been lost in the centuries since his death, much of it is still studied today. In theatrical terms, his greatest contribution was his *Poetics*, a piece of work exploring the nature of poetry and drama, specifically tragedy. The theories contained therein led to the development of the three unities of drama that were present in plays of the seventeenth and eighteenth centuries. These stipulated that 'a play should represent a single action taking place in a single day in the same setting'. This tenet had a great effect on European drama of this period, and played a role in the development of naturalistic theatre in the nineteenth century.

Greek theatre sought to make sense of the world; its playwrights took events which could not be explained by reason or by cause and effect — such as the plague — and tried to create some kind of order around the chaos. As a civilisation, the Greeks sought to order the workings of the universe through astronomy and the workings of the world through mathematics, but it was through poetry and drama that they sought explanations for the inexplicable.

Joe Keller in Miller's play *All My Sons* fulfils the definition of a tragic hero: he is amiable, generous and seen as a decent man in the community. He is not — in essence — a criminal. However, he has been guilty of a terrible error of judgement, which could be described as a 'frailty', by allowing the shipping of aeroplane parts he knew to be faulty. It is only when he realises and acknowledges the full magnitude of his actions that he commits suicide — significantly, off stage.

Miller on Greek tragedy

In *Timebends*, Miller describes himself as loving Greek tragedy the way a 'man at the bottom of a pit loves a ladder'. He felt that the writers of this genre 'sought to transform the vendetta and the blood feud into the institutions of law and justice'.

Joe Keller in Miller's play *All My Sons* fulfils the definition of a tragic hero. (Laurie Metcalf as Kate Keller and James Hazeldine as Joe Keller, National Theatre, August 2001)

In *Death of a Salesman*, the hero, Willy Loman, is a tragic hero: a man who is not 'eminently good or just', whose downfall is caused not by 'vice or depravity' but by frailties in his character. His weakness is not only his belief in the 'American Dream' but also his own inevitable inability to achieve it: the audience realises from the start of the play that Willy's all-important

The fatal flaw

In Greek theatre, the tragic hero's 'fatal flaw' or 'error' has usually been committed or manifested before the action of the play begins. Thus, at the beginning of *Oedipus Rex*, the citizens of Thebes are suffering the ravages of the plague because of crimes committed years before by Oedipus.

relationship with his elder son Biff has already been damaged before the opening of the action, although the reasons are not made clear. It is only in the final minutes of the play, when Biff's awareness of his father's adultery comes to light, that the audience understands the origins of the son's utter disillusionment with his father, and in return the father's seething resentment of his son.

Reversal of situation

There is an element of 'reversal of situation' in *The Crucible* — a dramatic device for tragedy which Aristotle refers to in the *Poetics*. An example of this in *Oedipus Rex* is the messenger's arrival — supposedly a source of comfort and reassurance to Oedipus about his mother, but in fact the moment that seals his doom.

In *The Crucible*, Proctor's survival is dependent on Elizabeth's willingness to testify to her husband's adultery. However, for the first time in her life she lies — in order to protect her husband — and thus she effectively ensures his condemnation.

The unities

Aristotle defined not only the tragic hero and the 'reversal of situation', but also certain conventions which he identified as the hallmarks of theatre. One of these is the use of 'unities': the unities of time, action and place.

According to Aristotle, the plot of a tragedy should:

 • take place over a 24-hour period (unity of time)
 • be continuous (unity of action)
 • be set in one area (unity of place)

In *All My Sons*, Miller follows the unities assiduously. The action of the play takes place over 24 hours in the yard of the Keller house, beginning in the sunshine of what seems to be a perfect August day. It ends with the revelation of a crime and the suicide of the main character, Joe Keller, before the day is out.

The structure of *Death of a Salesman* does not strictly follow the patterns established by the Greeks for tragedy, although, as we have noted, Willy Loman has the qualities of a tragic hero. Most of the play takes place within the Loman house. However, much of the second act — particularly the first half of it — takes place elsewhere in New York City, principally at Willy's office and a restaurant in town. The action does occur within 24 hours, but it is not strictly continuous: there are significant periods in the play during which the audience sees events from the past, as Willy relives the moments which have destroyed him. In this play, therefore, Miller is not using the Greek principles of staging as a rule book but rather as a useful and time-honoured guide. Shakespeare did no less in many of his tragedies, so Miller's is a scholarly approach based on a sound understanding of theatre practice.

The high-ranking protagonist

Tragedy, as presented by the Greek playwrights, and in its later incarnations in the sixteenth and seventeenth centuries, dealt with the lives of high-ranking protagonists of noble birth.

In 1949, the same year as the first performance of *Death of a Salesman*, Miller published an essay in the *New York Times* entitled 'Tragedy and the Common Man', in which he explained how and why tragedy is not exclusively the province of the high-ranking protagonist. For the twentieth century, Miller felt that such an exclusive use of the genre was limiting. In his essay, Miller makes the case for tragedy being a vehicle to explore a character's evaluation of himself, whatever his rank:

> Insistence upon the rank of the tragic hero, or the so-called nobility of his character, is really but a clinging to the outward forms of tragedy.

So for Miller, writing in the mid-twentieth century, tragedy should not preoccupy itself solely with the lives of nobility but should instead be made meaningful to the lives of more ordinary people. For him:

> ...the tragic feeling is evoked in us when we are in the presence of a character who is ready to lay down his life, if need be, to secure one thing — his sense of personal dignity.

There is a less obvious application of Aristotelian principles of tragedy in *The Crucible* (the action covers many months), but there is something of the tragic hero in Proctor, an 'ordinary man'; he does perhaps evoke in us Miller's 'tragic feeling'. We discover early on in the play that in a moment of weakness he has had sexual relations with his servant girl, Abigail Williams. On discovering this, his wife, Elizabeth, throws the girl out, and thus the seeds of Abigail's desire for revenge are sown. As Proctor endeavours, unsuccessfully, to save the community and himself from the vengeful Abigail, his struggles mirror the efforts of Oedipus. His attempts to discover the truth inevitably lead to his own downfall.

Naturalism

Greek tragedy was not the only cultural influence on which Miller drew in the creation of his plays. His work — in large measure — may be termed 'naturalistic':

August Strindberg (1849–1912)

Strindberg's works from the late nineteenth century are some of the earliest extant examples of naturalistic plays. As with many of his contemporaries, he began writing in other genres, preferring to compose stylised historical dramas and farces. However, alongside writers like Ibsen and Chekhov, he began to explore the effects of creating drama that presented a world much closer to that around us than previous style had allowed. His plays were littered with gender conflicts and displayed his personal disillusionment with intimate relationships. After a mental breakdown Strindberg ceased writing temporarily. When he returned, his works were more symbolic in style.

Anton Chekhov (1860–1904)

The work of playwright Anton Chekhov is inextricably linked with the ideas of Konstantin Stanislavski and the development of the Moscow Art Theatre in the late nineteenth and early twentieth centuries.

Chekhov's reflections on the lives of the fading ruling classes in works such as *The Seagull*, *The Three Sisters* and, perhaps most famously, *The Cherry Orchard*, are variously seen as irreverent and humorous or touching and poignant. This debate was often the subject of argument between writer and director, and there appear to be strains of both tragedy and comedy running through Chekhov's works.

Although Chekhov's plays have an exaggerated, almost melodramatic quality, the complex characters often demonstrate a frustrating inability to communicate their feelings or to make sense of the world they inhabit. Often (as in *The Cherry Orchard*), the harsh reality of the world overtakes the romantic preoccupations of the characters, leaving the audience feeling a combination of infuriation tempered with sympathy.

that is, his works deal with human beings struggling both to make sense of their environment and to survive.

Naturalism emerged as an influence on playwrights and novelists in the late nineteenth century and was a movement which, despite being essentially artistic, took its lead from science. Following his journeys around the world onboard *The Beagle*, Charles Darwin (1809–82) propounded his theory of evolution and 'survival of the fittest' (the first serious challenge to creationism) in his book *On the Origin of the Species* (1859). Here, Darwin argued that human beings had evolved over centuries and proceeded to trace them back through their evolution, relating them to earlier species and living organisms. That human beings were simply a product of, and struggling participants in, their environment was an idea dramatically at odds with the traditional Christian view that every human being was special and made in God's own image.

Meanwhile, with the major developments in the design of microscopes in the middle of the nineteenth century, the scrutiny of man's environment had never been more detailed. Following the example of Darwin, many playwrights and novelists decided to turn the writer's microscope on humanity in its contemporary environment — to study individual human beings' problems, weaknesses and strengths rather than producing comedy or heroic melodrama (the predominant literary/dramatic forms through the nineteenth century). Playwrights such as Strindberg (for example *Miss Julie*, 1887; *The Father*, 1888), Chekhov and Ibsen strove to present man struggling to survive in his natural, as well as societal, environment. They presented men and women facing crises of conscience, plunged into moral dilemmas from which they might or might not emerge wiser. In a sense, Darwin's theories were made visible on stage, and audiences were not always ready for the onslaught.

The naturalistic plays of Henrik Ibsen

Henrik Ibsen was probably the most influential of all naturalistic playwrights, and, according to his biographer and translator Michael Meyer, the most influential playwright since Shakespeare.

It was not only the credible depictions of his characters that established his reputation, it was also the enormously controversial themes and issues he was prepared to tackle. For many years his work was unsuccessful, and the theatre for which he wrote went bankrupt during the 1860s. However, his major success, which made him internationally famous, was *A Doll's House* (1879). Interestingly, he was over 50 years of age before he achieved this success, after half a lifetime of writing.

Perhaps significantly, Charles Darwin's *On the Origin of Species* was translated into Scandinavian shortly before Ibsen started work on *A Doll's House*.

A Doll's House

The principal character, Nora, is a pampered, pretty and somewhat air-headed housewife. However, early in her marriage she borrows money from an unscrupulous businessman, Krogstad, in order to take her husband, Torvald, abroad for a life-saving rest cure. Her husband believes Nora's father has given them the money for the trip. In fact, Nora forges her father's signature on the loan guarantee and is later blackmailed by Krogstad when he discovers the deception.

Henrik Ibsen (1828–1906)

As a playwright, Ibsen used theatre to challenge his audiences on personal, political and social levels. While he started his career with verse drama, and finished with more symbolic plays, it is his intervening naturalistic pieces which have had the greatest impact on theatre. Works such as *A Doll's House* and *Ghosts* broke standards of both the stage and society, by addressing taboo subjects through realistic characters and by avoiding conventions such as 'happy endings'. In their time, these works were considered scandalous and led to Ibsen leaving his native Norway to work abroad for the majority of his career.

By the end of the play, when Nora's activities have been revealed and she has been confronted by her irate husband, she decides she can no longer live with him. As Ibsen put it in a letter about the play, reported in the introduction to William Archer's translation:

> The wife in the play finds herself at last entirely at sea as to what is right and what wrong; natural feeling on the one side, and belief in authority on the other, leave her in utter bewilderment.

In the same letter, Ibsen remarks:

> A woman cannot be herself in the society of today, which is exclusively a masculine society, with laws written by men, and with accusers and judges who judge feminine conduct from the masculine standpoint.

It is Torvald's inability to understand Nora's needs and motives that leads her to leave him. (Anne-Marie Duff as Nora, New Ambassadors Theatre, January 2000)

Nora is so appalled at her husband's failure to understand her motives and is so torn between her feelings about what she has done and the views of society that she feels she can no longer stay with him. When Torvald remarks that she does not understand society, she agrees and says that one of the reasons for her leaving will be to discover who is right, 'society or I'.

This play caused a sensation among nineteenth-century European audiences. Divorce — especially at the woman's initiation — was a rarity bordering on the unheard of during the era in which Ibsen lived and worked. To make the argument of the play even more controversial to its contemporary audiences, the rationale for Nora's leaving is quite simply that she cannot stand to be with her husband any longer. He is not an adulterer, he is not physically violent; he has a good job and sees to it that Nora lives a luxurious and, so he thinks, insulated existence. It is Torvald's ignorance of his wife's true nature and inability to understand her needs and motives that lead her to leave him at the end, with no clear idea of her destiny.

Miller and Ibsen

Many of Ibsen's plays offer a clear message about how society has become corrupted and damaged by material interest, hypocrisy and bigotry. Miller confronts similar issues with an equal degree of passion and reformist zeal. In 1950, Miller even adapted one of Ibsen's most famous plays, *An Enemy of the People* (1882), the story of one man's struggle to uphold the truth and do the right thing as he sees it against extreme social opposition.

Miller's *The Crucible* also deals with the hypocrisy and crushing oppression that can be visited by one human being on another in the name of so-called 'values'. Just as Ibsen was prepared to incite disapproval from the establishment through the uncompromising nature of the content of his plays, so too was Miller through the uncompromising message of his work, none more so than *The Crucible*.

Naturalism and Shakespeare

Significantly, the second half of the nineteenth century saw the emergence of a new interest in performances of Shakespeare's full texts (as they have come down to us). Shakespeare was approached with a greater seriousness than hitherto. The interest in a scrutinising, critical, less celebratory view of life and society that accompanied naturalism at this time encouraged exploration of some of the more uncomfortable themes and images in Shakespeare's plays.

The famous nineteenth-century actor Henry Irving (1838–1905) was particularly known for performing in productions of Shakespeare's texts which had fallen from favour over the previous century. Irving was most active during the 1870s and 1880s, presenting, for example, a celebrated version of *Hamlet* in 1874.

Nahum Tate's sweetened Shakespeare

The playwright Nahum Tate (1652–1715) produced sweetened and sanitised versions of Shakespeare's plays during the 1680s to please the tastes of the audience of his day (adding, for instance, a happy ending to *King Lear*). These interpretations were preferred to the originals until the end of the eighteenth century. Even as serious and influential an actor as David Garrick (1717–79) favoured many of them over the master material.

Religion

A final point to be made about the cultural influences on the creation of *The Crucible* must be that of Miller's own religious background and the connection he himself makes between this and the world of Salem in the 1690s.

In his childhood, Miller remembered seeing his great grandfather taking part in a strange dancing ritual in the synagogue; this ritual was probably part of the Simchat Torah, celebrating the Lord's gift of the Torah to the people. When researching the witch hunts for *The Crucible*, Miller discovered some sketches in the Historical Society's 'Witch Museum' of the trials and of the hysterical reactions of the judges to the adamant denials of the accused. He wrote in *Timebends* (p. 338):

> Suddenly it became my memory of the dancing men in the synagogue… the same chaos of bodily motion — in this picture the adults fleeing the sight of a supernatural event; in my memory, a happier but no less eerie circumstance — both scenes frighteningly attached to the long reins of God. I knew instantly what the connection was: the moral intensity of the Jews and the clan's defensiveness against pollution from outside the ranks. Yes, I understood Salem in that flash, it was suddenly my own inheritance.

Contemporary influences on Miller

When exploring the cultural context of a piece of work, it is always important to investigate the cultural output of other artists working in the same social and historical context.

Tennessee Williams

Tennessee Williams was a contemporary of Miller. Both playwrights were of equal stature and dominated postwar American theatre. Williams's plays *The Glass Menagerie* (1945), *A Streetcar Named Desire* (1948) and *Cat on a Hot Tin Roof* (1955) were immensely successful — the last two becoming well-known films.

TopFoto

Tennessee Williams (1911–83)

Tennessee Williams was the pseudonym of Thomas Lanier Williams III. He was born in Columbus, Mississippi and is considered by many as one of the most prominent playwrights of the twentieth century. His college friends called him Tennessee because of his southern 'drawl'. He received many theatrical awards during his career as a dramatist, including the Pulitzer Prize for Drama for *A Streetcar Named Desire* (1948) and for *Cat on a Hot Tin Roof* (1955).

It is believed that his family provided him with the seeds of many of the characters in his plays. His father was a travelling salesman and an emotionally absent parent who was violent and abusive; his mother was the puritanical daughter of an Episcopal minister. His beloved elder sister, Rose, suffered from schizophrenia and spent most of her adult life in mental institutions. In 1937, in an effort to control her paranoia, her parents gave permission for a prefrontal lobotomy to be performed. The operation failed, and Rose remained incapacitated for the rest of her life. Williams never forgave his parents for allowing the operation, and Rose's situation perhaps influenced the 'mad heroine' theme that appears in many of his plays.

Tennessee Williams (pictured) and Arthur Miller dominated post-war American theatre

Williams's plays deal less with social issues and focus more on the darker recesses of human nature. Blanche DuBois — the faded southern belle who is the heroine of *A Streetcar Named Desire* — has sexual and romantic fantasies until confronted by the brutality of her brother-in-law, Stanley. In *Cat on a Hot Tin Roof*, Brick has turned to drink and cannot make love to his wife, Maggie, when faced with the confession of homosexuality and subsequent suicide of his best friend. In these plays, Williams explored issues of sexuality and sexual behaviours years before such ideas were a part of the general currency of the theatre. Consequently, his 'provocative' plays were often banned or severely edited.

Clifford Odets

The playwright who most immediately influenced Miller was the lesser known Clifford Odets, whose plays *Waiting for Lefty* (1935) and *Golden Boy* (1937) (later adapted into a film) contained strong socialist messages.

It was this strong flavour of socialism combined with a poet's craft that drew Miller to Odets. Here was a playwright responsible for 'disposing of middle-class gentility, screaming and yelling and cursing like somebody off the Manhattan streets' (*Timebends*, p. 229). The political affinity between Miller and Odets was clear, although in later years Miller would be more critical of Odets, seeing in him something of a contradictory character — one who would avow the cause of socialism (and who was more politically active than Miller) but who was also wooed by Hollywood and the champagne lifestyle.

Clifford Odets (1906–63)

Clifford Odets's earliest professional work was as an actor. After a series of small parts working in the theatre and on radio, he helped found the Group Theatre in New York in 1931 along with director and critic Harold Clurman (1901–80). Members held left-wing political views and wanted to produce plays that dealt with important social issues, for example Odets's first two plays *Awake and Sing!* and *Waiting for Lefty* (both 1935). Indeed, the earlier stages of his career as a playwright saw Odets become a major figure in American protest drama. His works were considered radical, using naturalistic theatre to object to the political situations in the USA. However, in later years he transferred to Hollywood as a writer and director.

Film noir

The mood of tension and pessimism that prevailed in the 1940s and 1950s influenced not only theatre but also cinema, giving rise to a genre of film known as 'film noir'.

Film noir has a melancholic, disillusioned feel. Some of the more successful of such films are adaptations of novels by writers such as Raymond Chandler, James M. Cain and Dashiell Hamett. The plots of these films — for instance

The Big Sleep (Howard Hawks, 1946), *The Asphalt Jungle* (John Huston, 1950), *Key Largo* (John Huston, 1948) and *The Postman Always Rings Twice* (Tay Garnett, 1946) — are dominated by violent crime, and both the hero and the villain characters are flawed, drink-dependent or corrupted. They live in worlds where moral structures have collapsed and been replaced by the bogus family values of the mob.

Although *The Crucible* is entirely different in genre and plot, it is possible to see the links between it and such films, especially when one considers the prevailing national condition of paranoia and suspicion in the aftermath of the Second World War.

Summary

A study of the cultural context of a play explores the society in which the play was written. It examines writers and artists who influenced the style as well as the content of the playwright's work.

However, a successful play is never solely a reflection of its life and times. It would be wrong to assume, for example, that *The Crucible* can only be seen as a reflection of the time of the HUAC and McCarthyism. A production of *The Crucible* was mounted in Shanghai in 1980, where many people seeing it for the first time assumed it to be a reflection of the Cultural Revolution and the purges undertaken by the former Chinese leader, Mao Tse Tung. Apparently, the role of teenagers as accusers was remarkably similar in both societies.

Discussion questions

1 What influences did the writers of Greek tragedy have on the work of Arthur Miller?

2 What are the links between the work of Henrik Ibsen and that of Arthur Miller?

3 What cultural connection is there between Miller's Jewishness and the themes of *The Crucible*?

4 What are the links between other cultural features inherent in 1950s America and *The Crucible*, e.g. film noir?

Essay questions

1 Chapters 1 to 4 complete the study of the context of *The Crucible*, written by Arthur Miller in 1953. In your own words — and using sources other than this book — write context notes for the play.

2 Using Chapters 1 to 4 as a guide, write notes on the contexts of the play(s) you are studying.

Hints

- Only include biographical details relevant to the plays.
- Try to maintain a balance of emphasis between the different sections of the context notes.
- Research the era in which the plays were written, as well as the periods in which the plays are set.
- Explore similarities between the style/genre employed by the playwright and those of other writers or artists he or she studied or was influenced by.

Chapter 5

Using language to bring the play to life

In his renowned work on the training of actors *An Actor Prepares* (1937), Konstantin Stanislavski observes that:

> At the moment of performance the text is supplied by the playwright, and the subtext by the actor... If this were not the case, people would not go to the theatre but sit at home and read the play. We are...inclined to forget that the printed page is not a finished piece of work until it is played on the stage by actors and brought to life by genuine human emotions...

Until the playwright's words are given expression by an actor, the play remains in an incomplete state. Reading the playwright's words can give you some insight into the expected delivery of the language and its meaning, but it is only when the words are spoken, and preferably spoken within the context of a rehearsed reading or performance, that the true meaning of the language can be understood fully. This is why when reflecting on the language of the playwrights you are studying you must always consider the impact the language will make when it is spoken on a stage, rather than the impact it makes on you as a reader.

In all your notes on drama and theatre studies, it is advisable to refer to practical activities you have completed, and your notes on language are no exception. To discuss the words as an end product in themselves is turning a study of drama into a study of literature.

In this chapter we will reflect on the language of Shakespeare and, to a lesser extent, on that of Harold Pinter.

Expressing ideas through language

Arguably, the language employed by a playwright in the expression of ideas is the most important part of the craft. Often the play's language reveals much about the traditions, social fabric and behaviours of its time, as well as the personalities of the characters. This is certainly true of Shakespeare and the writers of Restoration comedies. It is also true of melodrama.

Students (and others) often complain that the language Shakespeare uses is a barrier to understanding ideas and can complicate what may be a relatively simple message or plot line. This attitude fundamentally misunderstands the ways in which Shakespeare — perhaps more than any other playwright — uses the constructs of language to express the motives, thought processes and situations of his characters.

Hamlet

In the analysis of a playwright's use of language, the manner in which ideas are expressed is as important as the content itself. For example in *Hamlet* (*c.* 1600), the king, Claudius, addresses his courtiers, informing them of his recent marriage to Hamlet's mother, Gertrude, and the military ambitions of the young prince of Norway, Fortinbras:

Therefore our sometime sister, now our queen
Th' imperial jointress of this warlike state,
Have we, as 'twere with a defeated joy,
With one auspicious and one dropping eye,
With mirth in funeral and dirge in marriage,
In equal scale weighing delight and dole,
Taken to wife; nor have we herein barr'd

Your better wisdoms, which have freely gone
With this affair along. For all, our thanks.
Now follows that you know young Fortinbras
Holding a weak supposal of our worth,
Or thinking by our late dear brother's death
Our state to be disjoint and out of frame,
Colleagued with this dream of his advantage,
He hath not fail'd to pester us with message
Importing the surrender of those lands
Lost by his father, with all bands of law,
To our most valiant brother…   (I.2.8–25)

Claudius's speech conveys the essence of a prepared 'conference platform' address. It is the approach of a master politician. He conveys not only information but also an unhurried, prepared and statesmanlike impression.

Through the language and structure of this speech, important facets of the king's character are revealed. He begins by talking about his recent marriage to Gertrude, who only a month previously was married to the former king — Claudius's brother, whom he murdered. He then thanks his courtiers for offering him advice ('Your better wisdoms'); it seems that their advice has been given freely and that they therefore support his course of action in marrying Gertrude. Why then do they need to be told about his marriage to Gertrude? They do not, of course, but Claudius is at pains to implicate them in his decision to marry her by pointing out how important the 'advice' was.

He then continues:

Now follows that you know young Fortinbras

iambic pentameter

In English and most European languages, poets create poems with a certain number of syllables in each line to give rhythm and shape. The most common metre is known as iambic pentameter, which is ten syllables a line. Every even syllable in the ten is stressed (i.e. syllables 2, 4, 6, 8 and 10), but poets commonly play with the placing of the stressed syllables to create a distinctive, expressive rhythm.

Again, if his hearers already know about Fortinbras, what is the point in telling them about him? Simply, he is letting them know that not only is he aware of the threatening nature of the international situation but that he is also a strong ruler, and is taking steps to challenge Fortinbras and to deal with him. The speech is structured in iambic pentameter format and is, therefore, 'ordered'.

Contrast the regularity and almost predictable pattern of Claudius's speech with the opening of Hamlet's most famous soliloquy:

To be, or not to be, that is the question:
Whether 'tis nobler in the mind to suffer
The slings and arrows of outrageous fortune
Or to take arms against a sea of troubles,
And by opposing end them? To die, to sleep —
No more — and by a sleep to say we end
The heartache and the thousand natural shocks
That flesh is heir to: 'tis a consummation
Devoutly to be wished. To die, to sleep:
To sleep, perchance to dream: ay there's the rub,
For in that sleep of death what dreams may come
When we have shuffled off this mortal coil
Must give us pause: ...

(III.1.62–74)

The rhythm here is less predictable than in Claudius's speech. The irregularity of the metre indicates a mind in turmoil, a mind considering the benefits and pitfalls of suicide. There is nothing prepared about this; it is a spontaneous reaction to the moment.

The actor's task

The significant feature about the rhythmic feel to both these speeches from *Hamlet* is that they give clues to the actor as to the delivery of the verse. The well-ordered political verse of the opening of I.2 demands a calm, statesmanlike delivery, in contrast to the tumultuous, reflective ruminations of Hamlet's mind in III.1. The actor must use the rhymes of the verse effectively and carefully observe punctuation in the delivery if the interpretation is to bring Shakespeare's writing to life.

By comparing these two speeches, we can see that the distinctive features of the language are visible in the structure of the verse as well as in the content of the words. The actor must observe this; in certain genres of theatre, particularly non-naturalistic theatre, characters sometimes express themselves more through the way their language is constructed than through the specific meanings of the words.

The irregularity of the metre in Hamlet's famous soliloquy indicates a mind in turmoil. (Simon Russell Beale as Hamlet, National Theatre, July 2000)

Romeo and Juliet

One further example from Shakespeare that illustrates a useful point about use of language is a speech given by Lady Capulet in *Romeo and Juliet* (*c.* 1595). This verse seems, superficially, to be an example of inconsistent or even careless writing. When advising her daughter, Juliet, about what an attractive potential husband Paris is, Lady Capulet declares:

Read o'er the volume of young Paris' face,
And find delight writ there with beauty's pen,
Examine every several lineament,
And see how one another lends content
And what obscured in this fair volume lies
Find written in the margent of his eyes.
This precious book of love, this unbound lover,
To beautify him only lacks a cover.   (I.3.62–69)

Some literary critics have commented that this is an example of Shakespeare's early work being clumsy and naïve. After all, it is unclear whether Paris's face is in fact beautiful (although 'writ with beauty's pen') because it needs a 'cover' to 'beautify him'. The metaphors seem awkwardly contrived and the rhyming too obvious. However, this is not the case in performance.

The actor's task

The speech clearly reveals Lady Capulet's superficial concerns as she tries to convince Juliet of Paris's worth: she is attempting to lure Juliet into an arranged marriage with a high-ranking nobleman. From the Capulet family's point of view it would be a triumph and a mark of status, and would perhaps serve to improve their own fortunes as well as their relationship with the Prince.

In performance, it is important for the actor to realise that what, on the page, appears to be unconvincing writing can in fact be rendered effectively on stage, since it is Lady Capulet who is contrived, unconvincing and naïve, not Shakespeare.

This is an important example of the issues Stanislavski discusses in the quotation at the start of this section. The writing cannot be judged as a feature in itself. In this instance the subtext — the private motivations and ambitions of Lady Capulet — have to be explored if the actor is to do full justice to the language.

Hearing different voices

Finally, it is important when exploring the language of a play to remember that a character may not be the writer's mouthpiece.

How often have you heard a quotation introduced with the words 'As Shakespeare once said...'? For instance:

Neither a lender nor a borrower be.

Or from a few lines later in the speech:

To thine own self be true;
And it must follow, as the night the day,
Thou canst not then be false to any man.   (*Hamlet* I.3.78, 81–83)

Shakespeare wrote these lines for the character of Polonius, a skilful politician who later in the play orders a servant to Paris to spy on his son (to whom he has just imparted this advice). These words, combined with his actions, show that Polonius is something of a hypocrite and not completely honest. They cannot be said to represent Shakespeare's personal ideas or opinions.

The work of Harold Pinter

A modern example of the use of complex language and the importance of appropriate delivery is shown in the work of Harold Pinter. Pinter's work made a particular impact in the late 1950s and early 1960s, on television as well as in the theatre.

In one of his most famous plays, *The Birthday Party* (1957), two strange and intimidating visitors arrive at a seaside guesthouse where they meet and proceed to interrogate a permanent resident, Stanley. We cannot be certain what, if any, previous association they may have had, although one is hinted at during the interrogation scene in Act II.

Goldberg: Why did you come here?

Stanley: My feet hurt!

Goldberg: Why did you stay?

Stanley: I had a headache!

Goldberg: Did you take anything for it?

Stanley: Yes.

Goldberg: What?

Stanley: Fruit salts!

Goldberg: Enos or Andrews?

Stanley: En — An —

Goldberg: Did you stir properly? Did they fizz?

Stanley: Now, now, wait, you —

Goldberg: Did they fizz? Did they fizz or didn't they fizz?

McCann: He doesn't know!

Goldberg: You don't know. When did you last have a bath?

Stanley: I have one every —

Goldberg: Don't lie.

McCann: You betrayed the organisation. I know him!

Why should Goldberg want to know about Stanley's health or whether his headache remedy fizzed or not? What seems clear in the structure of this dialogue is that Goldberg is not actually interested in any response Stanley may make to his increasingly absurd questions. Neither do we assume that Goldberg is asking questions

Harold Pinter (1930–)

Harold Pinter is an English screenwriter, actor, director, poet and political activist, although his greatest impact has come from his work as a theatrical playwright. After publishing poetry as a teenager and acting in school plays, Pinter began his theatrical career in the mid-1950s as a rep actor, using the stage name David Baron. He is now considered one of the greatest living playwrights and is a formidable voice in modern drama. His writing is best known for its heavy subtext, alongside careful use of pauses and silences, which have given rise to the term 'Pinteresque'. He was awarded the Nobel Prize for Literature in 2005.

During a writing career spanning over half a century, beginning with his first play *The Room* (1957), Pinter has written 29 stage plays and 26 screenplays. His most famous works are *The Birthday Party* (1957), *The Caretaker* (1959), *The Homecoming* (1964) and *Betrayal* (1978), all of which he has adapted to film.

Despite frail health since 2001, he has continued to act on stage and screen and is very much an active practitioner, writing a screenplay adaptation of Anthony Shaffer's *Sleuth* in 2005.

Goldberg (Henry Goodman) and McCann (Finbar Lynch) interrogate Stanley (Paul Ritter) in a 2005 performance of Harold Pinter's *The Birthday Party*. (Duchess Theatre, London)

of any great significance. The important features here are the relentless pace and rapidity of the questions and the objective of Goldberg and McCann to confuse and intimidate Stanley. It is only at the end of this section of the interrogation that some previous knowledge of Stanley is revealed when 'the organisation' is referred to. We never know what the organisation is or what Stanley's role within it might have been, but of all the lines in this passage it is this one that hints most specifically at the previous association of the three men and the motives behind the interrogation.

This is an example of a text that is almost meaningless without the actor's interpretation giving life to the subtext. It is how the lines are delivered — their pace, their intensity and their conviction — that will translate the playwright's intentions to the audience.

Summary

The playwright's use of language is a vital tool in the dramatic make-up of a play. However, until that language is given a 'voice' by an actor, it remains simply words on a page. In articulating those words vocally, the actor must analyse and use the clues supplied by the playwright. The structure may convey as much as, and sometimes more than, the content. This may be especially true in terms of discovering the intention of a character. A clear example is Claudius's speech in *Hamlet* (I.2.8–25). Knowing that Claudius has killed his brother and married his brother's wife gives us an indication why his language is so carefully structured, political and courtly.

Discussion questions

1 Find a piece of Shakespeare in which you believe the structure of the language conveys as much information about a character as the content.

2 Act out the interrogation scene from *The Birthday Party* by Harold Pinter. What do you discover about the pace of the scene?

Essay question

Identify the vocal challenges for an actor playing either of the following roles:

(a) Stanley in *The Birthday Party*

(b) Claudius in *Hamlet*

Hints

♦ When discussing language, always quote the relevant section of the play.

♦ Consider language from the perspective of the audience (i.e. how it hears the lines) as well as the performer. This is more relevant and important to your studies than simply considering the impact on the reader.

Chapter 6

The language of Berkoff's *Metamorphosis*

In this chapter, we will investigate the ways in which the playwright Steven Berkoff constructs the language of his play *Metamorphosis* (1969). In so doing, all references to the language will be made in the context of possible ways to perform speeches and their impact on an audience.

Steven Berkoff (1937–)

Steven Berkoff was born in the East End of London and initially sought a traditional route into the world of theatre through drama school. However, finding the experience frustrating, he went to Paris and studied mime under Jacques Lecoq. He founded the London Theatre Group in 1968. Berkoff adapted a series of stories by Franz Kafka, most notably *Metamorphosis*. This allowed him to experiment with his ideas of a physically dynamic and verbally highly stylised form of theatre, which he called 'total theatre'. Other works by him include *Greek*, *Decadence*, *East* and *West*. A more overtly political piece entitled *Sink the Belgrano* emerged in the aftermath of the Falklands War.

The short story

The Metamorphosis was written as a short story by Franz Kafka (1883–1924) towards the end of 1912 and first published in a magazine called *Die Weissen Blätter* ('The White Leaves') in October 1915. It tells the story of a travelling salesman, Gregor Samsa, a young man worn down by the tedium of his job and his family's constant need for financial support. One morning he finds that he has been transformed into a gigantic beetle while sleeping in his bed.

The first instincts of his family are to hide the metamorphosis from the neighbours and to attempt to stop Gregor's Chief Clerk — who has arrived at their house to find out why his employee has failed to turn up for work — from spreading the word. Gradually, they learn to cope with Gregor in his altered state, feeding and containing him, but they begin to lose any sense that he was ever their son or brother. When they remove Gregor's belongings from his room, he tries to protest. However, his guttural screams terrify his mother and sister, and his father throws an apple onto his back, wounding him.

When lodgers arrive at the house, they are greeted with fawning enthusiasm by the family, who see them as being able, in part, to make up for the loss of income brought about by Gregor's indisposition. Gregor enters furiously when his sister, Greta, starts playing the violin for their amusement. The lodgers leave hurriedly, refusing to pay and threatening legal action. Greta, who has been the most compassionate of all the family towards Gregor, becomes suddenly deeply resentful stating, 'We must get rid of it!' Gregor, accompanied by his mother, crawls back to his room where he dies.

As the family recover themselves and take stock of their position, the father remarks how much his daughter, Greta, has grown and that it will soon be time to find a husband for her. The family's attention, therefore, is switched to Greta, and it is she who will now be expected to provide and to surrender her spirituality and individuality to the world of toil and duty.

Gregor Samsa awakes one morning to find he has been transformed into a gigantic beetle

The play

Kafka's story was adapted for stage by Steven Berkoff for his London Theatre Group in 1968 and was first performed at the Roundhouse. It was one of three adaptations he made from stories by Kafka, although *Metamorphosis* has emerged as the most famous and the most frequently performed. This is due largely to the daring feats of physical skill demanded of the actors, particularly the central role of Gregor Samsa in his beetle-like state. Celebrated performers who have attempted the role (apart from Berkoff himself) include Mikhail Baryshnikov, Tim Roth and Roman Polanski.

In his introduction to the play, Berkoff says that he came to Kafka on reading *The Metamorphosis*, seeing:

> …in him [Kafka] the most marvellous exertions of the imagination.

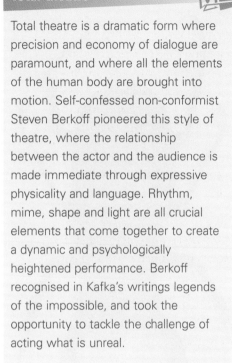

Total theatre

Total theatre is a dramatic form where precision and economy of dialogue are paramount, and where all the elements of the human body are brought into motion. Self-confessed non-conformist Steven Berkoff pioneered this style of theatre, where the relationship between the actor and the audience is made immediate through expressive physicality and language. Rhythm, mime, shape and light are all crucial elements that come together to create a dynamic and psychologically heightened performance. Berkoff recognised in Kafka's writings legends of the impossible, and took the opportunity to tackle the challenge of acting what is unreal.

Berkoff adapted the story using a highly stylised convention, as an example of what he describes as 'the theatre of the impossible' or 'total theatre'. He identifies Gregor's beetle-like transformation as the central idea that helps to define not only the dynamic of his adaptation but also much of his style of theatre:

> …an attitude deliberately taken to expressively show his inner-state, his naked dehumanised personality, a struggling insect.

This sense of exposing and expressing the inner state of humanity is often the hallmark of total theatre, effectively making the subtext of a character the most overt part of staging.

Before exploring the precise nature of the workings of the language in *Metamorphosis*, it is useful to reflect on Berkoff's influences in creating such a work. It is, after all, an artificial exercise to divorce the elements of language from an understanding of the convention as a whole.

Influences on Berkoff

Although Berkoff trained as an actor at a traditional British drama school, he found the lack of discipline frustrating. By the mid-1960s, he had become a reasonably established actor, working for both the Royal Court Theatre and the Royal Shakespeare Company. However, finding these experiences stultifying rather than liberating or challenging, Berkoff opted to continue his training in France.

Under Jacques Lecoq (1921–99), a French actor, mime and acting instructor, Berkoff improved and honed his skills as a mime artist. He combined this practice with a study of the works of playwright, poet, actor and director Antonin Artaud (1896–1948) and the mime artist, actor and director Jean Louis Barrault (1910–94). The philosophies of both Artaud and Barrault challenged the prevailing naturalistic conventions of theatre and set Berkoff on a quest to create a style of theatre which presented performance in an exciting, physical, non-psychological way.

Berkoff's view of naturalistic theatre was scornful. He described it in his introduction to *Metamorphosis* as:

> …a group of people screaming at each other the neurotic obsessions of the writer.

Berkoff's works show the influence of the theories of Artaud (see Chapter 13). We must be wary of assuming that all Artaud's principles were accepted wholesale by Berkoff, or any other practitioner for that matter. However, the links between the 'total theatre' which Berkoff aims to practice and the ideas of Artaud on language and gesture are undoubtedly in evidence. For instance, Artaud's biographer, Bettina Knapp, writes that (after seeing the Balinese Theatre in 1931) he was:

> …absolutely convinced that words are just incapable of expressing certain attitudes and feelings, and that these can be revealed only through gestures or sounds, symbolically felt.

Artaud himself wrote, in the first manifesto of his 'theatre of cruelty', that the combination of music, costume, chanting and gestures is as much a part of a play as the language:

> It runs through our sensibility. Abandoning our Western ideas of speech, it turns words into incantation. It expands the voice. It uses vocal vibrations and qualities, wildly trampling them underfoot… It aims to exalt, to benumb, to bewitch, to arrest our sensibility… Finally it breaks away from the language's intellectual subjugation by conveying the sense of a new, deeper intellectualism hidden under these gestures and signs and raised to the dignity of a special exorcism.

While there is an important narrative element in the language of *Metamorphosis*, there are also examples of Berkoff using words as incantation and chanting rather than ordinary dialogue, and including gesture and imagery following Artaud's ideas. All these elements combine to create the total-theatre impact. However, while Berkoff was clearly influenced by other practitioners and drama theorists, there was and remains something unique about his theatre.

Inevitably, in a style of theatre that seeks to express itself non-naturalistically (often using a chorus at its centre and relying on a focused, energised and highly disciplined ensemble) there are implications for the use of language both in the writing and in the delivery.

The language of total theatre

In what way is the language of *Metamorphosis* consistent with the style of total theatre or theatre of the impossible? It must be remembered that in this style of theatre, the text takes on a specific and unusual role. In a naturalistic style of theatre — for example the theatre of Arthur Miller (see Chapters 1–4) — there is a strong sense of subtlety and psychological realism, and characters are gradually revealed to an audience. This need not be the case in total theatre.

Physical and aural impact

In total theatre, there is a greater sense of immediacy about all aspects of performance. This includes the physical acting style, which relies — to a degree — on stereotype or representational acting.

In this way, Berkoff's theatre has links to the documentary or epic style of theatre of Bertolt Brecht (1898–1956) and shares, on occasion, some of his political ideals. In Berkoff's theatre, we are not interested in the hidden motivations or intellectual and emotional complexities of characters' psyches. We are concerned with their physical and aural impact on us as an audience. The conflicts and traumas of their lives are presented in an energised, physical manner, which is more of an enchantment or assault on the senses than a piece of theatre that evokes curiosity or intellectual debate.

The language in *Metamorphosis* is therefore simultaneously simple and complex: simple in that often the content of the family's contemplations is basic in its domestic nature (for example the scene where the family members argue about who should have the spare potato) but complex in the precise rhythms and poetic structure, requiring careful articulation by the actor.

Addressing the audience

Whether the play is by Shakespeare, Brecht or Berkoff, if a character acknowledges the presence of an audience by addressing it directly, he or she is at that moment acknowledging the essential 'unreality' of the play. This is a fundamental truth of all theatre.

Narration and 'chorus' comment

In the opening moments of the play, the language reminds us not only that we are dealing with a piece of work which is non-realistic but also that it is a piece of absurdity:

Mr S: As Gregor Samsa awoke one morning from uneasy dreams…

Mrs S: He found himself transformed in his bed into a gigantic insect.

Clearly, the absurdity of the play's central event will make an immediate impact on the audience, particularly as the narration is accompanied by the movement of the ensemble into a beetle-like image. However, the nature of the dialogue as narration serves to remind the audience that the actors — in this scene at least — are storytellers and represent the action; they are not impersonators who are trying to create an illusion of reality.

There are a number of other moments in the play when the characters turn to narration. At the height of the action in the first scene, Gregor at last emerges from his room and makes his first frightening appearance as 'the beetle', to the abject terror of his family and the Chief Clerk. The father seizes a brush and attempts to hurl Gregor back into his room. Suddenly, there is a hiatus and Gregor faces the audience:

Gregor: Gregor was quite unpractised in walking backwards and he was afraid of annoying his father even further by the slowness of such a rotation.

Mr S: His father for his part had no intention of making things easier by opening the door — but nevertheless wanted him out of the room as soon as possible.

Coming as it does at one of the most dramatically intense moments in the play, this seems an odd choice of language — suddenly to drop the dialogue and commence narration. No sooner is this exchange over than the character-led dialogue is restored and Gregor's sister, Greta, pleads with her father not to hurt him. However, the sudden dynamic of narration reminds the audience of the representative nature of the action and also provides a potentially comic contrast with the hysteria that has preceded it. It is like a dramatic moment 'in parentheses'. The action is paused while the characters are given an opportunity to comment.

In some respects, this moment reflects part of the traditional role of the chorus in Greek drama, especially in the uniformity of the family's response and the way in which they collectively create images. 'Chorus' is a recurring feature in much of Berkoff's work, and many of his adaptations include Greek tragedies, for example *Agamemnon* (1971) and more recently *Oedipus* (2000).

The role of the chorus in Greek tragedy

The chorus in Greek tragedy is a group of people affected by the action of the play but largely powerless to influence it. They narrate the action and pass comment upon it, helping the audience to follow the performance and showing an ideal reaction to the drama. Sometimes the chorus expresses to the audience what the main characters cannot say — for example, their fears and secrets.

Uniformity of character

Uniformity of character is explored through language in the depiction of the lodgers towards the end of the play. Such is the sense of the three lodgers defining only one character that it is a choice of many productions to have all three played as one by a single actor. However, the original script requires three actors, and through the language we can see how they may be presented, expressing a uniformity of thought and action.

1st L: We'd like to be called at eight o' clock.
2nd L: Prompt!
3rd L: Breakfast hot and ready at eight fifteen!
2nd L: Prompt!
1st L: Coffee, rolls and cheese.
2nd L: Marmalade, if you please.

While the dialogue is given to three characters, there is clearly a sense in which it is the expression of one mind. There is no significance in how the lines are divided between the three lodgers: it is immaterial whether the second lodger says 'prompt' or the first, and there are no subtle differences of motivation to be sought between the three of them. The characterisations are described succinctly by their label: 'Lodger'.

Assuming they are played by three people, there is also an essence of Greek chorus about the lodgers, perhaps even more so than the 'family chorus', since the lodgers possess no distinguishing characteristics.

The pattern of the dialogue, creating a rhyming verse, gives an indication of how a chorus of actors should play this scene. There is no subtlety here and certainly no subtext. The lodgers are presumptuous, rude and overbearing, and while there may be room for interpretation in terms of how that may be presented there are no issues of character interpretation. The swift pace of the dialogue and the volume of delivery alone should emphasise their demanding nature.

The structure of the language at this point is crucial. Accentuation of the rhyme, as well as the repetition of 'Prompt!' by the second lodger, will give the dialogue an insistent feel, while suggesting a uniformity of thought.

There is in this section the potential for humour, and this scene is often cited among Berkoff enthusiasts as a favourite. In the 1987 BBC version, directed by Jim Goddard and starring Steven Berkoff and Tim Roth, the late Gary Olsen performed the lodgers as one individual, using both voice and movement to great comic effect.

The alliance of dialogue and stage direction

An important moment of dialogue which occurs early in the play, and is later repeated with reference to the lodgers, is when the family members 'summarise' the uses Gregor has for them. It is accompanied by an important stage direction:

(A loud ticking is heard which continues throughout the next scene — **Gregor** marches behind his **family** who in time to the ticking call out **Gregor's** meaning for them. Double time for **Gregor** going about his work.)

Greta: Gregor!

Mr S: Cash!

Greta: Gregor!

Mr S: Shoes!

Greta: Gregor!

Mr S: Cigars!

Greta: Gregor!

Mr S: Food!

Greta: Gregor!

Mr S: Beer!

Greta: Gregor!

Mr S: Clothes!

Significantly, later in the play this section of dialogue is repeated but with Mrs Samsa calling out 'Lodgers!' instead of 'Gregor!', while Mr Samsa repeats his need for beer, cash and shoes and Greta expresses her need for clothes, food and books. The character of the dialogue again clearly demonstrates the non-naturalistic quality of the play, particularly in the repetition of the device. What is most important to notice is the way in which the insistence, greed and insensitivity of the family are expressed more by the manner in which the dialogue is structured than by the content of the dialogue itself. There is no explanation of the family's needs here, merely a crude, uncompromising and harsh exposition of them.

The stage directions require rhythmic ticking. This provides a background soundscape to the dialogue, giving it an extra relentlessness and supporting the actors in presenting a uniformity of need, differentiated only by the articles which most appeal to the characters ('beer', 'clothes' and so on). In this way, the audience is left in no doubt as to the meaning that Gregor, and later the lodgers, have for the family. The scene serves to express the truth of Gregor's relationship with his family more succinctly, dynamically and perhaps more accurately than a naturalistic passage of explanatory monologue or dialogue.

Vocal challenge

Later in the play, there is an entire passage which some productions present as almost indecipherable (see the 1987 BBC version). The stage direction for the actor playing Gregor supports this interpretation, reading:

Gregor: (Crying out — a guttural voice — a creature less than a human — his words become less and less distinguishable to them…)

Sir I'm just going to open the door — this very minute…slight illness — an attack of giddiness — kept me in my bed — getting up now — just a moment longer — sudden attack — be as right as rain soon…

Here is an example of where the impact of the sounds made by the actor is more important than the enunciation of the speech itself. Gregor pronounces the words in the way they would be heard by the rest of his family and the Chief Clerk, and as this is the first time the audience has heard Gregor speaking as the beetle, its impact must be terrifying and alarming. It is almost irrelevant whether the specific words are heard or not, although some of them might convey the message that Gregor is trying to deliver.

From an actor's point of view, the implication for the delivery of the language here is one of vocal technique. In order to communicate this guttural assault, exercises in breathing and an exploration of vocal range and projection must be addressed in rehearsal.

As Gregor (Gisli Orn Gardarrson) tries to speak in his metamorphosed state, he startles and terrifies his family. (Lyric Hammersmith, London, October 2006)

Real or surreal?

The possibility that a 'surreal' scene could actually be more reflective and expressive of the truth of a situation than a 'real' scene is the starting point for an interesting debate. In part, this idea sums up the frustration that innovators such as Artaud felt about the theatre of psychological realism. Artaud maintained that in naturalistic theatre, the audience is simply reduced to the role of 'Peeping Toms'. He stated in his first manifesto for the theatre of cruelty, in *The Theatre and Its Double*, that he wanted a theatre where dialogue was not entirely dispensed with but where words took on 'something of the significance they have in dreams'.

Dreams may not be realistic, but neither can they be dishonest: at the very least, they display part of the dreamer's unconscious mind, however disturbing that might be to confront. There is a brusque, almost nightmarish feel to the exchanges between Mr and Mrs Samsa and Greta quoted above, requiring an explosive, insistent delivery from the actors.

Realising the challenges of a play's language

It is vital to consider the challenges contained in the language of a play and how these may be met through rehearsal. You need to be aware of how you address these challenges in your own acting.

The language of the characters

Even in a piece as stylised as *Metamorphosis*, where characters are often part of a chorus or bordering on the stereotyped, language can be revelatory of character. When we explore the words used by the characters, there are some interesting features. While it is important not to try to invest the characters in *Metamorphosis* with any kind of psychological realism, it is possible to examine motives and behaviours through the language, in ways that will help performance.

The Chief Clerk

When the Chief Clerk speaks, his choice of words reflects his status and sense of self-importance. Referring to Gregor's illness, he says:

Whilst I hope it's not serious, I must say that in business one must ignore slight indispositions.

The choice of the expression 'slight indisposition' suggests fussiness and pomposity. We know from the stage directions Berkoff gives around this character that he is a figure of authority:

(**Clerk** moves menacingly in from L… The **family** shrink back on their chairs — freeze in attitudes of fear and oppression by authority represented by the **Chief Clerk**)

The actor playing the Chief Clerk can use both physical stance and posture to enhance the message of the self-consciously ornate language. He can speak with arrogance and influence: the Chief Clerk sees himself as 'high status', and the family members, by their reaction, show that they do too.

Gregor

Metamorphosis is not a play devoid of humanity. Indeed, one of the ironic features is that through his beetle-like state, Gregor once again finds his humanity. Alone in his room, he is left to his thoughts and looks out on the world after he has tried to speak to Greta and succeeded only in frightening her:

Gregor: I won't try to speak again — I know I'm repulsive and I'll go on being repulsive — how brave you are Greta to come here at all… It's growing dimmer — it looks like a desert waste of grey sky and grey land — everything's grey… Everything.

Here the language becomes calm, tranquil and reflective. The mood is clearly sombre and the audience should hear the actor enunciate Gregor's thoughts clearly and simply. Although the play has a distinctly absurdist feel, it would be a mistake to assume that there are no moments that an audience can find genuinely moving. We may not be able to identify with Gregor's literal state but we are able to identify with the feelings of melancholy and isolation this state entails. The text, expressing simple human sentiments, affords an opportunity to engage the audience emotionally.

Greta

Through their intolerance and inability to cope with Gregor's change of form, some members of the family lose their humanity as Gregor regains his. This is particularly true of Greta. When Gregor frightens the lodgers away and the family are thrown into anxiety as to how they might manage financially, Greta says with a simple yet ruthless conviction:

We must get rid of it.

This line is calculated to make a considerable impact on the audience, since it is Greta who throughout the play has pleaded on behalf of Gregor and, in the early stages of the play, struggled to come to terms with his altered state. Its delivery requires the actor to command the audience's attention, in order to convey the significance of what is being revealed about Greta.

Mrs Samsa

It is his mother who is with Gregor in his final moments. In this scene she is not a member of the 'family chorus' but an individual who shares with us surely the most touching moment of the play:

Mrs S: He looked at me — just as we closed the door — he turned his head — his eyes — Gregor's eyes, full of agony, looked at me in a way only a child looks at his mother as if to say — no more — no more pain… Be free, my little boy…free…free.

In his introduction to the play, Berkoff claims that audiences never fail to be moved when *Metamorphosis* is performed. It is clearly possible, and desirable, for the final moments of the play, as Gregor dies, to be delivered in a way that evokes an emotional response from the audience. Certainly the language in the final scene — touching, simple and sincere — helps to arouse such a reaction. Perhaps one of the reasons for the play's continued success is the depths of humanity explored within it.

Summary

In *Metamorphosis*, Berkoff uses a diverse range of dynamics of language to create a multi-faceted impact on his audience.

The play is undoubtedly surreal in many respects, and this is reflected in the Artaudian enthusiasm for incantation and chorus work, where the sound of the words is often more important than the content. In places, precise comprehension of the language is unnecessary; the essential role of Gregor's guttural screams is to reflect his desperate attempts to express himself. The discordant and disturbing sounds achieved by an effective performance would be sufficient to convey his state of mind and startle the audience.

Berkoff demands the use of rhythm and beats in some of his stage directions, and this stylised approach dictates how the actors deliver their lines and serves to further detach the onstage performance from reality.

However, there is a degree of interplay between surrealism and realism. Gregor's incomprehensible predicament must coexist with authentic and sentimental relationships between the characters. The use of reflective and sombre language, as Gregor contemplates his fate and his mother mourns his passing, leaves the audience with the feeling that although absurdist in many aspects, the play also, ironically, deals with central human emotional experience.

Discussion questions

1 What features of the language remind an audience that *Metamorphosis* is non-naturalistic?

2 What rehearsal techniques might you employ to assist a cast in meeting the challenges of the language in *Metamorphosis*?

3 What responses might the audience give to the differing uses of language in *Metamorphosis*?

Essay questions

1 When you have addressed the discussion questions, use the information in this chapter, together with your own research, to write language notes for Berkoff's *Metamorphosis*.

2 Focusing on the principal aspects of language covered in Chapters 5 and 6, complete notes on the play(s) you are studying.

Group activity

Reflect on your own work on bringing language to life in a play. Discuss roles that you have performed, comparing the vocal techniques you used and the challenges you encountered.

Hints

◆ Observe the structures of language in a play as well as the content of the words. Sometimes what a character says is less important than how it is said.

◆ The language of a play is meant to be spoken, not read. Most judgements about a play's language can only be made once it has been recited and heard.

◆ The playwright's language does not necessarily express his or her point of view. Make judgements about the character before making judgements about the playwright.

◆ When writing about the playwright's language, it is vital that you quote it, with scene references if you have the text in front of you. You must be specific about the point you are making and clear about its relevance to the text.

Chapter 7

The structure of Marlowe's *Doctor Faustus*

The purpose of this chapter is to discuss how a play's structure can influence the impact it has on its audience. The structure involves:

- the plot and subplot, and how both are revealed to the audience
- the balance of moments of dramatic intensity and moments of reflection, which serves to heighten the impact of key moments
- the setting of the action
- the way the playwright changes the focus on different characters

The setting of a play does not just provide a backdrop to the performance; it can and should influence the pace of the action and how the action is perceived by an audience.

The plot and subplot

On a simple level, the plot tells the main story of a play. A subplot is a secondary storyline — a subordinate or auxiliary strand of the main plot. Subplots may connect to main plots in time, place or in thematic significance. They can flesh out a story in a number of ways, placing the characters in context and allowing the plot to gain dimension and complexity. They can deepen characterisation by exploring a character's desires, relationships, vulnerabilities or growth, and provide a subtext to people's opinions and actions.

A theatrical plot can have different levels of significance. There are some plays, for example melodramas, where the plot is probably the most important feature. In a play like *Black-eyed Susan* (1829) by Douglas Jerrold (1803–57), a typical nineteenth-century English melodrama, there are adventures galore involving

There is virtually no plot in Samuel Beckett's *Waiting for Godot*. (Alan Howard and Ben Kingsley, The Old Vic, 1997)

impossibly heroic sailors and nasty villains, together with stoical damsels in distress. The plot gathers pace relentlessly, and there is almost a sigh of relief as all its strands are brought together and we reach an inevitably happy solution.

Conversely, there are some plays — particularly plays of an absurdist or expressionistic genre — where there is virtually no plot. In *Waiting for Godot* (1952) by Samuel Beckett (1906–89), two tramps wait by a tree for the arrival of Godot. Two other travellers, Pozzo and Lucky, pass by, but Godot fails to appear. At the end of the second act, a boy arrives and tells them that Mr Godot cannot come this evening but if they come back the next night he surely will. Essentially, that is the plot. There are no other events during the two acts of the play. At the time of its first performances, critic Vivian Mercier declared it to be the only play in existence where nothing happens twice.

Hamlet: lack of plot

In some of Shakespeare's plays, the plots are clearly not the most important feature of the drama. In *Hamlet* at the end of Act I, Hamlet knows that his father has been murdered. He asks the ghost of the murdered king to inform him as quickly as possible of the identity of the murderer:

Haste, haste me to know't, that I with wings as swift
As meditation or the thoughts of love
May sweep to my revenge.   (I.5.33–35)

The scene is set near the close of the first act, as though this were the plot for a revenge tragedy. Four acts later, however, Hamlet is still agonising over the manner, the methods, the justification and the means of his revenge. He has not taken any action at all. In a sense, the plot of the most celebrated play of all time collapses after the first act. This is not a defect of authorship. Some plays are dominated less by plot than by character or theme, and it is often the character or the theme that serves to manipulate the plot.

Revenge tragedy

Revenge tragedy was extremely popular in Elizabethan and Jacobean England. The most famous example is *The Spanish Tragedy* (*c.* 1590) by Thomas Kyd (1558–94). Its plot involves several violent murders, and one of its characters is a personification of Revenge. It has a 'play within a play' device, which is used to trap a murderer, and also a ghost intent on vengeance. Shakespeare uses both these elements in *Hamlet*. Thomas Kyd is often suggested as being the author of an original 'Hamlet' story that Shakespeare may subsequently have adapted.

Doctor Faustus

As a specific example of how the structure of a play works, we will examine Christopher Marlowe's *Doctor Faustus*, written in 1592. You may study this text for Unit 4, although the specific content of this section will be most useful for the completion of Unit 1.

Two versions of *Doctor Faustus* exist, one published in 1604 (known as text A), and the other — a longer version with a comic subplot, now generally held to be the original — published in 1616 (known as text B).

Text B is the version in common usage. The scholar J. B. Steane offers the explanation that the shorter version might have been a more manageable alternative used for touring or by 'a company with fewer resources', as text B is 'notably more spectacular'. Interestingly, Steane views text A as superior as it has:

> …everything essential to the presentation of the tragical history; the B text adds, for the most part, light simple-minded comedy, innocuous enough except that it distracts the mind from what is serious and valuable in the play; or rather it fails to occupy the mind at all.
>
> (*Christopher Marlowe: The Complete Plays*, 1969)

Steane's comments are purely a judgement on the text; the success of the comedy, or indeed any other feature of this play, is dependent, at least in part, on how it is realised by actors, designers and directors. Furthermore, the predominantly comic additional material of text B affects the audience's perception of

Christopher Marlowe (1564–93)

Christopher Marlowe was born in Canterbury in 1564 (the same year as Shakespeare), the son of a shoemaker. He received his early education at The King's School in the city, continuing his studies at the University of Cambridge at the age of 17. He received a bachelor of arts degree in 1584 and a master of arts degree in 1587.

Shortly after receiving his master's degree, Marlowe went to London, where he became known for his radical, bohemian ways and unorthodox thinking.

Marlowe's career as a poet and dramatist spanned only 6 years. Between his graduation from Cambridge and his death in 1593 he wrote only one major poem (*Hero and Leander*, unfinished at his death) and six or seven plays (one play, *Dido Queen of Carthage*, may have been written while he was still a student). Moreover, since the dating of several plays is inconclusive, it is impossible to construct a reliable history of Marlowe's intellectual and artistic development.

the play by providing a subplot to accompany the main plot and influencing the intensity of the audience experience.

Here then is the first important consideration for our understanding of the structure of *Doctor Faustus*: its tragic plot and comic subplot. The two extremes of emotion should be seen not separately but as part of the whole audience experience: the enjoyment of one will affect the horror of the other, and vice versa. This is the balance to be achieved between the dramatic elements that help shape the overall structure of the play.

Main plot

The main plot of *Doctor Faustus* is motivated by the arguments and state of mind of the eponymous character.

The significance of Wittenberg

Doctor Faustus is a scholar, and it is significant that the opening scene takes place in his study at the University of Wittenberg. Wittenberg was not only one of the most famous universities in the world and certainly the most famous in Germany; it was also the place where Martin Luther (1483–1546) had taught. Luther was a theologian and in his early days an Augustinian friar. However, he rebelled against the hierarchy of the Roman Catholic Church and felt that individual worship of God could be justified by faith alone, without the need of a priestly system mediating between men and God. This led, inevitably, to a break between Luther and the Church, and the foundations of Protestantism were laid. For many people in those days, Luther was a heretic. By placing Faustus in Wittenberg, Marlowe chose not only a famous seat of learning but also a place where faith, religion and belief were the subject of considerable questioning and scrutiny.

At the opening of the play, Faustus contemplates the world of academia and the various branches of learning. One by one, he rejects logic, medicine, law and finally divinity in favour of magic. He arrives at the conclusion that:

The metaphysics of magicians
And necromantic books are heavenly;
Lines, circles, letters, and characters;
Ay, these are those that Faustus most desires.   (I.1)

The significance of the good and bad angels

Faustus is visited by a good angel and a bad angel, the former desperately attempting to dissuade Faustus from his pursuit of magic, the latter gleefully encouraging it. To an audience in the 1590s, the presence of these spirits would be a reminder that Faustus's contemplations were no mere mind game, for heaven and hell were realities to the Elizabethans. Such presence would undoubtedly reinforce in the audience the feelings of tension that Faustus's dangerous arguments were building.

The move towards magic

Faustus reflects on how he will use his powers gained through magic. His ambitions are self-aggrandising and violent, and even at this early stage in the plot, the audience is thus alerted to the fact. Here he expresses his ambition to create new weapons of war:

Yea, stranger engines for the brunt of war,
Than was the fiery keel at Antwerp bridge,
I'll make my servile spirits to invent.   (I.1)

He is visited by Valdes and Cornelius, two scholars in magic who are only too delighted to encourage Faustus's pursuits in 'magic and the concealed arts'. At the end of the scene, Faustus triumphantly invites them to dine with him, vowing that:

This night I'll conjure, though I die therefore.   (I.1)

The next scene offers us an insight into the reputation of Faustus within the wider community of the university. When Wagner, Faustus's manservant, is approached by two scholars from the university, he informs them that his master is at dinner with Cornelius and Valdes — well known as dabblers in magic. The response by the first scholar reveals to the audience the fact that Faustus's frustrations with more legitimate areas of study and his growing interest in magic have been the subject of rumour about the university:

O Faustus,
Then I fear that which I have long suspected,
That thou art fall'n into that damned art
For which they two are infamous through the world   (I.2)

The relationship with Mephistophilis

As we move into the third scene, we see Faustus begin to conjure the presence of Mephistophilis, and to do so unaware of the presence of Lucifer and four devils. He begins his incantations and Mephistophilis appears in the shape of a dragon. Faustus dispatches him and requests that he appear in the form of a friar. This Mephistophilis does, giving the audience the impression that he is under Faustus's control. So begins a dialogue between Faustus and Mephistophilis about the nature of hell and damnation. It will strike an audience that during this scene two pieces of information emerge that are vital to the plot and Faustus's role within it.

First, Mephistophilis identifies hell not as a place but as the absence of God:

Faustus:
How comes it then thou art out of hell?
Mephistophilis:
Why, this is hell, nor am I out of it.
Think'st thou that I, that saw the face of God
And tasted the eternal joys of heaven,
Am not tormented with ten thousand hells
In being deprived of everlasting bliss?   (I.3)

To an audience, this part of the plot will seem startling: Mephistophilis sees his own existence as hell, and instead of encouraging Faustus to ally himself with Lucifer, as he might be expected to do, he is warning him *not* to do so.

Second, the audience soon realises that Faustus is not the standard tragic hero. Although in full the play is called *The Tragical History of the Life and Death of Doctor Faustus*, the protagonist's status is quickly called into question. As was discussed previously, the tragic hero is a victim of his own character flaws combined with fate. His destiny is often sealed even at his birth and there is nothing that he can do to escape it.

In the case of Faustus, the situation is clearly different. He is offered a number of opportunities during the play to avert the course of his destiny and to control his relationship with Mephistophilis. He is continually given warnings of the consequences of his actions, initially by Mephistophilis himself:

Mephistophilis (Jake Maskall) is summoned by the experimental necromancy of Faustus (Scott Handy). (Hampstead Theatre, London, October 2006)

Mephistophilis: O Faustus, leave these frivolous demands,
                    Which strikes a terror to my fainting soul.   (I.3)

As we have seen, Proctor in *The Crucible* tries his utmost to avert his destined fate and only embraces it when he realises that the sacrifice of his life means the restoration of his good name and his integrity. With Faustus, the opposite is true. He is knowingly sacrificing his life and his good name in return for earthly pleasure, fame and wealth.

Faustus asks Mephistophilis to put to Lucifer an agreement whereby he will enjoy unlimited power and fame for 24 years, at the end of which time Lucifer will receive his soul. Mephistophilis agrees and the scene ends with Faustus predicting how he will use his new-found powers to change geographical features of the world.

Subplot

A contrasting perspective

The next scene, which shows how Wagner recruits the clown Robin to his service, contrasts sharply with the theological debate of the previous scene but, echoes some of the momentous events of the play. In seeking Robin's service, Wagner remarks that he is so poor that he will sell his soul to the devil:

…for a shoulder of mutton, though it were blood raw.   (I.4)

Wagner has to coerce Robin into his (and thereby Lucifer's) service by conjuring two devils (Banio and Belcher) to torment him. The audience is therefore shown that even though Robin is a simple-minded, poverty-stricken clown, he refuses Wagner's money when he understands the condition on which the gift is based. This is that:

Wagner: …at an hour's warning whensoever and wheresover the devil
            Shall fetch thee…   (I.4)

Scholars sometimes criticise the comic subplot as a distraction from the main narrative, yet there are unmistakable links to aspects of the main themes of the play that stand scrutiny and create interesting highlights to the plot. If Faustus's intellectual greatness leads him to the appalling errors of judgement that it does, then the audience may feel that intellectual simplicity and a healthy fear of God is the better state of mind. Faustus and Robin may be poles apart academically, but faced with the same choice it is the academic who takes the wrong turn. For an audience, the irony of this moment, as well as its comic potential, should be clear.

Main plot

The moment of choice

At the beginning of the second act, we find Faustus in his study, expressing serious doubts about his actions. As he ruminates about his fate, the good angel and the bad angel once again appear, in order to affirm or thwart his doubts. However, having heard both, it is the bad angel's temptation of wealth that Faustus considers further. He invites Mephistophilis to bring him news from Lucifer. It is important to recognise that this is a moment when the plot is driven by Faustus's character.

Loss of control over Mephistophilis

Mephistophilis informs Faustus that Lucifer has agreed to his terms and that now Faustus must sign the pact in his own blood. Faustus once again asks Mephistophilis about hell, and although Mephistophilis makes no attempt to suggest that his hell is anything other than a place of suffering, torture and torment, Faustus arrogantly chooses to dismiss his warnings as 'mere old wives' tales'.

At the end of the scene, Mephistophilis promises to bring Faustus courtesans. At this point, the audience understands that for all his grand and worldly ambitions, Faustus is vulnerable: Mephistophilis is now pandering to his lust.

Subplot

Interlude

The following scene shows the two clowns, Robin and Dick, making mischief with one of Faustus's conjuring books.

This is the kind of subplot interlude that cannot be said to move the main plot along. However, there is a sense in which — like the previous scene from the subplot — it reflects in comic mood upon events and issues from the serious main narrative.

The use of humour in a tragedy can provide a stark contrast to the grievous decline and demise of the central character. It could be said that the clowning and childish conjuring of Robin and Dick mirror to some extent the vain and ultimately pointless conjuring of Faustus, or his behaviour in preferring courtesans to matters of destiny.

It is a matter for individual perception as well as directorial intention as to whether the use of humour makes the events of the main plot more or less terrible.

Main plot

Consequences of loss of control

At the start of the following scene, the audience is made aware that Faustus is feeling some loss of control over events: we see him, yet again, doubting his actions and resorting to blaming Mephistophilis for his fate. Mephistophilis appropriately and accurately retorts:

'Twas thine own seeking Faustus. Thank thyself.　　　　　　　(II.1)

On Faustus declaring that he will repent, the angels appear to him once more; yet again it is the bad angel's advice he eventually follows, dismissing the option of repentance. This choice is becoming a repetitive feature of the plot, determined in large measure by the dilemmas and constant mind-changing of Faustus. On such occasions the angels appear, and with every encounter, it is the bad angel who is the more persuasive and influential.

Faustus and Mephistophilis resume their discussion about astrology and the nature of hell. Mephistophilis, however, will not tell Faustus who made the world. Dissatisfied with this lack of response, Faustus once again doubts the course of his actions and dismisses the devil. With the good and bad angels once again in attendance, he cries out:

O Christ, my Saviour, my Saviour
Help to save distressed Faustus' soul!　　　　　　　　　　(II.1)

However, his appeal to the heavens results only in the return of Mephistophilis, Lucifer and Beelzebub. They inform him that because Christ is just, he has no interest in Faustus's soul, and that his cries to Christ cause them injury. In fear, Faustus asks their pardon, and as a reward for his renewed faith Lucifer conjures an image and parade of the Seven Deadly Sins, at the end of which Faustus declares that:

...this sight does delight my soul.　　　　　　　　　　　　(II.1)

Lucifer promises to show Faustus other delights from hell, and the scene ends with Faustus expressing gratitude to him. Faustus has now clearly lost control of his destiny and the plot is at a crossroads.

Moving the setting

At what is roughly the halfway point in the play, the chorus enters to describe the physical journey Faustus takes to see the wonders of the world, equipped by Lucifer with the ability to fly. This dramatic device is used to move the plot on and to inform the audience of events that would be difficult to stage.

At the start of the third act we are informed by the chorus that Faustus is now in Rome:

To see the Pope and manner of his court,
And take some part of holy Peter's feast,
The which this day is highly solemnised.

(III.2)

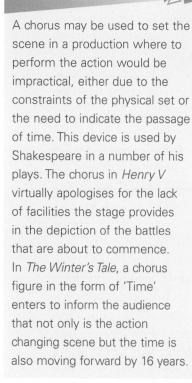

Using the chorus to set a scene

A chorus may be used to set the scene in a production where to perform the action would be impractical, either due to the constraints of the physical set or the need to indicate the passage of time. This device is used by Shakespeare in a number of his plays. The chorus in *Henry V* virtually apologises for the lack of facilities the stage provides in the depiction of the battles that are about to commence. In *The Winter's Tale*, a chorus figure in the form of 'Time' enters to inform the audience that not only is the action changing scene but the time is also moving forward by 16 years.

Why should such a device as the 'explanatory chorus' be necessary? Doesn't an audience expect that the location of a play may change as the plot develops? In fact, the application of Aristotle's three unities (see Chapter 4) was a crucial and much-used feature of Elizabethan drama. The setting of a play was rarely altered substantially and therefore an explanation from the chorus that the scene is now set in Rome was important to the audience's understanding.

The task of scene setting and informing the audience of events happening offstage continues into the substance of the scene as Faustus and Mephistophilis begin their dialogue. Not only does Faustus recount their travels but he also prompts Mephistophilis to explain where they are in Rome — the pope's privy chamber. Mephistophilis then informs Faustus about the splendour of Rome and its magnificent buildings and monuments. Thus, in the first speeches of Act III there is a substantial amount of information for an audience to assimilate. It is clear from the careful descriptions offered by both characters, as well as by the chorus, that Marlowe is making quite sure his audience fully understands the new location.

To a modern audience, used to the fast-moving experiences of film and television, this process may appear laborious. The level of reinforcement provided by Marlowe serves to remind us of how unfamiliar a sixteenth-century audience would have been with the notion of a play that shifts time and place so radically.

The significance of the popes

Faustus and Mephistophilis now witness the haranguing and trial of a rival pope, Bruno. This is not so absurd a situation as it might appear to a modern audience. For a period of about 40 years between the late fourteenth and early fifteenth centuries, there were two popes ruling simultaneously from different parts of Europe. The encounter between the two popes in this scene has no equivalent episode in history, but an informed contemporary audience would have been aware of the reference; even the less educated spectators might have heard about it.

Pope Adrian treats his rival, Bruno, violently, and he aspires to and enjoys power — like Faustus. Here is another echo of the main plot.

Bruno: Pope Adrian, let me have some rights of law:
I was elected by the Emperor.

Pope: We will depose the Emperor for that deed,
And curse the people that submit to him.   (III.2)

Later, when challenged again by Bruno, the Pope declares:

Is not all power on earth bestowed on us?
And therefore though we would we cannot err.   (III.2)

Pope Adrian is a character filled with hubris — abusing the principle of papal infallibility by believing he can do no wrong and aspiring to absolute power. It is not difficult, in plot terms, to see the similarities between the pope's arrogant rhetoric and Faustus's earlier rampant ambitions. The audience is likely to be aware of the significance of Bruno calling the pope 'Proud Lucifer'. However arrogant, corrupt and power-crazed Faustus himself may seem at points in the play, the depiction of a pope behaving equally tyrannically will surely leave its mark on an audience by casting doubt on the justice of the Roman Catholic Church: where therefore does virtue lie?

The significance of the Roman Catholic Church

The sacrilegious nature of Faustus's assault on and ridicule of the most senior member of the Christian Church was not necessarily offensive to the play's contemporary audience. The Roman Catholic Church was not publicly revered in Elizabethan England. Queen Elizabeth's father, Henry VIII, had declared himself head of the Church in England, disestablishing himself and the country from the authority of the Catholic Church in order to grant himself a divorce from his then wife, Catherine of Aragon. He plundered the monasteries and outlawed the practising of the Catholic religion. Although Catholicism was briefly restored during the reign of Elizabeth's sister Mary during the 1550s, by the time *Doctor Faustus* was written some 40 years later it was a discredited and outlawed religion once again. The ridiculing of the Pope would therefore have found easy favour with most people in contemporary audiences.

Descent into chaos

Disguised, Faustus and Mephistophilis purport to be two cardinals representing the synod of 'priests and prelates' bringing judgement on the emperor and Bruno and they declare that Bruno should be burned to death. The pope orders them to be taken to prison and announces a banquet in honour of St Peter's Feast.

During the banquet scene, Mephistophilis ensures that both he and Faustus are made invisible so they can work their mischief. It becomes clear that the previous judgement on Bruno and the emperor has been brought by impostors and that the two prisoners have, in fact, escaped. In the confusion that ensues, Faustus (still invisible) speaks to the pope and snatches his food away. In his fear, the pope crosses himself and, unseen, Faustus violently assaults him. He and Mephistophilis fling fireworks at the assembled friars and make their escape. At the end of the scene, the chorus enters once more to advise that Faustus makes his way home from Rome and impresses his 'friends and nearest companions' with his learned skill in astrology. He is now, the chorus informs us, at the palace of the Emperor Carolus the Fifth.

There is a sense of chaotic futility in Faustus's actions, which the audience, while enjoying the pope's discomfiture, will not have missed. Faustus has sold his soul in order to achieve fame, wealth and immeasurable power, and yet he chooses to squander it in practical jokes and fireworks. Compared to the megalomaniac aspirations of world domination he expressed at the opening of the play, his antics in these scenes seem childish.

An invisible Faustus (Scott Handy) and Mephistophilis (Jake Maskall) play a practical joke on the Pope (Jason Morell) by snatching his food

TopFoto

Subplot

Reinforcing the message of chaos

The foolery of Rafe and Robin in the next scene reinforces rather than contrasts with the theme of the previous scene: the audience understands that for all his intellectual greatness, the entertainment Faustus finds in magic is broadly similar to the behaviour of the clown-like characters in the play. In this scene, Robin steals a goblet from a vintner and attempts to use magic from a conjuring book stolen from Faustus to get away with it. His tricks go wrong and instead he conjures Mephistophilis, who turns Rafe and Robin into a dog and an ape respectively.

Main plot

Reinforcing the message of self-delusion

Faustus is now at the court of the German emperor and his guest, the newly-freed (other) pope, Bruno. The emperor requests to see a vision of Alexander the Great and his 'paramour'. Faustus creates this image and the emperor is suitably impressed. Faustus then punishes a doubting courtier, Benvolio, by having horns placed on his head, and only after the emperor's intervention is his normal appearance restored.

What is important to note here is that Faustus's vanity is developing. He is using magical powers to show off to great and influential people and is scornful of any doubt cast on his abilities. Yet they are not abilities that have been achieved through industry and learning; they stem only from gifts given to him by Lucifer. Therefore his proud rebuke to Benvolio, 'And hereafter, sir, look you speak well of scholars', is ironic. At the outset of the play, Faustus rejects the traditional aspects of scholarship; now he defends and celebrates his actions as being those of a scholar.

The inevitable delayed

The action becomes darker in the ensuing scenes, as Benvolio and his companions seek their revenge on Faustus. They think they have killed him, but because he has an agreement with Lucifer to remain on earth for 24 years he rises again and wreaks terrible revenge on his attackers:

Faustus: Go, horse these traitors on your fiery backs,
           And mount aloft with them as high as heaven;
           Thence pitch them headlong to his lowest hell.   (IV.3)

There is a clear sense that Faustus enjoys the violent exercise of the power that has been given to him. He is evidently not disposed to be merciful, as is obvious when soldiers in support of the courtiers try to arrest him:

Faustus: Then Faustus, try thy skill. Base peasants, stand!

For lo, these trees remove at my command,

And stand as bulwarks twixt yourselves and me,

To shield me from your hated treachery.

Yet, to encounter this your weak attempt,

Behold an army comes incontinent.

(**Faustus** strikes the door, and enter a devil playing on a drum; after him another bearing an ensign; and divers with weapons; **Mephistophilis** with fireworks. They set upon the soldiers and drive them out.)   (IV.3)

These moments do not offer the dramatic intensity expected from pivotal moments in other tragedies: Lear's madness in *King Lear*, and the deaths of Polonius and Ophelia in *Hamlet*, for example. They rely instead on engaging the audience's attention with staging and special effects. The tension comes from the audience's knowledge that Faustus's inevitable fate is only being delayed by such distractions.

It is interesting to note from a structural point of view that the heart of the play, Act IV, depicts Faustus at his most self-indulgent, least self-doubting and most vain, and the action is more that of a fantasy or comedy than a tragedy. The tension that is developed on stage surrounds the wonder of the visions and the impressive quality of Faustus's magic tricks. If we consider the plots of other well-known tragedies, their fourth acts often show us the depth of the tragic action. In *Antony and Cleopatra* (Shakespeare, *c.* 1607) and *The Duchess of Malfi* (John Webster, 1614), both Antony and the Duchess meet their respective deaths in Act IV, while the remaining act resolves the rest of the action. In *Julius Caesar* (Shakespeare, 1599), the war between the forces of Brutus and Antony is at its height, and in *Romeo and Juliet* the (apparently) dead body of Juliet is discovered on the morning of her wedding. By contrast, the fourth act of *Doctor Faustus* shows a character drunk with arrogance but using his magical powers simply to have fun.

Descent into farce

The mood of mischief continues through Act IV, as Faustus encounters a horse courser who, feeling that Faustus has tricked him in the sale of his horse, pulls at his leg until it comes off. Seeing Faustus subsequently with two healthy legs, the courser assumes the other leg to be false.

The action here is almost farcical — physical humour involving clowns and tricks. Faustus impresses yet more high-ranking friends as he provides visions of castles in the air for the Duke of Vanholt, much to the latter's delight. Faustus renders the horse courser and the other clowns dumb before the duke and duchess, who declare at the end of the scene and the end of Act IV:

Lady: My lord,
We are much holding to this learned man.

Duke: So we are, madam, which we will recompense
With all the love and kindness that we may.
His artful sport drives all sad thoughts away.   (IV.7)

Here then, at the end of the penultimate act, we have a testimonial to Faustus. It is almost as if he has sunk to the status of court jester or entertainer, little more than a circus clown himself. For all his intellectual curiosity about magic, he uses it ultimately to impress powerful friends. He does not even aspire to great heights of power in these actions, to bring about military victories or to break new ground in academic research. He has become a social climber, a corporate magician. He provides tricks for the rich and the powerful who are duly impressed. At this stage of the play, the tragedy is less to do with a tortured conscience than with a pathetic spectacle of lost opportunity.

The final choice

The final act changes in tone and content from the outset. Wagner informs us that he believes his master will die soon since he has made a will in his favour. There is implicit in this monologue the idea of time passing and the suggestion that Faustus's 24 years are almost up.

A group of scholars emerges with Faustus from his study, discussing the world's most beautiful woman. They have decided, on the basis of their research, that Helen of Troy is the most beautiful woman in history and they request Faustus to conjure her image, which he duly does. As the scholars marvel at her presence, Faustus is visited by an old man who warns him:

Oh gentle Faustus, leave this damned art,
This magic that will charm thy soul to hell.   (V.1)

Faustus has not been given a warning over his choice for some time, and this is the most personal and lengthy. The old man speaks to Faustus as a friend and assures him that his exhortation is not made in anger but:

in tender love,
And pity of thy future misery.   (V.1)

Chastened, Faustus bemoans his fate and prepares to die so hell can claim his soul. The old man, however, reassures Faustus by telling him that it is not too late and that he should 'call for mercy'.

Alone, Faustus expresses his dilemma: should he turn towards the forces of good or continue to give in to the temptations of the forces of hell? Mephistophilis rebukes him as a traitor and threatens to tear his flesh. Immediately, Faustus repents and reaffirms his vow to Lucifer.

Here, in the final act, the plot returns to the torments and temptations of Faustus, with the tension increasing as the hour of his doom approaches. Increasingly the audience sees a man who appears incapable of choosing his fate but instead capitulates on each occasion to his worst fear. He fears Lucifer and eternal damnation and wants to heed the words of the old man, but in turn he also fears the vengeance of Mephistophilis. Faustus is now trapped and out of control of his own destiny. He tries to regain some control at the last moment by asking Mephistophilis to bring him Helen of Troy as a mistress, and fleetingly we hear Faustus attempt to invoke his former bravado:

Instead of Troy shall Wittenberg be sacked,
And I will combat with weak Menelaus,
And wear thy colours on my plumed crest…   (V.1)

It is his final hurrah; a piece of magic not designed to impress anyone or entertain some crowned head of Europe. Nor is it mischievous or violent. Instead, we see a weak, frightened and vulnerable man approaching death, trying to find some comfort in a kind of synthetic love by taking as a lover a legend, a vision. As Faustus exits with his love, the old man reappears and declares Faustus 'Accursed'.

The denouement

It is clear in the final scenes that whatever opportunities Faustus may have had for redemption have now been lost. Mephistophilis appears to take no pleasure in the forthcoming fate of Faustus. Scholars gather to speak with Faustus and he informs them of his pact with the devil. They express sympathy and exhort him to 'call on God'. However, Faustus believes that he is beyond forgiveness and can no longer turn to God to repent. The scholars leave, assuring him that they will pray for him, and Faustus is left to his fate. The good angel and bad angel appear, but not, this time, to attempt to persuade him away from or into the path of righteousness. It is clear from the words of both that Faustus's fate is sealed. As he is left alone, we hear his final agonies as he prepares for hell. As midnight strikes, the devils appear to take him to eternal damnation.

In the final scene, the scholars who had offered Faustus some comfort the previous evening find his severed limbs and give him a Christian burial. The chorus appears in the epilogue and advises those who are curious only to:

…wonder at such unlawful things,
Whose deepness doth entice such forward wits,
To practise more than heavenly power permits.   (V.4, epilogue)

Summary

Doctor Faustus is not plot-led; there is no involved, episodic story. Contrast the plot of this play with the developing and tense storyline of *The Crucible*. Instead of a progressive narrative, the audience is offered a series of vignettes — individual moments where new characters join Faustus for a brief period and then depart. It is almost as if these scenes are subplots, along with the clown scenes involving Robin, Wagner and Dick. They illustrate the stages of Faustus's journey as he continues on his inevitable path to damnation. There is almost the feel of a 'road movie' about *Doctor Faustus*. Some of the episodes are barely connected, save that they are part of Faustus's spiritual decline.

Summary of plot features

- Faustus, the main character, is the dominant figure of the play and, consequently, the plot.

- Part of the plot is taken up with the intellectual reflections and subsequent spiritual decline of Faustus. These moments may be described as 'internal action'. These contrast with the events of the play — the entrances and exits of characters — which may be referred to as 'external action'.

- Some of the other characters represent their own subplot, for example Pope Adrian, Benvolio and Helen of Troy. These subplots are linked to the fate and adventures of Faustus, although he is their only link.

- There is also a persistent subplot involving the clown-like characters of the play. This subplot reflects some of the features of the main plot, particularly in the way that magic is used for practical jokes and tricks. The characters of the main plot and the subplot only come together towards the end of Act IV, when Faustus renders some of the clown-like characters dumb.

- The plot does not provide a narrative through-line, other than the fate of Faustus. The story of Faustus and his journey is both literal and metaphorical — his 24-year journey through spiritual decline.

♦ The audience is informed of changes in time and place during the action through both the dialogue of main characters and narrative speeches given by the chorus. This is particularly important at the outset of Act III, when the action moves to Rome.

♦ There are a number of exciting climactic moments in the plot, for instance the appearance of the characters from hell or Faustus's decision to sell his soul. Later, climaxes are provided in the 'special effects' moments, for example when Faustus throws fireworks at the pope. The final climax is when Faustus faces his ultimate doom.

♦ There is an increasing sense that Faustus's fate is sealed. As he immerses himself further in the indulgent activities of his magic, he questions himself less and less until the arrival of the old man in the final act. By then he is too atrophied by fear to make a rational decision regarding his own fate.

Summary of plot structure

♦ The play is a five-act tragedy, a structure typical of the Elizabethan and Jacobean eras.

♦ The opening of the play is quiet and contemplative, featuring the central character at his studies. This contrasts greatly with the scenes of spectacle and adventure later in the play.

♦ In the earlier stages of the play, the subplot featuring the clown-like characters provides some relief from the agonised dilemmas of Faustus. The juxtaposition of such scenes — the ridiculous and essentially harmless buffoonery of the clowns followed by Faustus's more sinister dabblings — allows the audience to witness both similarities and contrasts between the seemingly disparate character types and their actions.

♦ The structure helps to emphasise the philosophical moments of the play: it begins and ends with a monologue from Faustus. The first scene shows him at his most curious, the last at his most emotionally distraught.

♦ The plot structure allows the intellectual development of Faustus's beliefs and doubts to dominate the first half of the play, especially by virtue of his discussions with Mephistophilis. Much of the second half reveals the results of Faustus's ambitions and is governed by action rather than talk. The final act combines intellectual and physical denouement with an inevitable resolution to Faustus's necromancy.

Discussion questions

1 How does the structure of *Doctor Faustus* influence the action of the play?

2 How does Marlowe structure individual scenes to develop dramatic intensity?

3 How does the structure of the scenes affect the pace of the play?

Essay question

Comment on the action in *Doctor Faustus*. Reflect on how the contrast between non-verbal action and action led by dialogue affect the overall audience experience.

Chapter 8

Characterisation in Marlowe's *Doctor Faustus*

Although a play may use many actors, it is not necessarily the case that all these actors portray distinct and identifiable characters. There are many plays which describe characters simply by their function — 'messenger', 'prisoner', 'guest' and so on.

Martin Crimp (1956–)

Martin Crimp is noted for the astringency of his dialogue and his interest in theatrical form and language rather than narrative. Before turning to drama, he published a collection of short stories and a novel. His most innovative play, *Attempts on Her Life*, has been translated into 20 languages. It challenges the notion of what constitutes a play and questions whether a person has any reality beyond the ideas about them constructed by others.

Six of Crimp's plays have been presented at the Royal Court Theatre, London, where he was writer in residence in 1997.

In a piece of naturalism such as Miller's *The Crucible*, it is demonstrably the case that the play's success relies on our belief in the characters and, on the whole, they may be described as well-rounded and believable people. Indeed, Miller based them on actual citizens of Salem in the late seventeenth century.

By contrast, the script of an ensemble piece such as *Attempts on Her Life* (1997) by Martin Crimp identifies neither time, place nor characterisation. There is a series of (apparently) unconnected scenes, in which violent events and acts of terrorism are depicted involving a personality called Annie. How the play is presented is left entirely to the creativity of the director and the skills of the performers. It is suggested that the company of actors should be represented by a multiplicity of cultures and races.

Crimp's approach to characterisation is echoed in *4.48 Psychosis* (1999), the last play written by Sarah Kane, in which the 'dialogue' is continuous and no characters are specified at all. Because of the nature of the dialogue, we 'hear' arguments and voices responding to each other.

The play was first performed by three actors but it can be performed, theoretically, by any number. There is undoubtedly a central 'character', but it is usually the case that the contrasting and conflicting aspects of that character are played by many actors.

Another example of a play where characterisation is far from realistic and there is a greater reliance on ensemble work is *Interview* (1964), the first part of the trilogy *America Hurrah* by American playwright Jean Claude Van Italie. In the opening scene, we see four interviewees arriving simultaneously at four different job interviews conducted by four different interviewers. Much of the opening section deals with the rituals of interviews. The following extract exemplifies the format and the characterisation:

First interviewer: How do you do?
Second interviewer: (sitting) Thank you, I said, not knowing what.
First interviewer: Won't you sit down?
Second applicant: (standing) I'm sorry.
First applicant: I am sitting.
First interviewer: (pointing) There. Name, please?
Second applicant: (sitting) Jane Smith.
First applicant: Jack Smith.

Sarah Kane (1971–99)

4.48 Psychosis is an exploration of mental disorder written while its author was in the depths of a depressive illness which ultimately led to her suicide. Although some people felt that the play read like a suicide note, Sarah Kane's family vehemently defended the work as a legitimate piece of theatre rather than a *crie de coeur*. When it was staged posthumously, the play was a resounding success and has emerged as one of her most popular works.

Although Kane's first work, *Blasted* (1995), was largely derided by the critics, playwrights such as Harold Pinter and Martin Crimp came to her defence. Kane, in turn, openly admired the work of Crimp and acknowledged his influence in the writing of her penultimate play, *Crave* (1998).

As you can see from the excerpt, this play is non-naturalistic and the dialogue intersects between one interview and another. Later in the same scene, the dialogues from all four interviews intersect with each other. Here characterisation is immediate, recognisable and, to a degree, functional. During the interviews, the characteristics of individuals emerge. Later in the play we see each of the characters in a specific, if surreal, setting.

Characterisation in Doctor Faustus

In *Doctor Faustus*, Marlowe uses characterisation in a number of ways, encompassing both the functional and the more rounded approach.

Principal character: Faustus

It is not always the case that the eponymous character in a play is given such dominance as Faustus. Hamlet is obviously the major character in the play to which he lends his name, but it would be foolish to treat characters such as Claudius, Polonius and Ophelia as in some way minor. In *Julius Caesar,* while the title role is a dominant force and influences all the action (even though Caesar himself dies in Act III), this is only one of four major roles. Faustus, however, dominates the action throughout Marlowe's play, rarely leaving the stage except during the comic scenes of subplot and moments of intervention by the chorus.

Marlowe uses the technique of soliloquy throughout the play to allow Faustus to reveal his innermost thoughts to the audience. (Jude Law as Faustus, the Young Vic Theatre, March 2002)

The relationship Faustus establishes with the audience is crucial. Marlowe uses the technique of soliloquy throughout the play to allow Faustus to reveal his innermost thoughts to the audience. The relationship changes as he moves from expressions of hubris — self-important pride — to doubt, from mischievous practical jokes to pathetic anguish. Through his various journeys — both physical and emotional — the audience follows his changing fortunes and responds to them accordingly.

We might compare the characterisation of Faustus with that of Edmund in *King Lear* or Iago in *Othello* — villainous characters who take the audience into their confidence through soliloquy.

Overwhelmingly, *Doctor Faustus* is a play about one character — his choices, his dilemmas, his temptations and his ultimate fate. All the other characters either provide functions which help him to achieve what he wants, spur him on to take the decisions that he does or advise him to take a different course of action. Some of these characters reflect his behaviour, some challenge him and others provide him with easy targets to hone and practise his trickery to comic effect. However, it is his character that emerges as the one well-rounded person for whom the audience develops concern and for whose fate, however deserved, the audience feels sympathy.

Major character: Mephistophilis

Perhaps the second most prominent character in the play is Mephistophilis, the agent from hell who is dispatched to secure the sacrifice of Faustus's soul. In one sense, we may see Mephistophilis as another way of finding out about the principal character, as he is, like the audience, Faustus's confidant.

Faustus: Sweet Mephistophilis, thou pleasest me.
      Whilst I am here on earth let me be cloyed
      With all things that delight the heart of man.   (III.1)

However, Mephistophilis is also a messenger character and fulfils an important dramatic function in providing a link between Faustus and the forces of hell. Thus it is Mephistophilis who carries the message to Lucifer of Faustus's intentions and he who returns to Faustus with Lucifer's response. Consequently, his motives as a character are determined by the desires and ambitions of both his masters — Lucifer and Faustus. It is clear, therefore, that there is much that is subservient about him — a character who carries out and reflects the wishes of others.

Another element to his character emerges when Faustus questions him about hell and its occupants. Mephistophilis tells Faustus that he is one of a number of 'unhappy spirits that fell with Lucifer', and a moment later he makes an anguished outburst to Faustus, confessing that the risks he is taking 'strike terror to my fainting soul'.

This is an unexpected complexity in the character. For an actor playing Mephistophilis, these contradictions are an important feature to focus upon when preparing for the role. It is not possible to stereotype the character of Mephistophilis purely as a symbol of hell, a character of undiluted evil and mischief. There is evidence of a soul in anguish who is still subject to the contradictory forces of good and evil. In a sense, the characters of Faustus and Mephistophilis are similar: both of them are captivated by the forces of magic and hell, but in the case of Mephistophilis the enchantment is over and he is already in hell. Mephistophilis could be seen as the foil for Faustus — a character of a similar disposition but whose experience gives him the insight to respond to Faustus's questions.

Powerful cameo characters

A cameo role is generally small, but even though the character may only be on stage for a few scenes, he or she has a dominating effect on the action. Such a character in *Doctor Faustus* is Lucifer.

Lucifer possesses a threatening hold over Faustus and significantly influences Faustus's activities and state of mind, sometimes through his servant Mephistophilis. While we can hardly describe Lucifer as a psychologically well-rounded character, his impact and influence are such that it is difficult to portray him effectively as a stereotype.

It is likely that Lucifer will make a visual impact on the audience, depending on the nature of the production and the choices made by the designer and the director. When he arrives on stage near the start of Act II to remind Faustus of his sworn loyalty to him, his physical presence should be truly frightening as he declares:

Christ cannot save thy soul, for he is just.
There's none but I have interest in the same…   (II.2)

His impact is immediate: Faustus quickly moves from expressing his penitence towards Christ and, instead, offers it to Lucifer:

Pardon me in this,
And Faustus vows never to look to heaven,
Never to name God or to pray to him,
To burn his scriptures, slay his ministers,
And make my spirits pull his churches down.   (II.2)

Functional cameo characters

Characters such as Pope Adrian or Benvolio are less influential in the play and perform more functional cameo roles. They may thus lend themselves to a stereotyped interpretation in performance. They are character types rather than psychologically complex individuals.

The pope is a bully and a blusterer — pompous and proud. His function is to provide an overbearing character that is an easy target for Faustus and his mischief. It is not hard for an audience to enjoy the ridiculing of such an unappealing character.

Benvolio is a buffoon, a nobleman who doubts the powers of Faustus and who sets himself up as his challenger. Even before we meet him, we hear of his drinking exploits. Again, he is set up as a character on whom Faustus can practise the more mischievous side of his magical powers, for example making horns appear on his head. We feel little sympathy for Benvolio, since it is difficult to take his character seriously.

Stereotype characters

The characters who appear in the subplot can largely be described as stereotypes. While their scenes are important in the structure of the play, and require dexterous, imaginative physical theatre and good comic timing from the actors, as characters they are one-dimensional creations and do not provoke in the audience any kind of concern for their fate.

Functional characters

Functional characters may be described by the purpose they provide — the 'good' angel imparting sound and well-meaning advice, the 'bad' angel fulfilling the opposite function. It could be argued that Mephistophilis, as a 'messenger', is, to a degree, a functional character.

Summary of characterisation

- There is one principal character in *Doctor Faustus* — that of Faustus himself.

- The next most important character is Mephistophilis. As he is a character who has fallen from grace and languishes in hell, there is a sense in which he has previously faced the decisions and temptations that Faustus now faces. This indicates that Mephistophilis is in some ways a parallel character and, as such, a foil for Faustus.

- There are powerful cameo characters, such as Lucifer. They are not major characters in that they do not appear frequently, but they have an important impact on the action.

- There are functional cameo characters — such as the Pope and Benvolio — who provide unsympathetic targets for Faustus's mischief.

- Characters in the comic scenes are stereotypes. Their antics often rely on physical comedy and wordplay. Their scenes may provide comic relief or a humorous reflection of the behaviour of Faustus.

- Some characters may be described only by the function they provide.

Discussion questions

1 For each of the plays you are studying for Unit 1, identify the principal characters in the action.

2 Are there any powerful cameo characters — that is, characters who may dominate or be prominent in the action for the brief period of time they are on stage?

3 Are there any characters who may be described as stereotyped — that they have one overriding characteristic which marks them out as comical or extreme?

4 Are there characters who fulfil functions and are described as their functions (e.g. 'servant', 'horse courser', 'vintner' etc.)?

5 Are there characters who provide dramatic functions? (Examples in *Doctor Faustus* are the pope and Benvolio, who become suitable targets for the action perpetrated by Faustus.)

6 Are there characters who might contribute to the comic nature of the play or provide a series of humorous moments in the play, even if it is not specifically a comedy?

Essay question

Using the model of *Doctor Faustus* and some of the examples in the introduction to this chapter, describe the types and natures of characterisation as explored in your chosen plays for Unit 1. Remember, it is important not to force labels onto any character.

Section B

Shaping the play

The work of influential directors and devisors

The identification of the director as a single functionary role in theatre is a relatively modern concept.

The nineteenth-century actor Henry Irving exemplified the 'actor-manager' style of running a company, which relied on one individual undertaking several important roles. The actor would form the theatre company, choose the plays he wanted to produce, play the leading roles in said plays and manage the company's business arrangements.

Only towards the end of the nineteenth century did the notion of the director emerge, with the Duke of Saxe-Meiningen and his colleague Ludwig Chronegk, arguably, being the first.

Although Irving saw the work of the Duke's company on its visit to London in 1881, he was not the kind of individual to relinquish his position of star actor in favour of an ensemble approach. However, the young Konstantin Stanislavski — future artistic director of the Moscow Arts Theatre — was suitably impressed by the company when it performed in Moscow in 1890.

The Duke of Saxe-Meiningen and the Meiningen Players

The Duke of Saxe-Meiningen George II (1826–1914) was a wealthy aristocrat and head of a small German principality. In 1866, he established his own court theatre group, known as the Meiningen Players. He recognised the importance of central artistic control and undertook several roles: producer, director, financial backer and costume and scenery designer. Influenced by contemporary English theatre, he insisted on realistic lighting, speech and stage mechanics and historically accurate costumes and sets. The Meiningen Players toured Europe from 1874 to 1890, inspiring theatrical reforms wherever the group performed.

The growing notion of the ensemble company gradually moved the theatre away from the Irving 'actor-manager' model. Creating an ensemble of players meant that a thorough period of exploration was needed during rehearsal, and the process was therefore made considerably longer than had previously been the case. It involved a more detailed analysis of how design could be used to emphasise the themes of the play. The figure of the director — as the artistic conduit of this process — came into being.

Essentially, the exclusive role of director as the pivotal position in the play/production-making hierarchy finally emerged around the turn of the twentieth century.

What does a director do?

Although the idea of the director as a leader of the theatre-making process is now widely accepted, the approaches of individual directors can be and often are radically different.

On a simple level, the director is responsible for:

• putting the play on stage
• guiding a group of actors through the process of rehearsal
• ensuring that the technical staff involved in the production have fulfilled their functions

However, there are so many ways of conducting the above processes and so many different styles of theatre that it is impossible to define the nature of directing. A great deal depends on the philosophy of the director and the aims of the company for which he or she works. Moreover, the nature and the genre of the play also influence the rehearsal process and, therefore, the directorial interpretation.

This section explores the work of some key directors who have helped to shape the development of theatre throughout the twentieth and twenty-first centuries. Any list will be incomplete, but the purpose of each director's profile is to inspire further study. In particular, it is essential to consider how the texts you are studying might have been or might still be interpreted by the director or devisor under discussion.

We will reflect on some practitioners whose work is almost always new and who may be more accurately regarded as devisors than as directors. It is important to approach each of these practitioners as openly as possible, identifying the likely advantages and disadvantages of their approaches while acknowledging that they represent radical and revolutionary ideas far more than restrictive blueprints or rulebooks. In no case is this truer than the first individual whose work we will examine — Konstantin Stanislavski.

Chapter 9

Konstantin Stanislavski

There is probably more written about the ideas and work of Konstantin Stanislavski than any other theatre practitioner. This chapter aims to distil the available information down to a manageable size. However, it is essential that you use the chapter as a springboard into further research, rather than reading it as an end in itself.

Konstantin Stanislavski (1863–1938)

Konstantin Stanislavski came from a wealthy family in Russia. He was born Konstantin Sergeievich Alexeiev 'Stanislavski' was a stage name that he adopted in 1884, in order to keep his performance activities secret from his parents. The prospect of becoming a professional actor was unthinkable for someone of his social class; at that time, actors had a low social status in Russia.

From childhood, he developed an obsession with acting and the theatre, performing initially in a converted building on his family's estate. He founded the Society of Art and Literature in 1888 and later the Moscow Art Theatre in 1897 with Vladimir Nemirovich-Danchenko. Stanislavski is credited with being the originator of naturalistic acting and strove to create a sense of truth on stage, adapting and revising his ideas constantly. His system of acting is often linked with, but should never be confused with, the 'Method', whose practitioners include Lee Strasberg and Stella Adler.

An ambition to act

Stanislavski's career as a director is inextricably linked with his aims as a teacher of acting. In order to gain a true appreciation of his theatrical endeavours, it is essential to understand the historical and social context into which he emerged and in which he worked. You should also note that Stanislavski was, principally, an actor and a director. He was not a playwright.

Stanislavski was born into great wealth in the latter half of the nineteenth century and his family fortune enabled him to practise his art. In his youth, Stanislavski performed in many plays and sketches, and his desire to be a good actor — often the source of painful frustration in his adolescence — became a lifelong ambition.

Stanislavski's initial attempts to refine his talent as an actor through drama school in the 1880s brought nothing but further frustration.

The training was largely imitative, delivered with the idea that there was only one way of rendering poetry, only one acceptable manner of sitting on a chair or playing a particular 'type' of character. It did not offer him what even at this early stage he felt he needed — an approach to understanding and conveying the internal forces and feelings of the characters.

It has been argued that if Stanislavski had possessed a natural talent in acting then he might not have spent most of his life trying to hone and develop an approach to acting. However, the failures and successes he experienced in performance served to set him on course to identify a defined system to help actors in the preparation of roles.

The Society of Art and Literature

In his twenties, Stanislavski founded the Society of Art and Literature, which sought to promote an ambitious repertoire of plays and develop a more realistic style of acting. Stanislavski describes the state of Russian theatre in the late nineteenth century in his autobiography *My Life in Art* (1924). According to his account, and the accounts of others, the world of theatre was paralysed by a 'star' system and by the emphasis on declaiming speech beautifully, often with substantial help from the prompt.

The idea that Russian theatre had always been a vehicle for the vain 'ham actor' is, however, far from the truth. A generation earlier, the great actor Mikhail Schepkin (1788–1863) and the novelist and playwright Nikolai Gogol (1809–52) had both emphasised the need to create a greater sense of truth and realism in theatre.

Schepkin had been the lead actor at the Maly Theatre — the national theatre of Russia — for nearly half a century. However, since his death (he died coincidentally in the year Stanislavski was born, 1863), the standard of Russian theatre had seriously declined. Through his work at the Society of Art and Literature, Stanislavski sought to recreate the spirit of Gogol and Schepkin by emphasising a more considered approach to acting.

Star system

In the star system, individual talents dominated the theatre, often to the detriment of a production. In Britain, the staging of a play was often built around the celebrated appearance of a star individual, such as Edmund Kean or Henry Irving. In such productions, the performances of other actors were subjugated to the needs of the star player and his relationship with the audience.

Such an approach runs counter to Stanislavski's emphasis on the importance of ensemble. He referred rather disparagingly to the star system he saw in evidence in the Russian theatre at the start of his own career: 'In spite of my great admiration for individual splendid talents, I do not accept the star system; collective creative effort is the root of our kind of art.'

Although technically an amateur institution, the society eventually became a focal point for quality theatre in Moscow. High-profile actors and directors such as Aleksandr Fedotov and Fiodor Kommisarjevsky were attracted to the society to work, and Stanislavski's own reputation as an actor grew throughout the 1890s.

Moscow Art Theatre

In 1897, Stanislavski and his colleague Nemirovich-Danchenko (1858–1943) founded the Moscow Art Theatre. This offered them the opportunity not only to produce excellent theatre but also to identify and practise a disciplined philosophy in acting and repertoire.

The decadent days of the Russian theatre — with its emphasis on ornate décor, actors and audience arriving fashionably late and its upholding of the 'star' system — were now over. The ambitions of the two men were nothing less than to create the most professionally rigorous theatre in the land. However, they were not intellectually or socially elitist and despised the way the theatre had become a club where wealthy Muscovites could meet and socialise. Their initial idea was to call the theatre 'The Moscow Art Theatre — open to all'.

Konstantin Stanislavski with the Moscow Art Theatre troupe of actors in the 1930s

TopFoto

Naturalism and realism

Naturalism as an artistic movement came to prominence initially in the nineteenth-century French novel; the term was invented by the French novelist Emile Zola. His works were a conscious refutation of romantic fiction and often depicted low-born characters struggling to survive in adverse environments.

The classic example of this is *Germinale* (1885), the story of a group of miners in northern France struggling against starvation and oppression. Conveying a sense of 'gritty' realism, Zola explored the idea of inherited characteristics. The central character, Etienne, is shown to possess strengths and weaknesses bequeathed by his ancestors. Zola deliberately took a more scientific approach to the creation of characters and the exploration of their behaviour in specific environments.

As we have seen in Chapter 4, the scientific advances of the nineteenth century, most notably the evolution theories of Charles Darwin, inspired novelists and playwrights to take a more analytical, often harsher view of humanity and its ability or inability to survive. Thus it is that plays of the nineteenth century that can be said to be part of the naturalistic movement often take a deeply unromantic, even if sympathetic, view of humanity.

It is essential to acknowledge the inherent problems with terminology such as 'realism' and 'naturalism': these terms are not always used with consistency and are subject to individual interpretation (and, in this case, translation). Stanislavski himself drew a distinction between the terms. He used 'naturalism' as a more pejorative expression, meaning merely the imitation of surface-level behaviour, whereas 'realism' described 'natural truthfulness'. He wrote in *An Actor's Handbook*:

> Those who think we sought naturalism on the stage are mistaken. We never leaned toward such a principle… We sought inner truth, the truth of feeling and experience.

However, those who believe that Stanislavski is a slavish exponent of realism at the expense of imagination should recognise the distinctions he makes between 'scenic' and 'literal' truth. Stanislavski was at pains to point out that what happens on a stage is not real but the product of an imagination. Therefore, when attempting to create truth in acting (scenic truth), the preoccupation is with the sense of purpose and believability established by the actor, not with making sure that the props are authentic or the set completely realistic. Furthermore, it is entirely possible to create a sense of truthful acting in a piece that is surreal (not bound by the limits of realistic truth), hence the distinction between scenic and realistic truth.

For Stanislavski, the danger of applying a philosophy such as naturalism to acting was to threaten the potential individuality of a character and, therefore, the truthful playing of that character. He identified the need for an actor to avoid extremes of theatrical excess and exaggeration of the truth.

As he went on to say in *An Actor Prepares*:

> Naturalism on the stage is only justified by the inner experience of the actor.

Stanislavski stressed that even if a character is described as 'peasant', it is the inner characteristics of that particular peasant rather than the outer stereotypical, instantly recognisable characteristics of the concept of peasantry that should be of concern to the actor.

In *An Actor's Handbook*, he draws a useful example from the 'death scene', which he says should not be concerned with 'cramps, nausea, groans, horrible grimaces' at the expense of preoccupation with 'the last moments of the human soul'. He says that:

> Truth on stage must be real but rendered poetic through creative imagination.

A director's theatre

Stanislavski, as a director and a coach of actors, as well as an actor himself, had to find a system which could lead to convincing and credible productions through this subtle approach to playmaking and characterisation. His sense of the importance of the work of the Meiningen Players (see page 85) lay in their ensemble playing and coherent production methods as much as in their acting. He was aware that he was watching a company that was disciplined, organised and concerned to demonstrate the authenticity of a play through accurate design features created specifically for each new production. By contrast, in the Russian theatre of Stanislavski's youth it was not unusual to see the same elaborate sets and costumes brought out time after time.

The Meiningen Players' acting, which was workmanlike rather than vain and did not include a specifically emphasised star performer, could perhaps be more accurately described as a 'director's theatre' than an 'actor's theatre'. This too attracted Stanislavski's attention. His detestation of the star system and the kind of simultaneously overblown and amateurish production commonly to be seen on the Russian stage in his youth emerges clearly in his autobiography *My Life in Art*:

These performances seemed to be created for the purpose of showing the primary importance on the stage of the actor himself and the entire lack of necessity of the whole production and all beautiful scenery in the absence of the most important person — the actor… What is important to me is that the collective creation of all the artists of the stage be whole and complete and that all those who helped to make the performance might serve for the sake of the same creative goal and bring their creations to one common denominator.

Stanislavski's ideas

Many of Stanislavski's ideas on acting can be found in his published works *An Actor Prepares* (1937) and *Building a Character* (1938). However, two points must be borne in mind when reading these:

- Much of Stanislavski's writing is still unpublished and in its original Russian.
- There is substantial evidence to suggest that his ideas on acting were constantly changing. Revision notes found after publication of these works and after Stanislavski's death confirm this. While *An Actor Prepares* was published during his lifetime, other works were published posthumously and reflect thoughts and ideas at specific moments during his life and career. According to those with whom he worked, these were always subject to revision.

Consequently, Stanislavski's writings should never be seen as a rule book or a dogma, as many of his critics have sought to insist. They are, instead, a guide, an attempt to help the learning actor. Stanislavski's need to provide theatrical works of distinction and, above all, to impart authenticity and a

Stanislavski's writing should not be seen as a rule book or a dogma

sense of truth meant that his work as a director at the Moscow Art Theatre combined with the role of acting coach.

It would be a mistake to believe that at its inception the Moscow Art Theatre brought with it a coaching programme consistent for every production and adhered to by all the practitioners in the theatre. Stanislavski's work as a director, actor and acting coach over the decades provides many examples of trial and error.

However, accepting that the written guides we possess are not definitively reflective of Stanislavski's practice — since it was constantly changing — there is still a sufficiently robust philosophy for practitioners to apply.

Seeking ways forward

By 1906, Stanislavski had reached something of a crisis point in his work. He had just played Thomas Stockmann (the central character) in Ibsen's *An Enemy of the People* (1882). Response to much of the theatre's repertoire over the 9 years since its foundation had been positive and the Ibsen production was likewise well received. Stanislavski and Nemirovich-Danchenko's ambition of a theatre dedicated to excellence was on its way to being realised. However, for Stanislavski these apparent successes were not enough. He constantly sought ways to improve his practice.

He had established — under the directorship of Meyerhold — the 'First Studio' company, dedicated to experimental work in both styles of acting and repertoire. However, this had not been a success and he was afraid that the company would stagnate unless new and successful ideas could be implemented. In particular, he was concerned with how to identify a process for actors which could help them to achieve a successful performance, even if it could not *guarantee* such an accomplishment. He recognised the moments of success in his own and other actors' careers but could not define how that success had been achieved. Too often it was a matter of luck whether a performance was successful or not.

He was also concerned that, as the senior actor and director at the Moscow Art Theatre, his work was imitated. He knew from his disastrous time in drama school in the 1880s that learning through copying a demonstration of another's work could only be a partially successful activity, lacking in creativity and depth.

Realistic sets

Much of the way in which Stanislavski tried to activate a sense of truth in the imaginations of his actors was by providing the stimulation of a realistic set. Mention has already been made of the poor practice in Russian theatre of using and reusing the same artefacts to create sets. Part of the philosophy of the Moscow Art Theatre was to make theatre design a central concern. This approach, however, had once again achieved only partial success. According to Stanislavski's biographer, Jean Benedetti, one notable production of *Julius Caesar* succeeded in achieving archeological and historical authenticity while failing to offer anything but dull drama. Instead, students of history were reputedly taken to see the production simply because of its accuracy in recreating the environment of ancient Rome.

Development of emotional or sense memory

Stanislavski became aware that in order to create believable acting it was necessary to stimulate feeling — that is, to work on the internal thoughts and motivations of the actor. His problem was to find a way of stimulating feeling that an actor could use at will. To dictate to an actor what he or she should be feeling would be counter-productive: the actor could simply demonstrate the required feeling through behaviour without genuinely connecting with the sentiment.

Stanislavski realised that the strength of an individual's will and the ability to concentrate on personal performance without being distracted by an audience or other external forces were crucial. This in turn prompted his interest in psychology, although the subject was in its infancy. The work of the French psychologist Théodule Armand Ribot (1839–1916) had particularly caught his attention, as it put forward the theory that all memories are stored in the nervous system rather than forgotten and that stimulation can reawaken those memories. Such stimulation may be merely a touch or a smell or a sound: the memory comes flooding back, bringing with it the associated emotion.

Stanislavski felt that if an actor, through will, could find ways to trigger appropriate memories during acting, then the emotion produced would be genuine. It was important for the actor to be fully aware of the emotions attributed to the dramatic persona, in order to associate with them and create the appropriate response.

Emotional memory versus incoherent emotion

The process of recalling emotional memory is not, as some have interpreted it, the ability to cry copious tears on cue. The challenge of the process is in fact for actors to understand the emotion of their character, to use their will to reawaken the appropriate personal memory and to draw on that memory to express the emotional dimension of the character without exaggeration. Mere histrionics result in a lack of truth and the kind of 'over-naturalism' to which Stanislavski frequently refers.

It is important to understand the distinction between the disciplined, creative process of drawing on emotional memory and the somewhat indulgent method of producing hysterical, incoherent emotion for emotion's sake. There have been many 'successors' to Stanislavski, most of whom have defined their allegiance in the context of the execution of emotional- or sense-memory acting. However, this is perhaps one of the most common areas of misunderstanding and misinterpretation of Stanislavski's system. Emotional truth does not necessarily mean emotional outpouring; indeed, the canon of plays produced by the Moscow Art Theatre in most instances demanded a subtle, discriminate and measured application to acting.

In *So You Want to be a Theatre Director* (2004), Stephen Unwin argues that while there has been much mystification of the process, emotional memory is an essential part of acting and is constantly used by good actors and good directors alike.

The 'circle of attention'

Through his meticulous note-taking and scrupulous awareness of his own fallibilities and strengths as an actor, Stanislavski realised the important link between concentration and successful performance. He also realised that the more he concentrated his focus on himself during performance, the more relaxed he was. If he allowed his attention to wander to extraneous matters, such as distractions from the auditorium, his muscles tensed and his performance became nervous and artificial.

Stanislavski therefore defined the 'circle of attention' — the confined and specific area of focus with which the actor should be concerned, the world of the play on stage. If an actor can maintain that focus, Stanislavski argued, the audience members will be drawn into the world of the play and the actor's hold will 'force them to participate actively in his artistic life' (*An Actor's Handbook*, p. 24).

This 'circle of attention' can be enlarged or reduced depending on the nature of the action taking place on stage. However, if an actor is to be successful, he or she must control the nature of the circle and not allow anything to distract his or her attention.

Units, objectives and obstacles

During rehearsals, Stanislavski would break up a play into 'units'. Each unit would be defined by a piece of action or an event. As Stanislavski put it in *An Actor's Handbook* (p. 154) 'a core…a thing without which it cannot exist'.

Within each unit, an actor will have to meet a particular objective for the character he or she plays. In Act I scene 2 of *A Midsummer Night's Dream* (c. 1595), for instance, the unit may be said to concern the casting of the play. The actor playing Peter Quince must realise his character's objective of seeing to it that all the other characters know the role they are to undertake and are supplied with the script. However, it may be the case that another character's objective might be to provide an obstacle to Quince's objective — and so it proves to be. Bottom, who has been cast as Pyramus, has the objective of playing all the other parts too. This hampers Quince, who ultimately has to assert himself vigorously:

No, no. You must play Pyramus.   (I.2.42)

It would be impossible for both characters to achieve their objectives, as they are mutually frustrated by the disparate intentions. It is Quince who wins the argument, although his subsequent mollifying words to Bottom suggest that perhaps he has an additional objective, that of ensuring that Bottom is happy with his role and not sulky:

You can play no part but Pyramus, for Pyramus is a sweet-faced man, a proper man, as one shall see in a summer's day: a most lovely gentlemanlike man: therefore you must needs play Pyramus.   (I.2.63–65)

It is important for actors to understand the objective of their character, in order to appreciate their motivation and to recognise whether the objective is finally achieved or whether an obstacle — usually another character's objective — has prevented it from being accomplished.

Super-objective and through-line of action

The super-objective is the ultimate ambition of the character and may be linked to the fulfilment of immediate objectives. Thus, to use the example of Peter Quince again, it may be argued that while his immediate objective in the unit of Act I scene 2 is to cast the play, his super-objective is to put on a fine production for the entertainment of Duke Theseus. The objective of Act I scene 2 is merely a small part of that super-objective.

Stanislavski explained how the fulfilment of each objective leads to the next objective as the 'through-line' of action. The actor must navigate his or her way through the play using the immediate objectives and individual units almost as a sailor might use marker buoys. However, as Unwin has argued in *So You Want to be a Theatre Director?* (2004), the super-objective is by no means certain in each case and is often subject to change. Quince's super-objective may not just be the achievement of a fine production; he may also wish to become a full-time poet so that he no longer has to work as a carpenter.

Hamlet's ultimate super-objective is to avenge his father's death by killing his uncle. However, at the beginning of the play he is not aware of the circumstances of his father's death and his initial super-objective is to find any means possible

TopFoto

While the immediate objective of Peter Quince in Act I scene 2 of *A Midsummer Night's Dream* is to cast the play, his super-objective is to put on a fine production for the entertainment of Duke Theseus. (Linbury Theatre, November 2005)

to end what he sees as a desperate and heartbreaking existence. His only means of escape — having discounted suicide — is to go back to Wittenberg University. However, even this objective cannot be achieved, as his uncle and his mother both put pressure on him not to return.

Recognition of the super-objective is a useful way for an actor to determine the character's ambition and motivation. The fact that this may be linked to how the actor interprets the role, as well as how the playwright has written it, makes the notion of the super-objective no less valid.

Given circumstances

Stanislavski felt that an actor must have a fundamental awareness of 'the story of the play'. This awareness should take in not only the facts that are contained within the script, but also the context of the character — social, historical and political — and his or her specific condition. Knowledge of these 'given circumstances' cannot be achieved without a thorough exploration of the text and a sound understanding of the director's interpretation.

Arthur Miller's *Playing for Time* (1980) — a play based on the autobiography of Fania Fenelon, a Parisian Jewish singer who was deported to Auschwitz during the Second World War — tells the story of how she and other inmates survived by forming an orchestra to entertain the Nazi hierarchy. The context here, therefore, is not only specific but also particularly graphic and violent. Obviously, it is vital for everyone in the company of actors to understand and appreciate the extreme nature of the context, but not just in political or historical terms. In addition, the actors need to have a sense of the characters in terms of their backgrounds before entering Auschwitz. They must explore their characterisations beyond the label of 'Jewish prisoner'.

Actors must also explore the more visceral of the given circumstances, such as how it must feel to be permanently hungry and to know that each day could well be your last. In this sense, the given circumstances of the character are linked with the emotional preparation that the actor must make and the development of truth and credibility in performance. It is not possible to 'bluff' through a script which offers so many challenges and which deals with the bravery of individuals in one of the most appalling episodes of human history. In plays such as *Playing for Time*, the assimilation by the actors of the given circumstances of the characters is necessarily a respectful as well as a professionally expedient practice.

Magic or creative 'if'

The idea of 'magic if' is concerned with the actor's appropriate and effective use of imagination. While a situation such as the one cited above in *Playing for Time* may be beyond his or her experience, the actor must try to imagine what life would be like 'if' he or she was in that situation.

Inevitably, this idea is linked to that of emotional memory. It is highly unlikely that any actor taking part in this play can compare experiences in his or her own life with what he or she is being asked to enact. Actors may be able to conjure memories of fear through the emotional memory technique but they will need to engage a developed sense of imagination to place themselves in that specific situation. Imagination will need to be supported with research — led by the director — into the historical details of the situation.

The notion of the 'magic if' comes with a health warning. It is sometimes argued that it is necessary to lose all sense of self and to believe that you *are* the character that you are playing. For an actor to render a role with complete believability, it is vital for him or her to believe that he or she is genuinely inhabiting the world of the play, rather than simply performing on a stage.

It should be stressed that while there may be exponents of the above method who believe such a theory, Stanislavski was opposed to such a technique. He did not believe that the actor should 'give himself up to hallucination…quite the contrary… He does not forget that he is surrounded by stage scenery and props' (*An Actor's Handbook*). To try to indulge the kind of hallucination Stanislavski refers to is to lose control as an actor and to move from a process of creativity to one of abandoned self-deception. On the contrary, it is the word 'if' that acts as a lever to lift the actor from the real world into the world of his creativity. Stanislavski did not engender any notion in his actors or his students that they were to believe they had actually become the character they were playing.

Stanislavski and politics

When Stanislavski's work is discussed, comparisons are often drawn with the work of other practitioners, most notably Bertolt Brecht. One important and obvious distinction, however, is that Brecht was principally a playwright and Stanislavski was not. It is also often argued that while Brecht was a political and theatrical revolutionary, Stanislavski was a more establishment bourgeois figure, from a background of privilege and wealth, who had no interest in politics.

Such a judgement is partial and unfair. Stanislavski lived and worked in a politically volatile society: early twentieth-century Russia. During a performance of Ibsen's *An Enemy of the People* in 1905, Stanislavski, playing the lead role, experienced an unusual audience reaction. Earlier in the day, a troop of imperial guards had opened fire and massacred unarmed civilians protesting over food shortages in Kazansky Square in Petrograd (now St Petersburg). The audience in attendance at the Moscow Art Theatre's production in Petrograd that night was largely made up of middle-class, middle-aged members of the intelligentsia who were in angry mood and revolutionary spirit. They identified with many moments of the production. When the principal character Stockmann (played by Stanislavski) put on his coat — torn during an assault on him — and declared 'One need not put on a new coat when one fights for truth and freedom', this was too much for them. In *My Life in Art*, Stanislavski relates:

> The spectators in the theatre connected this sentence with the massacre in Kazansky Square, where more than one new coat must have been torn in the name of truth and freedom. Unexpectedly my words aroused such pandemonium that it was necessary to stop the performance... The entire audience rose from its seats and threw itself towards the footlights... I saw hundreds of hands stretch towards me all of which I was forced to shake... That evening I found out through my own experience what power the theatre could exercise.

Russia was subjected to two further revolutions in 1917, resulting initially in the removal of the tsar as head of state and ultimately in the success of the Communist Party led by Lenin and later Stalin. As the head of the foremost theatre company in Russia, Stanislavski would have been subjected to the keenest scrutiny by government officials. That both he and the company survived through this time when many did not (his successor at the Moscow Art Theatre, Vsevolod Meyerhold, was tortured and shot by the authorities in 1940) is a tribute to Stanislavski's considerable skill and courage when dealing with the Communist Party and, on occasion, Stalin himself.

In his biography of Stanislavski, Benedetti points out that his approaches to Stalin smack of political naivety. However, it is unfair to suggest that he was in any sense a 'part' man or a mouthpiece of government propaganda. In fact, Stanislavski did not pursue an overtly political line in either the choice of repertoire at the theatre or in his interpretation of the repertoire as a director. Indeed, he was clear that the actor should not try to project a political message. He felt that while political messages may emerge from the work, there should be no attempt to compromise the artistic integrity of the production by substituting honest and truthful acting with preaching. However, by promoting the work of Chekhov, Gorky and Ibsen, among others, he was consciously placing an emphasis on the work of the most prominent playwrights of the era who, as we have seen, were part of the naturalistic vision. As such he was presenting plays which were often critical of both society and its leaders.

With regard to the work of Chekhov, the official party line was to interpret the plays as being critical of the old tsarist order. However, Stanislavski often found himself at odds with the aims of the official censor. There is no doubt that as a theatre director, Stanislavski saw that he had a spiritual and educative duty to the ordinary people of Russia; that he used this position to promote some of the finest and most socially-conscious playwriting in theatre's history should not be overlooked.

Summary

As we have seen, it is misguided to interpret Stanislavski's ideas on acting as a permanent and rigid set of training principles. Even in the area of emotional memory, which some see as being the defining element of his ideology, Stanislavski moved in the later part of his life towards a belief that emotion could be more effectively triggered by a method of physical actions:

External action acquires inner meaning and warmth from inner feeling, and the latter finds its expression in physical terms.

(*An Actor's Handbook*, p. 8)

Nonetheless, irrespective of his ability to move on to other ideas, the principles of acting we have inherited from Stanislavski are enormously useful, especially in approaching a work of realism. The next chapter is devoted to attempting to apply these principles to a proposed production of a suitable play.

Activity

Select a scene for performance from either a play you are studying or one of personal interest to you. The play needs to be of a realistic nature and involve rounded characters. Before you attempt the scene, focus on your character (A) and another character (B) with whom he or she is particularly close, for example Hamlet and Ophelia, Romeo and Juliet, or Proctor and Elizabeth. Go through the script, asking the following questions:

- What does character A say about character B?
- What does character B say about character A?
- What does character A say about himself or herself?
- What does character B say about himself or herself?
- What does character A say to character B about him or her?
- What does character B say to character A about him or her?

While this may seem an exhaustive and almost fussy process, it requires you to consider how characters respond to one another and reveals the honesty or frank-ness with which they address one another about their feelings. On this basis, you can start to consider your character's motives with regard to the other character, and perhaps engage in some emotional preparation.

Chapter 10

Applying Stanislavski's principles

An Inspector Calls by J. B. Priestley

An Inspector Calls was written in 1944 by J. B. Priestley. It is probably his most famous play, although *Dangerous Corner* (1932), *Time & The Conways* (1937) and *When We Are Married* (1938) are all well known and respected standards of British theatre, albeit less frequently performed.

J. B. Priestley

John Boynton Priestley (1894–1984)

J. B. Priestley was an author, novelist, playwright, broadcaster, scriptwriter and social commentator — a 'man of letters' whose career spanned the twentieth century. His first theatrical venture was an adaptation of his novel *The Good Companions* in 1931. This was followed by the thriller *Dangerous Corner*. A committed socialist, his best-known play is *An Inspector Calls*, which depicts a complacent and well-to-do family, all of whom have contributed to the death of a local girl but fail to take responsibility for their actions. However, Priestley was also an adept writer of comedy, and his farce *When We Are Married* is still frequently performed.

The plot

An Inspector Calls is set in the fictional industrial town of Brumley on a spring evening in 1912. A well-to-do family, the Birlings, are finishing dinner, and the mood is clearly one of celebration. Sheila, the daughter of the household, is getting engaged to Gerald Croft, a similarly well-to-do young man but from an even more important local family. There is an atmosphere of cheerfulness, and perhaps even smugness, about their situation.

After proposing a toast to the happy couple, Mr Birling begins to make a speech. He tells his family that they are lucky to be living in such a time of progress and prosperity and that, despite all the rumours and scaremongering, there is no chance of war. There is simply too much at stake and the Germans are as unenthusiastic about war as the British. Furthermore, one of the signals of progress is the building of a new and unsinkable ship of over 40,000 tons, and equipped with every luxury and named *The Titanic*. Later in the same scene, he tells his son and prospective son-in-law to ignore all the nonsense spoken about community because a man has to make his own way in the world.

Into this complacent world a police inspector named Goole unexpectedly arrives. He is investigating the death of a young girl named Eva Smith, who has killed herself by drinking disinfectant. Finding letters and diaries in Eva's room, the inspector is pursuing an inquiry which involves all the members of the Birling family and Gerald Croft too. One by one, the inspector reveals how each of them has contributed to Eva's downfall and suicide. Mr Birling sacked her from his factory when she was one of a group of young women who led a strike for higher wages; Sheila, his daughter, had her sacked from her next job working in a clothes shop. Gerald had a relationship with her after she fell into prostitution and kept her as his mistress, but ended the relationship when it no longer suited him. Eva then met Eric, the Birlings' son, and had a brief relationship with him, which ended when she became pregnant by him. Finally, Mrs Birling rejected Eva's appeals for help when she came to her charitable organisation pregnant, abandoned and destitute.

The inspector warns that unless people like them learn the lesson that we are not alone, that our fates intertwine, that we are all part of one community and responsible for each other, there will come at time of 'fire, blood and anguish'.

We discover ultimately that there is no Inspector Goole (possibly a play on 'ghoul', meaning ghost) and that no girl has died. As Mr and Mrs Birling and Gerald all breathe a sigh of relief on the assumption that they have been the victims of an elaborate hoax, the phone rings. Mr Birling receives the news that a girl has just died from drinking disinfectant and that an inspector is on his way to ask some questions.

A piece of naturalism?

In many respects, the play is a piece of naturalism, most notably in that it explores the behaviour of people in a specifically defined social context. The historic context of the play is in fact not 1912 but the mid-1940s at the end of the Second World War, also a time of 'fire, blood and anguish'.

Some would argue, however, that *An Inspector Calls* is not a wholly naturalistic play because of the 'supernatural' quality of the inspector's character and because of his polemical statements about society and shared responsibility. His involvement gives the play something of a didactic, political quality.

The play does not attempt to break with the conventions of naturalism and the reality of the inspector is completely accepted by the other characters, even if they find his behaviour unorthodox.

Applying Stanislavski's system

Stanislavski's system can help actors in a production of *An Inspector Calls* in a number of ways.

Working with emotion and sense memory

Each of the characters endures an emotional journey during the course of the play, with the possible exception of the inspector. Even though he differs from the other characters in this way, it is clear that he becomes increasingly impatient with Mr Birling's blustering defence of his actions and the others' attempts at excusing their behaviour.

All the characters experience a moment of recognition when they remember what has happened between them and Eva Smith. Each actor must therefore consider carefully his or her character's reaction to the news that Eva is dead.

Sheila

When Sheila is shown the photograph of Eva and recognises the young woman she has caused to be dismissed, the stage direction reads:

She looks at it closely, recognises it with a little cry, gives a half stifled sob, and then runs out.

The stage directions do not necessarily have to be followed exactly here, but there is a clear expectation that Sheila reacts to the photograph with extreme shock. Later she discovers that her fiancé, Gerald, has been unfaithful to her with Eva and she gradually learns of the involvement of the rest of her family in the death of the girl.

If this emotional journey is to be played with a convincing sense of truth and with credibility, the emotion which the actor playing Sheila displays must be genuine. While the actor in question may not know what it is like to discover that she has contributed to a young girl's suicide, it is possible to isolate the emotion of shock she experiences at this point by remembering a time when she personally received shocking news. If the memory can be recalled vividly, this will make the effect all the more potent. In order to evoke a powerful recollection, the actor should aim to recall the place where the shocking news was received, the way in which the news was delivered, the smells in the air and so on. In this way, the shock is stimulated from distinct memories rather than from vague recollections.

Gerald

The way in which an actor experiences shock or grief may differ from the way his or her character does — it is not just a case of reliving the emotion, but of recounting it and making it part of the creative process. Thus the actor playing Gerald must assimilate the information that his character has had a close relationship with Eva, may even have been a little in love with her, and admits to being:

rather more upset by this business than I probably appear to be.

Gerald perceives himself to be responding to the news of his former lover's death with stoicism, but there is still a need for the actor to stimulate emotion — in order to then conceal it. That is why it is important — as stated earlier — that emotional truth is not simply about emoting liberally on stage. Far more important is the task of cultivating the appropriate level of emotion and using knowledge of the context (the character and his or her situation) to judge how that emotion should be expressed.

The inspector

The role of the inspector is more challenging. Can emotional or sense memory help an actor to play a character who is supernatural? Much depends on the interpretation made by the actor playing the role and the director of the production. If there is something of the mystic about the inspector — a figure of authority with a spiritual message he feels impassioned to communicate — that could lead to a delivery of some emotional intensity. The actor could draw on experiences of frustration or impatience, or of trying to convince a sceptical audience of a deeply-held conviction.

There is an unsettling and disturbed quality to the frequency with which the inspector recalls seeing the dead body of Eva Smith — an image he recalls quite graphically. Although we discover that, at the time of the inspector's visit, no girl has been brought into the infirmary, we infer that the inspector has foreseen this event and knows the harrowing nature of the image he describes. The description may be enough to enable the actor to visualise what he describes so that no extra help is needed from his emotional memory. However, recalling a response to a distressing image — even an image of death from television news — might help the actor recreate the sense of anger and helplessness required here.

There is something of the mystic about the character of the inspector, and this can influence an actor's delivery. (Niall Buggy at the Playhouse Theatre, London, September 2001)

Using the 'circle of attention'

Unlike a musical or a play with narration, this is a play which requires no acknowledgement of the presence of the audience. The audience should be drawn into the world of the play and, therefore, the actors' concentration should be directed entirely within the stage environment.

The circle of attention for the actor playing the inspector may enlarge sufficiently to encompass all of the other characters, as it does immediately before his final exit early in Act III. However, it may also be limited to a direct address to one character, as during his interrogation of Mr Birling or Gerald for example.

When Mr Birling makes his optimistic and complacent speech about progress at the beginning of the play, his circle of attention is still the world of the play, but more the world — or his interpretation of it — beyond the immediate action of the stage. At this point, Mr Birling's attention is focused on the world of business and enterprise, of unsinkable ships and eternal optimism, of prosperity and triumphant capitalism. Although still focused on his dramatic audience (the other characters on stage), the actor playing Mr Birling can afford to allow his imagination to conjure the images the character describes and to create a focus which assimilates the world of the play with the world beyond the confines of the stage.

Identifying units

The play has a three-act structure, but there are clear and almost predictable units as the plot progresses. After a while, we almost anticipate that the inspector will move on to the interrogation of another member of the family. It is as if each character is assigned a personal unit in which his or her relationship with Eva and the portion of his or her guilt are revealed.

The plot has something of a murder mystery about it. Agatha Christie's stories — Poirot or Miss Marple — work in this forensic way to investigate each of the suspects until the identity of the murderer is revealed. However, there is little mystery about *who* is responsible for Eva's death; the mystery is *how* they were responsible and how one person's responsibility links to another's.

Identifying objectives

Since the behaviour of the characters alters drastically during the course of the action, it is challenging to identify each persona's objective.

At the outset of the play, the immediate objective of each character seems to be simply to enjoy the occasion, and in each instance that objective is being fulfilled. However, there is perhaps a little more detail to be drawn into these objectives; much depends on the interpretation of the actors and the director.

Mr Birling

Mr Birling is concerned to make a good impression on Gerald, being conscious that Gerald is of a higher ranking family than his own. He is also aware, perhaps, that his son is inclined to drink too much and that he is a likely source of embarrassment. Eric's behaviour is, therefore, a potential obstacle to Birling's objective.

Eric

Eric may have a different objective from simply enjoying himself. As we see later in the play, he has stolen money from the firm in order to help Eva as he knows she is pregnant. His level of anxiety is therefore more intense than anyone else's at the outset of the play. Both he and Gerald know that they have done something which must remain secret if a way of life is to be sustained and its relationships are to remain unaffected.

Alteration of objectives

The arrival of the inspector alters each of the characters' objectives. Mr Birling's initial objective is to see to the inspector as quickly as possible and then go back to enjoying himself. Clearly, the inspector's behaviour provides an obstacle to that objective being achieved.

As the inspector works through the characters' accounts of their personal acquaintance with Eva Smith, his objective is to get each individual to tell the truth. In each case, he succeeds in eliciting confessions from the characters about their involvement with Eva, even if they remain resolutely unrepentant, as do Mr and Mrs Birling. Indeed, there are few real obstacles to the inspector realising his investigative objective, apart from Mrs Birling's rather feeble accusation of impertinence and Mr Birling's somewhat superfluous interjections of 'Now, look here, inspector'.

Arguably, it is a weakness of the play that the inspector extracts the confessions too easily, and that at no point is any witness accused of committing a crime. However, it is clear from Sheila's response to the inspector that any actor undertaking the role should give him qualities which prompt each of the characters to

TopFoto

The inspector's objective is to get the other characters to tell the truth. (Diane Fletcher, Niall Buggy and Emma Gregory; Playhouse Theatre, London, September 2001)

disclose information about their involvement and face up to their responsibilities in contributing to Eva's death.

Following the exit of the inspector, the objectives of each character change again. Mr Birling is concerned with how to avoid a scandal and protect his prospective knighthood. Eric and Sheila, however, have radically different objectives from their father. Their social consciences have been awakened and they are concerned that the inspector's words are heeded. They demonstrate sincere regret over what has happened and they feel frustration and anger towards their parents as they witness Mr and Mrs Birling's efforts to disprove the inspector's words and confute his authenticity. The realisation of the children's new-found objective is frustrated by the attempts of Gerald and Mr and Mrs Birling to protect themselves and solve the mystery.

Staging objectives and obstacles

Making observations about characters' objectives and obstacles is only of use if interpreted practically for work on stage. For example, a director recognising the ways in which the inspector's objectives provide obstacles for other characters should allow this realisation to influence staging ideas.

On his entrance, the stage directions describe the physical presence of the inspector as 'creating a sense of massiveness, solidity and purposefulness', although it also mentions that he need not be a big man. During the play, the inspector dictates a lot of the action, at points allowing people to leave the room and at others preventing them from doing so, particularly Eric. Although it would be inappropriate to have the inspector using any physical force in his dealings with the Birling family, his physical presence could be used in such a way as to present a physical obstacle to a character's exit. Certainly the stage direction offered by Priestley — that he stares at a person before asking them a question — is a useful device in meeting the objectives discussed.

There are also other methods of staging that can be used to explore the dynamics between the characters and their objectives. There is a sense of binary opposition between the inspector and the other characters, and this should be explored on stage. For example:

- The inspector is the hunter — the other characters are the hunted.
- He is shabby — they are glamorous.
- He is direct and purposeful — they are noncommittal and obfuscating.

This binary opposition would translate well into physical terms, for instance:

- The inspector is sitting — the other characters are standing.
- He is calm and still — they are moving and gesturing.

Super-objectives

The inspector's super-objective is to hold all the other characters accountable for the death of Eva Smith and to make them acknowledge their involvement.

The super-objectives of some characters alter following the unexpected arrival of the inspector: while Mr Birling's super-objective at the beginning of the play could be interpreted as the securing of his daughter's engagement to Gerald, by the end it is to rid himself and his family of the inspector and to avoid a public scandal.

Characters' super-objectives do not change immediately with the arrival of the inspector, however. For a time, Mr Birling sees his unexpected guest merely as a temporary inconvenience — an obstacle, perhaps, but not a permanent obstruction to the achievement of his super-objective.

Subtext super-objectives

It may also be argued that Mr Birling's (and Mrs Birling's) super-objective at the outset of the play is to use the evening to better his chances of receiving a knighthood or of being re-elected as Lord Mayor.

It is important to realise that such a super-objective is reliant on personal interpretation and decisions made by actors and the director. The script is not the ultimate determinant. In this regard, there is an element of subtext in the establishment of both objective and super-objective. The text itself, as Stanislavski argued, is a piece of work in progress and can only be completed when given life on a stage. A play, therefore, may lead to many varied and diversified productions, dependent on actor and director interpretation.

The through-line of action

In this play, there is really only one character with a clear through-line of action, and that is the inspector. However, the through-line of action is important in order to establish for each actor a sense of purpose and urgency in the communication and achievement of their character's super-objective:

* How urgent is Mr Birling's desire to secure the partnership with Gerald and/or his knighthood? How does the audience witness this degree of urgency in the actor's performance?
* How important is it to Eric to get through the evening without detection? Is it his super-objective just to anaesthetise himself with alcohol and to leave at the earliest possible moment? If that is his super-objective, how urgent is it for him to achieve it and how will the urgency show in the actor's performance?

Ultimately, the character's objectives and super-objective will only be of cursory interest to the audience if the portrayal of them is not linked with the physical, vocal and emotional decisions of the actor.

Given circumstances

An Inspector Calls has a specific set of given circumstances and it is impossible to act in or direct this play appropriately without a thorough understanding and awareness of its backdrop.

The play is set clearly in 1912; there are references in the play to dates and events of the era, making it virtually impossible (and pointless) to set the play in any other period of history. Moreover, there can be no doubt about the intentions of the playwright in writing the play at the end of the second of the major world wars and setting it on the eve of the first: the setting of the play might be 1912, but the historical context is 1945. Priestley's point is that the attitudes and social injustices of the early part of the twentieth century are so entrenched that they have led to more than 30 years of 'fire, blood and anguish'. There is a didactic message here: that the reign of 'fire, blood and anguish' is reaching its height at the time of writing (1944–45) and that it will not die away until lessons of the past have been learned.

However, if the play is actually set in 1912, should the performances — according to a Stanislavskian interpretation — show any kind of awareness of the social upheaval to come? Not only would this be rather difficult to achieve, it would also seem to run counter to the ideas of Stanislavski that the actor should invest belief in the circumstances of the play. The 'magic if' requires actors to assimilate the given circumstances of their characters within the social context of the setting.

Nevertheless, setting and interpretation are ultimately down to directorial adaptation.

Given circumstances: character versus setting

Stephen Daldry's landmark revival of Priestley's play in 1992 for the National Theatre afforded a revision of the usual naturalistic delivery set in the Birling family's dining room. Instead, Daldry embraced both historical eras and set the Edwardian world of the Birlings in a doll's-house-like structure on stilts on the stage, while ragamuffin children from the 1940s played in bomb craters around it. At the moment of the inspector's 'fire, blood and anguish' speech, the doll's house spectacularly collapsed and the speech was delivered straight to the audience.

Can Daldry's interpretation, or indeed any expressionistic interpretation of a play, remain consistent with Stanislavski's principles regarding realistic performance? Certainly it seems feasible. Despite the imaginative and unorthodox setting of the play, the reality for the characters remains the same. We have seen how Stanislavski's attempts to stimulate realistic performances from his actors by supplying a completely authentic set ended in frustration and partial failure.

Stephen Daldry (1961–)

Stephen Daldry entered the world of the stage via a traditional route, spending part of his formative years performing youth theatre in Taunton. While at Sheffield University he excelled in dramatics, becoming chairman of the university drama society. After graduation, while most of his friends sought jobs as assistant stage managers, he took up an apprenticeship with Italian clown Elder Milletti and worked alongside him in a Romany circus in southern Italy. From 1985 to 1988 he served an apprenticeship at the Crucible Theatre in Sheffield, before heading to London, where he trained at the East 15 Acting School. While there, he began to garner attention for his work at the Gate Theatre (1990–92).

In 1992, Daldry was appointed artistic director at the Royal Court Theatre. He went on to direct the long-running, Tony-Award-winning revival of J. B. Priestley's *An Inspector Calls* and David Hare's monologue *Via Dolorosa*. He has also directed several films, including *Billy Elliot* (2000) and an adaptation of the Michael Cunningham novel *The Hours* (2002).

The acceptance of the given circumstances for each character does not undermine or challenge a more experimental array of choices for design or production. Daldry's production proved this: critical reactions to his interpretation pointed out that the complacency of the Edwardian world of the Birlings coupled with the devastation of the 1940s, when the play was written, served to underpin rather than detract from the play's major themes.

Therefore, whatever the nature of the production, the facts the actors need to assimilate for their characters remain the same. The characters' circumstances are in most cases quite clear.

Mr Birling

The actor playing Mr Birling must identify himself with the specific circumstances of the character in the play. He is a wealthy industrialist with no reason to be anything other than completely happy. He sits at the head of his table, having enjoyed a good dinner, and is now indulging himself with speech making. One assumes that as he has had experience in local politics, speech making is not something he finds difficult. He is confident in his opinions and clearly enjoys airing them.

Eric and Gerald

In the cases of Eric and Gerald, their guilty secrets are an important part of their given circumstances. Gerald is celebrating an engagement, knowing that he has cheated on the girl he intends to marry. Eric is aware that his theft could be discovered by his father at any moment. Therefore, their happiness is possibly tainted.

The inspector

It is more difficult to establish the inspector's given circumstances, since he is possibly an unearthly or ghostly figure. How can an actor interpret Stanislavski's ideas when the character he is playing arguably does not occupy a reality in the pragmatic sense? Can we think in terms of motivation and given circumstances for a character who, in all probability, is not a real inspector?

Again, it is important to think of reality in the context of the play. The inspector certainly has a stage reality that is accepted by the other characters until he leaves, and the conviction of his arguments leaves the audience in no doubt that he is heartfelt in his determination to secure the confessions of the Birling family. The circumstances that necessitate his visit are real, even if his character is a supernatural or mythical presence. It is the social evils committed by the Birlings that provide the actor with the important given circumstances on which the reality of his character is based.

Summary

J. B. Priestley's *An Inspector Calls* can lend itself to interpretations other than the purely naturalistic, as Daldry's expressionistic revival demonstrates. If Stanislavski could have directed *An Inspector Calls* (he died 7 years before it was written), his production would almost certainly have looked different from Daldry's. However, it would be a mistake to assume that because a production embraces techniques or design ideas that take it beyond the province of naturalism, its conception is inconsistent with Stanislavski's ideas.

The importance of the sense of scenic truth, which needs to be projected in this play, and the need for psychological understanding of the characters by the actors still hold good and are consistent with Stanislavski's key principles.

For both actor and director, Stanislavski's advice on concentration, units, objectives, obstacles and sense memory will surely prove useful.

Summary of Stanislavski's ideas

♦ Stanislavski was the first practitioner to identify a form of actor training. It was embedded into his work as artistic director of the Moscow Art Theatre.

♦ He believed in a theatre which promoted a sense of truth in acting.

♦ He drew clear distinctions between naturalistic theatre and realism. When discussing Stanislavski, it is important to distinguish the two.

♦ His ideas about acting and his dramatic practices changed and developed across a career spanning almost 60 years. It is essential not to interpret his ideas as a rule book.

♦ He and the Moscow Art Theatre promoted the work of some of the most important playwrights of the day, for example Chekhov, Ibsen, Gorky and Bulgakov, as well as revivals by Shakespeare.

♦ Although not politically motivated, Stanislavski felt a sense of social responsibility as a director and believed that theatre had educational and spiritual virtues. He often directed the works of playwrights who were politically motivated.

♦ He sought to create a style of theatre which undermined the 'star' system and the vanity of theatre.

♦ He set up studios to experiment with more expressionistic and non-realistic styles of acting.

Discussion questions

1 Reflecting on the plays you are studying, which of Stanislavski's ideas might prove useful in the preparation of one or more roles?

2 What plays have you seen where you think the director or actors may have used some of Stanislavski's ideas in their preparation?

3 Have you seen a play where you have been critical of aspects of the acting? Would the application of any of Stanislavski's ideas have helped? If so, which ones and with which performance(s)?

Essay questions

1 Plan a rehearsal of a play you are working on. Show how you might introduce some of Stanislavski's ideas, either through text or off-text work.

2 Focusing on one of the plays you are studying, make the case for a director requiring a realistic approach to the acting but not necessarily to the design of the set.

3 Name a style of play where the ideas of Stanislavski might not be useful. Explain your answer.

Chapter 11

Bertolt Brecht

Aside from Konstantin Stanislavski (and possibly Antonin Artaud, see Chapter 13), Bertolt Brecht is the most influential figure in twentieth-century theatre. Brecht and Stanislavski are often contrasted with one another, since it is generally supposed that their intentions and their ideas were in complete opposition.

TopFoto

Bertolt Brecht in 1954

Bertolt Brecht (1898–1956)

Bertolt Brecht was a German poet, playwright and theatre director. He studied philosophy and medicine at the University of Munich before becoming a medical orderly in a German military hospital during the First World War. After the war, Brecht returned to university but eventually became more interested in literature than medicine.

His first play to be produced was *Baal* (1922). This was followed by *Trommeln in der Nacht* (1922), a play about a soldier returning from war, *Im Dickicht der Städte* (1923) and *Mann ist Mann* (1926).

Brecht developed a new approach to the performance of drama, trying to dispel the traditional make-believe of the theatre. Brecht required detachment from the audience, so that he could communicate his version of the truth.

The Berliner Ensemble

Despite the supposed polarity of their aims, what Brecht and Stanislavski have in common is that they were both outstanding directors who cultivated a particular tradition and discipline with specific theatre companies — in Brecht's case with the Berliner Ensemble, which he founded in 1949.

Brecht's rebellion against the established theatre was not necessarily a rebellion against the specific ideas and practices of Stanislavski, although there were many elements of the theatre of realism that he criticised. Neither is it the case that all his work as a playwright and director makes use of his theories about theatre.

John Willett — generally acknowledged as the foremost British scholar on Brecht — makes the valuable point that some of Brecht's later productions with the Berliner Ensemble achieved critical acclaim without being specifically 'Brechtian' in style. In *The Theatre of Bertolt Brecht*, he cites Sam Wanamaker (1919–93, the actor and restorer of the Globe Theatre in London), describing the performance by Brecht's wife Helene Weigel (1900–71) in *Mother Courage* (1939) as 'indistinguishable from a superb Stanislavski-trained actress'. Just as with Stanislavski, it is important not to adopt a formulaic or rigid approach when exploring Brecht's ideas for theatre.

The principal difference between the two men — not in terms of their political aspirations, which we shall come to, but in their practical activities — is that whereas Stanislavski was an actor as well as a director, Brecht was primarily a playwright, essayist and poet.

This is a crucial consideration. Although Stanislavski wrote daily, and copiously, he did so for the purpose of personal reflection, self-analysis and observation, in order to improve his own practice and the practice of those in his charge. His work was essentially note-taking. Brecht, on the other hand, was a writer of academic essays. He was a Communist and a supporter of the revolutionary ideals of Karl Marx. He wrote about theories of performance and presentation in order to contribute publicly to a political debate as much as to express coherent practical ideas of theatre procedure. There has, therefore, been a tendency by some teachers and directors to interpret his ideas too literally and ignore the political context in which he offered them. Stephen Unwin states the situation succinctly in *So You Want to be a Theatre Director?*

> Brecht is his own worst enemy. His essays have led generations of actors and directors into a theoretical jungle, in which superficial aesthetic ideas have been mistaken for substance — above all the much disputed 'alienation effect' — and crude demonstrative acting is excused on the grounds that it's 'Brechtian'. But Brecht's writings on theatre need to be seen as provocations at a particular time and place, a reaction against the headlong embrace by half of Europe's theatre-goers of the ghastly stupidity of fascism. And they can be exceptionally useful.

Brecht's ideas

If Brecht's ideas are to be 'exceptionally useful', as Unwin suggests, then they must be applied with understanding and discrimination. This means, as much as anything, the realisation that those ideas will not work for every play and that, indeed, they will not even necessarily work for every play by Brecht.

Before we identify a suitable text which might be explored effectively in production using Brechtian theory, we will first pinpoint the major elements of the theory and then explore how they were developed in practice.

Epic theatre

Brecht's style of theatre is often referred to as 'epic theatre'. 'Epic' is a term originally coined by the Greek philosopher Aristotle with reference to poetry. The poetic tragedy, Aristotle argues, should consist of one series of events taking place over a definable and contained period of time (see the discussion of Aristotle's 'unities' on pages 26–27). On the other hand, the epic poem may depict a number of events that happen simultaneously, to 'add mass and dignity to the poem'.

There is in the 'epic' creation, therefore, a sense of scale or a 'capacity for enlarging its dimensions'. It is this sense of scale that has meaning for us today when we describe a play — or more usually now a film — as epic, referring to its length or the complexity of its setting. Many of the films of the mid-twentieth century made by the British film director David Lean have been described as epics, for instance *The Bridge on the River Kwai* (1957), *Lawrence of Arabia* (1962), *Doctor Zhivago* (1965) and *Ryan's Daughter* (1970).

The epic poem

An epic poem is a long narrative poem, often detailing the heroic exploits of an individual. The first epic poems would have been created and transmitted orally, often by travelling poets, and were not written down. Many ancient Greek epics (for instance Homer's *Iliad* and *Odyssey*, poems centred around the siege of Troy) date from between the eighth and the sixth centuries BC, and were probably originally oral. The Old English poem *Beowulf* is an example of a Dark Ages epic poem that was probably oral in origin (c. 700 AD) but later written down (c. 1010 AD). It is over 3,000 lines long. A more recent example is John Milton's famous epic poem in ten books, *Paradise Lost* (1667).

Doctor Zhivago (1965) has been described as an epic film

Brecht's use of the term 'epic' bears some relation to Aristotle's definition, in that he did not wish to be constrained by the unity of time, which Aristotle had identified as being an essential ingredient of tragedy. He wished to have the freedom to depict events happening in an irregular time frame. This is why many of Brecht's plays contain a large number of short episodic scenes that do not necessarily take place in a chronological order.

Part of Brecht's desire in moving away from the unity of time was to eliminate what he saw as the hypnotic qualities of theatre — those elements that might seduce an audience into becoming too engrossed in the story rather than engaged by its social issues. Short, punchy scenes, often punctuated by music and covering a series of events that might be taking place simultaneously, would keep an audience's attention and 'jerk' its members into the role of an observers rather than passive witnesses.

Brecht and silent film

Brecht was impressed by early silent cinema (from around 1895 to the late 1920s), particularly some of the comic work of Charlie Chaplin (1889–1977) and Buster Keaton (1895–1966). Silent film comedy shows episodic structure and the use of strong, immediate physical humour.

Epic theatre versus dramatic theatre

Brecht used the term 'epic' to distinguish his work from 'dramatic' theatre. In his introductory notes to *Rise and Fall of the City of Mahagonny* (1927) — a political-satirical opera by Kurt Weill to which he wrote the libretto, first performed in Leipzig in 1930 — Brecht usefully offers definitions to clarify his understanding of the two types of theatre. Some of them are reproduced in Table 11.1.

Table 11.1 Epic theatre versus dramatic theatre in Brechtian terms

Epic theatre	Dramatic theatre
Narrative	Plot
Turns the spectator into an observer	Implicates the spectator in a stage situation
Arouses the spectator's capacity for action	Wears down the spectator's capacity for action
Forces the spectator to take decisions	Provides the spectator with sensations
The spectator is made to face something	The spectator is involved in something
Argument	Suggestion
The spectator stands outside, studies	The spectator is in the thick of it, shares
The spectator is alterable and able to alter	The spectator is unalterable
Social being determines thought	Thought determines being

If you compare the two sides of the table, you will begin to understand the essential differences between Brecht's own epic theatrical aims and his perception of the theatre of realism ('dramatic theatre').

The importance of audience

The aims shown in Table 11.1 are particularly useful for a discussion of the importance of audience. It is interesting to note that while Stanislavski, in his writing, clearly respects the audience and takes seriously his role as a provider of culture and education, he does not make the audience a part of the dramatic process. Brecht, on the other hand, views the audience as a pivotal part of the process of theatre, and this process is geared towards making the spectator respond. Not only should man be seen as a being who can reach decisions as a result of witnessing theatrical productions, the theatre that he sees should force him to make such decisions.

Brecht's aim, therefore, is to inspire his audience to take action. Having identified in simple terms the aims of epic theatre, what techniques does Brecht employ in order to achieve these aims?

The alienation effect

Of all the techniques and theories propounded by Brecht, undoubtedly the so-called 'alienation effect' (or '*V-effekt*') is the most controversial and often the subject of misunderstanding or misinterpretation.

The word 'alienation' in this context is a translation from the German term *Verfremdung*, thus the concept is often referred to as the *Verfremdungseffekt* or the *V-effekt* (you should note that 'alienation' is an imperfect translation for *Verfremdung*).

In essence, we should see the alienation effect as being the means by which we can look critically at events and people in a fresh and perhaps unfamiliar light. To illustrate the idea, Brecht gives the example how one might regard one's mother as a wife:

> To see one's mother as a man's wife one needs a *V-effekt*; this is provided, for example, when one acquires a stepfather. If one sees one's form-master hounded by the bailiffs a *V-effekt* occurs: one is jerked out of a relationship in which the form-master seems big into one where he seems small.
>
> (Willett, *The Theatre of Bertolt Brecht*)

Practical application in performance

The common misperception of the alienation effect is that it requires an actor to perform without emotion or even expression. Reflecting on Wanamaker's view of Helene Weigel's performance in *Mother Courage* (see page 117) — a performance captured on film and clearly one of emotional complexity and depth — it is difficult to sustain the view that the alienation effect somehow means that the actor should emotionally neuter his or her performance. What then is meant by 'alienation' in the context of performance, and why is it misinterpreted in this way?

The alienation effect does not entail estranging the audience in the sense of making its members hostile to the performance they are watching or the views being expressed by the play. Rather, it is an attempt to reveal drama in a fresh light, where events and relationships should not be taken for granted. Therefore, Mother in *Mother Courage* should not simply be seen as a mother who loses three children in the war but as a woman who puts business before her children and loses them as a consequence. The alienation here is an attempt to distance the audience from the obvious interpretation of the character as a grief-stricken mother. The emotional complexity of the role should not deter the actor from exploring the social implications of the play and the strong political message that underlies it. The playing of the role should reflect this 'concrete truth' and not become a performance that is purely about the bereavement of a mother.

The alienation effect, then, prevents an audience establishing too intimate or one-dimensional a relationship with an actor's interpretation of a character. An actor should explore the social elements of the character — in conjunction with the director — to ensure that his or her interpretation demonstrates an understanding of the character as a feature of society, not just a figure of human emotion. That is why one of the major distinctions between the 'epic' theatre of Aristotle and the 'epic' theatre of Brecht is the lack of empathy between audience and actor: for Brecht, members of the audience must not be hypnotised into losing themselves in the performance of the actor and so surrendering their critical faculties. They must remain alert to the issues of the play, make decisions about them and then act on those decisions.

This does not preclude the idea that the action may be presented with emotion by the actor, but this emotion should not distract from the playwright's message, the substance and content of the play.

Gestus

Gestus is, perhaps, an even more difficult German term than *Verfremdung* to translate into an equivalent English expression. As the word suggests, it is connected with the gestures an actor might make. However, it also describes the attitude and gist of a scene or a role and is, therefore, expressed in a number of ways.

Gestus, either through words or movement, helps the actor to simplify the role and condense it into its recognisable essential elements. It defines appropriate action rather than subtext and psychological preoccupation.

Practical application in performance

The sense of distilling a role to its essentials is reflected in Brecht's craft as a writer, choosing as he does to adopt an economic poetic style rather than create expansive or elegant speeches and dialogue. A good example is Peachum's opening song in *The Threepenny Opera* (1928):

You ramshackle Christian awake!
Get on with your sinful employment.
Show what a good crook you could make.
The Lord will cut short your enjoyment.

Betray your own brother, you rogue
And sell your old woman you rat.
You think the Lord God's just a joke?
He'll give you His Judgement on that.

The language in this extract is simple, the meaning and attitude abundantly clear, assisted by a punctuated, sharp rhythm. There is no subtlety in these lines and they leave little room for doubt about the character and motives of Peachum.

However, in its crudest and most misguided interpretation, *Gestus* has been used to suggest character through a series of limited and repeated gestures. In a recent production of Brecht's *Señora Carrar's Rifles* (1937), the director had clearly instructed the actors to choose about three gestures each and stick to them rigidly. Given that this particular play is, arguably, a rare example of Brecht experimenting with a more Aristotelian approach, the sight of actors constantly having to repeat a series of awkward and contrived gestures was alienating to the audience in precisely the manner Brecht did *not* intend.

Gestus can be helpful to actors and director alike in attempting to discover the essential heart of a scene or an onstage relationship. To impose the notion of *Gestus* as a rule which restricts movement or gesture is to miss the point entirely. At its best, it can be used as tool of discovery and simplification; at its worst, it can confuse, obstruct and over-complicate.

Music

Brecht often used music in his plays. His most notable collaboration was with the composer Kurt Weill in *The Threepenny Opera* (1928), an adaptation of *The Beggar's Opera* written by John Gay in the early eighteenth century. The role of the music here is not to hypnotise or charm the audience, as is often the case in the modern musical, but instead to jerk them into consciousness.

The songs in *The Threepenny Opera* have been described as 'interruptions', and the actors in the original production were chosen because of their acting ability and not their prowess in singing. In his notes for *The Threepenny Opera*, Brecht writes:

> Nothing is more revolting than when an actor pretends not to notice that he has left plain speech and started to sing… As for the melody, he must not follow it blindly: there is a kind of speaking-against-the music which can have strong effects; the result of a stubborn, incorruptible sobriety which is independent of music and rhythm.

For Brecht, music is not there to provide an emotional peak to a play or scene but instead to create a moment when a character might speak messages or tell stories through the song. We must not confuse Brecht's use of music, therefore, with the use made of it by writers of popular musical theatre, where music is used to seduce or thrill an audience — for example, the title theme in Andrew Lloyd Webber's *Phantom of the Opera* (1986).

It is open to question whether the intention not to seduce or thrill was truly realised, given the success and appeal of some of Weill's music — most notably 'Mac the Knife' from *The Threepenny Opera*, which has since been recorded by Bobby Darrin, Ella Fitzgerald and Frank Sinatra. The big production treatment afforded to this and numerous other versions of the song would have appalled Brecht, who used a simple chamber orchestra production sung by an actor with an untrained singing voice. For him, the music had to deliver the text and was, therefore, subservient to it. Brecht's lyrics were part of his notion of *Gestus*; they were economical and poetic but efficient and constrained. They were not lyrically expansive and beautiful.

Among other collaborators, Brecht worked somewhat unsuccessfully with the composer Paul Hindemith on the *Lehrstück* (1929), a series of short didactic plays. While Hindemith's work is often far from easy listening, it can be chillingly atmospheric and Brecht was concerned that it might interfere with or overwhelm the sharply didactic nature of the text. Hindemith, on the other hand, was reluctant to provide music which was always going to be subjugated to the text — designed to deliver the written word rather than to enhance it as an equal partner.

Practical application in performance

In Brechtian theatre there should be little or no attempt to disguise the musicians from the audience. Hence musicians can appear on stage beside the actors, rather than being hidden away in an orchestra pit. In some Brechtian productions, the actors may also serve as musicians, ensuring that the illusion of their characters' reality will be broken for the audience as soon as they pick up their instruments.

Music in Brecht's plays, it has been argued, is part of the alienation effect, since it cannot fail to remind the members of an audience of the theatrical nature of what they are seeing and subvert any temptation they may feel to accept that the representation they are witnessing is fact — it is an obvious part of the mechanics of theatre. However, the role of music is more profound and defining than simply that of a reminder to the audience of the theatrical devices at work. Rather, it is an attempt by Brecht to punctuate his language — sometimes quite harshly — and affords characters the opportunity to report on the action and to tell stories to the audience that are relevant to the action and often didactic in tone.

Education and 'entertainment'

Many people assert — understandably, given the nature of some of his essays — that Brecht firmly believed the theatre should be a place of education and not of entertainment.

In his notes on *Mahagonny*, he identifies the distinctions between dramatic and epic theatre and also expresses the need to redefine the theatre generally:

> Thus to develop the means of entertainment into an object of instruction, and to change certain institutions from places of amusement into organs of public communication.

This statement has a somewhat authoritarian tone to it and perhaps provides us with an example of how Brecht's theory can differ from his practice. There is little doubt that his plays of the time *were* entertaining — often containing significant elements of verbal and physical humour — and it seems strange that he would advocate the complete scrapping of the role of entertainment. Brecht's theories do at times differ from his practice, and it is necessary to remember that he was writing from the viewpoint of a polemicist and his expressed views are, therefore, deliberately provocative.

Auditorium atmosphere

In his notes to accompany *The Threepenny Opera*, Brecht describes the auditorium atmosphere he aspired to have as:

> …that boxing-ring attitude of smoking and observing.

Clearly Brecht felt that the audience should be relaxed and in an informal environment, conducive to discussion and reflection. The members of the audience should be able to see all the mechanics of theatre — musicians, stagehands, all the work of acting and singing. No attempt should be made to persuade them that the theatre experience is mimicking reality. The theatre, in other words, should be a place of representation rather than illusion, and the theatrical environment one in which the working man should feel comfortable, not awkward.

Changing theory of entertainment

In 1949 Brecht wrote an important document called 'A Short Organum for the Theatre', in which he refers once again to the theme of entertainment. The 'Organum' was deliberately written in the style of Aristotle, whose original 'Organon' had been his treatise on logic.

Just as Aristotle had sought to define areas of theatre, so too did Brecht, offering revised versions of his earlier ideas. Instead of suggesting the scrapping of entertainment, as he had once done in the introductory notes of *Mahagonny*, he now wanted to embrace it:

> Let us treat theatre as a place of entertainment…and try to discover which type of entertainment suits us best.

However, this new emphasis on entertainment was not quite the radical shift which it first appears. Nor should it be thought that by embracing entertainment Brecht now saw theatre as a place of frivolity. In the postwar era, Brecht was concerned that theatre should be seen as part of the new scientific age. Willett argues in *The Theatre of Bertolt Brecht* that the pleasure gained from the entertaining elements of theatre is the pleasure one might feel from seeing a highly efficient and beautiful piece of mechanics at work, or from hearing a social issue expressed with clarity and analytical precision: 'Science and art meet on this ground, that both are there to make man's life easier…'

The Organum is a development of Brecht's earlier writings, being rather less polemic and less politically motivated. This is understandable, since it was written after the defeat of the Nazis. Many of his earlier ideas regarding the use of lighting and singing remain unchanged. However, it is important to point out that even the *Organum* contains elements of theory that Brecht did not try out. The majority of Brecht's productions were not held in factories or centres populated by only working people. They were often performed in the centre of Berlin or on tour, and frequently to appreciative middle-class audiences. So far as his untried theories were concerned, Brecht put this down to a lack of readiness in the audience. Although the members of his audiences lived in a scientific age, he said, they themselves were not scientific enough to be exposed to his new ideas.

Brecht's theories applied

The point should be clear now that one should not apply the work of theorists formulaically. When you visit the theatre, although you might do so with a critical perspective, your first response to a production will probably *not* be to ask yourself whether it has been influenced by the ideas of either Brecht or Stanislavski. It is not contradictory for a production to be influenced by both practitioners. The practice of trying to force Stanislavski and Brecht into a 'boxing ring', where the work of one is diametrically opposed to the work of the other, is as pointless as it is inaccurate. However, there are principles and practices of Brecht which may be applied usefully and successfully. To illustrate this idea, we will look at two plays, one of which is unmistakably Brechtian in tone and style and another which is open to broader interpretation.

Approaching a production of 'Oh! What a Lovely War'

In preparing any text for production, it is important for a director to consider his or her concept for the play. *Oh! What a Lovely War* (Joan Littlewood, 1963) is a play with a number of specific requirements. It is the story of the First World War, staged as an 'end of the pier' Pierrot show. All the actors, therefore, are intended to be dressed in white clown-like costumes over which they add extra elements of theatrical attire.

Oh! What a Lovely War is staged as an 'end of the pier' Pierrot show. (Regent's Park Open Air Theatre, 2002)

It is, of course, possible to vary this presentation. In 1963, when the play was first performed, Pierrot shows would have been in the living memory of some members of the audience — such shows were on the rise at the time of the First World War (1914–18). However, a modern director may feel that Pierrot is too remote an image for an audience of the twenty-first century and therefore wish to adapt or amend the nature of the play's presentation.

Oh! What a Lovely War depicts the major events of the First World War in a series of episodes, and delivers its message through music and dance as well as dialogue. In what ways could this play be seen as typifying the elements of Brechtian theatre?

'Character' in the play

It is impossible to become embroiled in the fate of one major character in this piece — there aren't any. At the start of the play, the members of the cast sing a well-known 'music hall' song of the era, 'Johnny Jones'. The Master of Ceremonies enters, wishes everyone a good evening, tells a few corny jokes and introduces 'the ever popular war game'.

The 'characters' of all the major countries involved in the war now enter and explain their tense relationships. Germany believes it should have more say in world affairs. The MC blows a whistle and announces the second part of the war game, and — against the background of German music — the German generals discuss their plans for war. As they do so, an image of the 'Schlieffen Plan' (Germany's ultimately disastrous blueprint for winning the war in a matter of weeks) is projected onto a screen by a slide projector. One by one, the other nations announce their plans for war and for striking the all-important knockout blow.

As the play continues, we see the progress of the war through a series of scenes, some more realistic than others.

Towards the end of the first half, the scene is set in the trenches of the Western Front on Christmas Eve 1914. A dialogue develops between the soldiers from the German and the British trenches and eventually they meet and shake

Pierrot shows

The character of Pierrot, in his familiar white baggy costume, was created by Giuseppe Giratoni in France in the middle of the seventeenth century. Pierrot arrived in England in 1891, and his popularity was established by his appearance in a French mime play which ran at the Prince of Wales Theatre. The first English Pierrot troupe was set up around 1895.

Pierrot shows pioneered a new form of public entertainment in England, consisting of songs, dances, comic sketches and occasional monologues. The shows were performed in the open, and gained the English name 'concert party'.

By 1910, troupes were taking their Pierrot shows on tour rather than remaining in one resort for the summer season. By the end of the 1920s, permanent wooden staging was often used for the alfresco shows, offering proper seating for the audience. These shows continued to flourish through the 1930s and 1940s, after which their popularity waned.

hands in the middle — in 'no man's land', the patch of ground between the two sets of trenches. The famous First World War song 'Goodbyee' is played. The end of the first half seems to arrive at a tranquil, almost ironically peaceful mood when the sound of an exploding shell is heard and the last line of the song is rendered inaudible.

The following links with Brechtian theory are important:

- During the play, the projection of images and statistics relevant to the war involves modern technology. The use of powerful factual imagery and information underpins the dramatic action, and serves to remind the audience that the performance on stage represents a reality that reaches far beyond the world of the theatre.

- Although written nearly half a century ago and depicting events of nearly 100 years ago, the play is still remarkably popular, particularly with community and youth groups. It is not uncommon for modern productions of *Oh! What a Lovely War* to use photographic and video images from more recent wars and to employ multiracial casts in order to afford a more contemporary feel to the piece. Thus Brecht's ideal of a play which does not constrain its audience within an individual plot is preserved, and a modern audience may still bear witness to the narrative of an anti-war statement.

- Although there is a chronology to the war, to which the slogans and on-screen projections largely adhere, the episodic structure of the play prevents an audience being drawn into a plot line. The arms dealers' shooting scene at the start of Act II is not significant from the perspective of plot (this scene could have been placed almost anywhere in the play); it is the potential impact on the audience that is important.

- The first act ends with the scenes in the trenches on Christmas Eve 1914, demonstrating the basic humanity of the soldiers — the men are not naturally enemies. The opening of the second act is almost a parody of this revelation, showing arms dealers from the various sides in the war enjoying the camaraderie of the grouse hunt and celebrating the wealth that the continued hostilities bring them.

- In the second half of the play we meet the only character other than the Master of Ceremonies who could be said to have a major role. Field Marshall Haig was the commander of all British troops from 1916 to the end of the war, and we see him frequently throughout the second half. However, he is presented as a compassionless individual, ordering men to certain death and contemplating that 'the loss of say another 300,000 men could yield some really great results'. There is little danger of an audience being drawn into his story or identifying with him — quite the reverse. This undoubtedly one-sided view of Haig's character (and indeed of other characters and events) led some to criticise the play. But again, this is a reason why it is suitable for a Brechtian treatment. Brecht's theatre is not balanced — there is always a strong political or social message. The message of *Oh! What a Lovely War* is clearly an anti-war statement, and there is no attempt to create a balanced piece of theatre. It is in the nature of political theatre that it presents a cogent viewpoint, not a representation of all sides of the argument.

◆ Further examples of characterisation in *Oh! What a Lovely War* are also consistent with Brecht's style of presentation in that they are described by their functions — 'officer', 'nurse', 'chaplain' etc. The characters are immediately recognisable and relevant to the social and violent context in which they are presented. An ensemble of actors would be expected to play all the parts and would be identifiable in each role they played.

Practical application in performance

How might a performance of *Oh! What a Lovely War* demonstrate elements of Brecht's theories as previously discussed?

First, a production should not be created as a vehicle or showcase for any practitioner's work; such elements should be used only if they help to enhance the production. This was the case for the original adaptor and director of *Oh! What a Lovely War*, Littlewood, and her Company of the Theatre Workshop. They had a clear artistic policy, underpinned and defined by a socialist view of the world. In this regard, they therefore had much in common with Brecht and the work of the Berliner Ensemble. Indeed, Littlewood would almost certainly have seen examples of the ensemble's work when it toured Britain. The broad ideological aims and the nature of the piece they wanted to create meant that many of Brecht's devices for presentation were relevant. For a company producing this play today, there are equally many elements of Brecht's theories which might be useful.

The alienation effect and *Gestus*

The alienation effect is found in the nature of the characterisation, in the use of music and singing and in the short *Gestus*-orientated scenes. *Gestus* is employed in the sense that every scene has a particular gist to it, making it distinctive. For example, the scene featuring Mrs Pankhurst clearly articulates the suffragettes' view of the war and the abusive response of many of the ordinary men and women to her. The sight and sound of her embattled pleas as she speaks to an increasingly dubious and hostile crowd gives the scene a specific dimension and angle.

There is no attempt to explore the psychological impact of the crowd's hostility towards the character of Mrs Pankhurst, nor is there an intricate description of the motivations of each of the characters on stage with her. Such features are unnecessary because it is easily discernible within the action of the scene that one of the effects of the war was to polarise the spirit of patriotism and the aims of the suffragettes, so that the suffragettes were seen almost as traitors and, as a consequence, their cause lost momentum.

There is a definite *Gestus* character to the party scene involving the generals, as they dance with their wives or mistresses to the gentle sound of a palm court orchestra and play power games with and against each other. Such an event may never have taken place, but the purpose here is not to recreate or replicate reality. Rather, there is a higher reality or 'concrete truth', which is that titled and wealthy generals vied for positions of power and influence while sending other men to the Western Front, where they died horrible and premature deaths. The *Gestus* is clear, and a director and actors will find this helpful in developing the characters.

While the nature of the *Gestus*, in this particular context at least, may lead to choices that are stereotypical (for instance, making the character of a general an 'upper-class twit'), that does not make the anger of the piece any less valid or dramatically justified.

The 'boxing ring' atmosphere: audience reaction

It would surely be impractical to stage *Oh! What a Lovely War* in a boxing ring atmosphere, with audiences smoking, observing and commenting on the action; perhaps this would be taking Brechtian theory a step too far.

However, the important quality for a production of this play is that the anger and anti-war sentiment are made abundantly clear to the audience. Even though it is a piece about the First World War, the message should be relevant to the modern world, and the audience should feel a strong reaction.

The director might feel, for instance, that the absurdly nationalistic arguments of the generals professing that 'God is on our side' are reminiscent of the attitudes of a number of politicians over recent years. The members of an audience may well make that connection for themselves, but a director — perhaps one known for his or her strong political stance — might use imagery, scenery and costume to make that connection more concrete for them.

Just as performances in Brechtian-style theatre may have an emotional content, the audience response may legitimately be emotional too. Ask yourself why the audience of *Oh! What a Lovely War* might be weeping. To weep for the loss of a fictional character — for example the death of Leonardo DiCaprio's character in the film *Titanic* (1997) — is an example of the kind of cathartic response that Brecht found repellent. On the other hand, for the audience to weep at the injustice and horror of war is a sign of the play's success, since it is that emotional reaction which may lead the audience to want to change the society that brought about the war in the first instance.

The use of technology

While the original productions of Brecht's plays were given simple settings by his designer, Caspar Neher, Brecht valued the use of technology. His belief in the aesthetic pleasure of seeing efficient technology at work could be incorporated into a modern production of *Oh! What a Lovely War*. Of course, the sophistication of theatre technology has increased enormously since the first production in 1963. It would not be necessary, therefore, to use excessively complicated and expensive technology to enhance such a production, in order for it to qualify as 'Brechtian'. However, it is arguably illogical not to use computerised lighting boards, digital sound systems and PowerPoint-generated images, following a misguided view that any invention that has emerged since Brecht's death is not 'Brechtian'.

Effective use of lighting can certainly support specific moments in the play. For example, a change in lighting, which Brecht advocated when a character sings, could be used to dispel any notion of reality. However, this play is performed successfully in a variety of venues by companies with vastly different budgets. In production, its effect depends more upon clarity of performance and swiftness of scene change than technical wizardry.

Comparison with 'Journey's End'

Does *Oh! What a Lovely War* make its point more effectively than *Journey's End* (1928) by R. C. Sherriff (1896–1975) — a much more naturalistic play on the same subject?

Journey's End is set in a dugout on the Western Front, and the action takes place over the period of a few days in March 1918 during the German offensive. In the course of the play, we become familiar with each of the characters. Stanhope, the young but prematurely aged captain, presides over the officers in his platoon as one by one they fall victim to the enemy onslaught. Does the audience's emotional involvement with the lives and deaths of the officers in *Journey's End* mean that it might lose sight of the issue of the rights and wrongs of war? Some would argue that the naturalistic style of *Journey's End*, in allowing the audience to witness the suffering of individuals, brings home the horror of war more effectively than the Brechtian style of *Oh! What a Lovely War*.

It is ultimately a matter of individual audience experience and the skill of those involved in particular productions as to which play is regarded as more successful. It is not possible to argue conclusively that an issue-based piece of theatre which avoids naturalism is definitively more successful at communicating a 'message' than a piece of 'epic' theatre.

What can be argued with these two examples is that while the element of human suffering is uncompromisingly clear in both plays, the anti-war politics of *Oh! What a Lovely War* are unmistakable. It would be tenable, therefore, to draw the conclusion that *Journey's End* is more of a humanist play and *Oh! What a Lovely War* more of a political one. The message conveyed is no less powerful; it is simply that the emphasis is different.

Does the naturalistic style of *Journey's End* bring home the horror of war more effectively than the Brechtian style of *Oh! What a Lovely War*?

Summary

When evaluating Brecht's theatrical ideas, it is important to remember that he was principally a playwright and a director, not an actor. Furthermore, he did not always put his own ideas into practice. As an essayist, he put forward theories of theatre and staging that were, at least in part, defined by a belief in Marxist ideology. Brecht argued his Marxist standpoint most vociferously while his native Germany was under the tyranny of Nazism.

Brecht identified comparisons between his own works and theories of performance and those of Shakespeare, specifically in the use of verse and soliloquy, and the extensive use of epic action. During his career, Brecht directed a number of Shakespearean productions and was critical of many standard productions of the time.

Group activities

1 The best way to explore Brecht's ideas is to rehearse a scene from one of his plays: look especially at *Mother Courage* and *Caucasian Chalk Circle*, or at some of the shorter plays in *Lehrstücke*, such as *The Exception and The Rule*.

2 If you are using Brecht's ideas as a model for devising, you could attempt the following activity about the story of the Good Samaritan in the Bible (Luke 10:25–37). In this story, a Jewish man is set upon by thieves and left for dead. A lawyer and a priest pass him by, but a Samaritan helps him and takes him to a place of rest.

It is important to note that Samaritans were despised by the story's target audience, the Jews. To recast the story in a more recognisable modern setting, instead of a Jew being helped by a Samaritan, one could have a racist helped by a member of the race he or she hates, or a sexist man helped by a woman.

Rather than concentrating on the graphic reality of the attack, play the scene ensuring that the views of the participants are clearly known. Each character should use narration to explain his or her actions or the lack of them. An audience should be left in no doubt as to (a) the motives of the individuals in their actions and (b) where the sympathies of the group lie.

Do not necessarily follow the religious implications of the story. For example, you may want to slant the story to the thieves' point of view and focus on their motivations. Or you may wish to suggest that the Samaritan has reasons other than simple 'goodness' in carrying out his actions. The important feature should be that the members of the audience are engaged in a debate and feel challenged by what they have witnessed.

Chapter 12

Applying Brecht's principles

Macbeth by Shakespeare

Brecht directed a number of Shakespeare's plays in addition to his own work, and it has been argued that there are some interesting links between the crafts of the two men. These were links which Brecht himself identified:

* Brecht argues that his plays *Life of Galileo* (1938/1945) and *Mother Courage* owe elements of their structure and their use of clear historical contexts to some of the great works of Shakespeare. Many Shakespearian plays are set in specific time periods or based on real characters from history.

* Shakespeare's use of monologue or soliloquy, usually in verse and addressed directly to an audience, is echoed in some of Brecht's rhythmic verses, likewise delivered directly to the spectators. Shakespeare used soliloquy to confront an audience with a particular view or a passionate declaration, designed to provoke an unexpected response. For example in *King Lear*, the audience does not expect to sympathise with 'the bastard' Edmund when he confides his plotting against his brother and his father. However, having heard Edmund's soliloquy, the audience is forced to take a view about his behaviour. Is he simply a devious and malicious villain, or should we have some sympathy for his case?

In *The Theatre of Bertolt Brecht* the translator and scholar John Willett (1917–2002), who is famous for translating Brecht's work into English, identifies the qualities which drew Brecht to Shakespeare:

Actual events, actual relations, clearly-defined actions, a sort of running fight in which each successive issue is plain: Brecht had aimed at such goals...and in Shakespeare he saw them attained. In Shakespeare but not in the average Shakespeare production.

Brecht also described how he considered Shakespearian plays to be more 'epic' than 'dramatic'. When discussing the structure of *Coriolanus* (*c.* 1608), Brecht claims:

> ...all these great and small conflicts thrown on the scene at once; the unrest of the starving plebeians together with the war against their neighbours the Volsci; the plebeians' hatred for Marcius, the people's enemy — together with his patriotism; the creation of the people's tribunes — together with Marcius's appointment to a leading post in the war. How much of that do we get in the bourgeois theatre?   (*idem*)

Presumably Brecht believed that most Shakespearian productions did not meet the demands of the play because they failed to reflect 'these great and small conflicts' all at once.

Brechtian elements in productions of Shakespeare

Barrie Rutter

Since the early 1990s, Barrie Rutter's company Northern Broadsides has produced a large number of Shakespeare's plays. Rutter usually employs actors from the north of England who use northern accents. His settings are simple, with plays staged in real working environments. Such an approach has definite links with the aspirations of Brecht and the kind of settings he wished his plays to have.

Productions of Shakespeare often have a specific political flavour, which gives the plays an earthy, angry pugnacity. Rutter's 1992 production of *Richard III* (*c.* 1592–94), for instance, opened with an argument between Richard (played by Rutter) and the Lady Ann which had a fierce, gutteral, confrontational quality about it — a ringing, uncompromising clarity and an unmistakable *Gestus* of anger and guile.

Barrie Rutter (1946–)

Born in 1946, the son of a Hull fishworker, Rutter grew up in the fishdock area of Hull. At school, an English teacher frogmarched him into the school play because he had 'the gob for it'. Rutter's future direction was thus determined.

After leaving school, he studied at the Royal Scottish Academy of Music and Drama and then spent many years in the National Youth Theatre, culminating in his role as Douglas Bagley in the television drama *The Apprentices*

Barrie Rutter often employs Brechtian elements in his productions of Shakespeare's plays

(Peter Terson, 1968), a role specially written for him. His natural talent for acting has resulted in many other roles being written for him throughout his career.

Seasons at the RSC in Stratford, London and Europe completed the 1970s. In 1980, he joined the National Theatre; at this time he met and worked closely with the poet Tony Harrison. Rutter performed in all three of Harrison's adaptations, all written for the northern voice: *The Oresteia* (1981), *The Mysteries* (1985) and *The Trackers of Oxyrhynchus* (1988). In *Trackers*, the part of Silenus was written especially for Rutter. It was this experience of performing in the northern voice that germinated the idea for his company, Northern Broadsides.

Northern Broadsides was founded in 1992 and has developed a reputation for high-quality productions of Shakespeare and classic adaptations. The productions are often simply staged, sometimes using working settings such as textile mills or boatyards, to emphasise a 'workman-like' approach. The style has endured; Northern Broadsides is one of the country's most respected theatre companies, and Rutter himself has emerged as an important director in British theatre.

Michael Bogdanov (1938–)

Michael Bogdanov has produced, written and directed for both theatre and television during his successful career, but his primary interest is in the theatre. He received a Director of the Year award in 1979 for his RSC production of *The Taming of the Shrew*. He has also directed productions of Shakespeare's plays internationally, including *Hamlet* at the Abbey Theatre in Dublin, *Romeo and Juliet* at the Imperial Theatre in Tokyo, *Measure for Measure* at Stratford, Ontario and *Julius Caesar* at the Deutsches Schauspielhaus in Hamburg. In 1992, he directed a pioneering version of *Macbeth*, which travelled to four African countries.

He also created and directed a 12-part series for Channel 4, *Shakespeare Lives*. He co-founded the English Shakespeare Company with actor Michael Pennington in 1986.

Bogdanov was instrumental in establishing the Wales Theatre Company and has continued to enhance his reputation through successful productions of *Under Milk Wood* (2005) and Mal Pope's *Amazing Grace* (2006).

Michael Bogdanov

An example of a political approach to Shakespeare is Michael Bogdanov's production of *The Merchant of Venice*, staged by the English Shakespeare Company (1991).

In this production, the distinguished actor John Woodvine played a tall, dignified Shylock in a Venice set in Mussolini's fascist and anti-Semitic pre-war Italy of 1938. The persecution of Shylock at the hands of the Christians was therefore lent extra venom and political savagery.

Ian Brown

Ian Brown's 2002 production of *Hamlet* at the West Yorkshire Playhouse was not specifically set in a particular period of history, but the use of silent film and uniforms suggested an inter-war setting — perhaps the 1920s or 1930s. The gloomy high walls of the set, with many entrances set at different levels, suggested a place of secrets, rumours and paranoia. Claudius, the king, was dressed in a grey military uniform, suggestive of a totalitarian regime such as Hitler's Germany or Mussolini's Italy. Hamlet himself, played by Christopher Eccleston, was angry, ill at ease and seemingly stifled by an atmosphere of suppression and claustrophobia; he was a trapped poet, suffocating in the politicised, military environment of his uncle's court.

The character of Hamlet in this production, therefore, is not realised simply as a grieving son lamenting the loss of his father and the traitorous actions of his mother. Instead there is a realisation of Hamlet — an emotionally and intellectually vigorous individual — finding himself in a context where individuality may be regarded as dangerously subversive. As such he is a threatened and depressed figure. The production thus had a political as well as an emotional dimension to it.

Macbeth

We will examine here some of the questions which you might consider as the director of a production of *Macbeth* (*c.* 1606) who wishes to make use of Brechtian ideas.

Your production need not, of course, obey all the 'rules' of what is sometimes seen as a traditional Brechtian production. These include actors getting changed in view of the audience, slogans being projected on screens, actors wearing black and white costumes and musicians being visible on stage. The reality of a production can be far more subtle and may share features with the work of other practitioners.

Background

The plot of *Macbeth* is convoluted. We are first presented with the setting: Scotland, a country ravaged by war from a combination of Norwegian forces and the traitorous Thane of Cawdor. Before any of the political plot-laying

'Deadly theatre'

If a production of Shakespeare offers only beautiful spoken verse and the starring performance of a famous actor, the potential strength of the play with its complex social message can be lost. It becomes what the British theatre and film director Peter Brook (1925–) referred to in *The Empty Space* as 'deadly theatre'. A successful production should be a living theatre experience, where members of an audience become involved, where they identify with the characters' emotions, and where they emerge with a heightened awareness of important universal themes.

commences, we are confronted with the witches' scene, presaging their meeting with Macbeth 'on the heath'.

The swift-moving opening, which takes us from the witches to the king to Macbeth and Banquo, presents us with a series of simultaneous events; the audience is not introduced to a single plot. While we may subsequently be drawn into the world of Macbeth, it is clear from the events of the play that it is about far more than one man's demise — it is concerned with the consequences of abuses of power and the social destruction those abuses wreak.

With its themes of power, ambition and tyranny and the use of violence to achieve political ends within greater and smaller conflicts, this play is potentially a revolutionary piece.

Historical context

Do you wish the production to use images and settings from a specific period in history? If you create a specific setting, do you want the war which is being fought at the beginning of the play to be a recognisable war from the past or, indeed, the present?

Presenting the context on stage

Given the multiplicity of scenes and different environments of the play, how will you treat your setting? How will your set be more conceptual than realistic, and how will it serve the aims of the play and the production? How will you achieve part of the *Gestus* of your production through setting? (Hint: remember the high walls of the set in Ian Brown's production of *Hamlet*, referred to on pages 136–37. Consider how that set decision influenced the play's themes and how the audience might have received these themes.)

Advising the actors

Macbeth

What is the driving force of Macbeth's ambition that makes him kill a king? This question must be linked to the world of the production, not just to individual psychological motives. So, the question for the actor and the director becomes not 'What kind of a man will kill a king to achieve his ambitions?' but rather 'What kind of world is it — and how has that world affected Macbeth — where a man will kill a king?' The character of Macbeth should not simply be presented as a Scottish nobleman who decides on the basis of a supernatural encounter with witches to kill his monarch; crucially, he is part of the violent political world of the play.

The alienation effect is useful to both the actor (not just the actor playing Macbeth — this applies to other roles as well) and the director when considering the elements of the character that society has shaped and how this affects behaviour.

The witches

It is important that the witches are related to the world of the setting — one of political intrigue, violence and ambition — rather than resembling an absurdist 'add on'.

- How do the witches connect with Macbeth, and what is it about them that exerts influence on him?
- Are they part of his nightmare, for example, or a manifestation of sexual fantasy?

These are not psychologically-based questions, but rather a prompt to consider what part of the world of the play the witches occupy. Are they part of its belief system?

The witches in a 1996 production of *Macbeth* at the RSC

Showing social consequences

How do you ensure that this play shows the social consequences of the behaviour of the rulers?

The implication of this question is not that you should contrive a series of vignettes revealing beggars and perpetrators of street violence. On the other hand, it is important to find ways to show how the tyranny of Macbeth has infiltrated society.

How, for example, do you portray the violence of the play? The murder of Lady Macduff and her young child is probably one of the most brutal scenes in Shakespeare. Do you want the audience to feel that this is a terrible one-off event or symptomatic of the world in which the Macduffs are living? How, in other words, do you present violence as a daily reality?

Using technology

Your decisions about the social and historical setting will influence your use of technology.

- How could you use lighting not just to illuminate the events, but also to affect and influence audience perception?
- How could lighting contribute to the *Gestus* and alienation effect of each scene and of the whole production?
- Is technology a part of the play as well as a contributing element of production? For example, do you want the technological influence of armaments to be a perceptible part of the production?

Summary of Brecht's ideas

- Brecht developed a theory of performance, referred to as 'epic theatre', that challenged Aristotle's concept of 'dramatic theatre'. Epic theatre aimed at disputing the dramatic unities of Aristotle and presenting an audience with a series of simultaneous events rather than a single plot line.
- Brecht's ideas were aimed at motivating the members of an audience to action, rather than seducing them with an intricate plot or emotional hypnosis.
- Brecht's theatre is not, as some suggest, devoid of emotion. However, the audience should not feel emotion in the sense of emotional empathy with a character. The emotion conveyed should motivate the audience to take some action.
- Brecht's theories acknowledge and proclaim the social function of theatre — the ability to change things by changing people.
- Brecht had important (and, over the years, changing) views about the role of entertainment in theatre.
- Brecht used music and singing extensively in his plays, not to charm the audience with beautiful melodies but to interrupt the play and allow his characters to tell stories.
- Science and technology played important roles in Brecht's productions.

Using sound and music

Remember that music in the world of Brechtian theatre is important not as a means by which to charm or seduce an audience but rather to jerk its members into a response and to allow a character to tell a story or share his or her thoughts.

The link has already been made between Brechtian song and Shakespearian verse and soliloquy. Is there a similar role for music in your production, to punctuate or intensify moments in the play?

Discussion questions

1 Reflecting on the plays you are studying, which of Brecht's ideas might prove useful for a director preparing a production?

2 What plays have you seen where you think the director or actors may have used some of Brecht's ideas in their preparation?

3 Have you seen a play where you have been critical of aspects of the production? Would the application of any of Brecht's ideas have helped? If so, which ones?

4 Are there any styles of play where the ideas of Brecht might not be useful? Explain your answer.

Essay questions

1 Plan a rehearsal of a play you are working on. Show how you might introduce some of Brecht's ideas on alienation effect or *Gestus* to your cast, either through text or off-text work.

2 Do you believe it is possible to incorporate the ideas of both Brecht and Stanislavski into one production? How would this work and with what play(s)?

Chapter 13

Antonin Artaud

There is an important difference between Antonin Artaud and the two practitioners we have studied so far: while Stanislavski and Brecht achieved recognition as great artists in their lifetime, Artaud — aside from a small, intensely loyal following — did not. Indeed, most of his experiments with theatre ended in failure, and his ideas were not accepted by his theatrical contemporaries. However, his influence on modern theatre practice is significant.

What is Artaud's style and why did he struggle so much to convey his ideas to both his audiences and his peers? What is his impact today and how might his practice be implemented?

A 'disease of the mind'

In his early twenties, Artaud submitted some poetry for publication to Jacques Rivière, editor of *La Nouvelle Revue Française*. Rivière rejected the submission. He liked Artaud and thought him talented but was critical of the poems' literary merits and commented on their 'divergent images'. Artaud informed Rivière that he was wrong about the literary merits of the poems, and that the problem was in fact a 'disease of the mind'. The ensuing correspondence revealed Artaud's ability to analyse his own deficiencies. Rivière was so captivated and impressed by the content of these letters that he chose to publish them instead.

Self-obsession and genius

It might seem an insult to refer to someone as being self-obsessed, as it implies complacency, but the nature of Artaud's self-obsession did not cause him any pleasure. At times during his life he was in a state of tortured and unrelenting anguish. As a child, he had suffered a near-fatal attack of meningitis, and although he recovered he was blighted by headaches for the rest of his life.

However, it was Artaud's anguish and mental torment that provided, in many respects, the source of his genius as well as his frustration and — at least during his lifetime — his failure. These elements are also at the heart of his work, in both his performance and his writings.

It is important to understand Artaud's frustration with the inadequacy of language: for him, words were not enough, even though he used them powerfully to explain his own mental illness. He wrote copiously but still was unable to express clearly either the agonies of his existence or his theories of theatre practice.

However, in his compendium of essays and articles *The Theatre and Its Double* (1938) he did articulate his theatre manifestos, and from these it is possible to discern the essence of his approach.

Antonin Artaud (1896–1948)

Antonin Artaud was a French playwright, poet, actor and director. Born in Marseilles — his father a wealthy shipbuilder, his mother of Greek heritage — he suffered a lifetime of ill-health, both physically and mentally debilitated by a near-fatal case of meningitis when he was 5 years old. He was educated at the Collège du Sacré Coeur in Marseilles, and at the age of 14 founded a literary magazine. Still in his teens, he began to suffer from depression and experience sharp head pains, which continued throughout his life. Around his early twenties, he began taking laudanum (a solution of opium in alcohol) for his pains, and continued to use opium, heroin and other drugs until his death.

Antonin Artaud's influence on modern theatre practice is significant

As an avant-garde theorist of revolutionary theatre, Artaud is famous for his influence on the way writers, directors and actors comprehend the production and the purpose of theatre. He was the progenitor of a provocative form of theatre, the aim of which was to disconcert and radically transform its audience. He sought to dispense with rational drama, masterpieces and psychological exploration, instead advocating a 'theatre of cruelty', drawing on psychoanalytic theory and the Balinese Theatre.

Early career

Artaud worked briefly as a stage performer for the French actor and director Aurelien Lugné-Poe (1869–1940), but this was not a success. He was too consumed by his own agonies to be able to assume another role effectively. He attended classes with Charles Dullin (1885–1949), an actor, theatre manager and director who trained a whole generation of French actors. Dullin admired Artaud's presence and fervour but found nothing but frustration in attempting to direct him. Artaud found it almost impossible to interpret a role in a realistic manner and on one occasion played the Emperor Charlemagne by crawling on all fours. When Dullin upbraided him, Artaud exclaimed in exasperation 'Oh, well if you want the truth!'

The Théâtre Alfred Jarry

At the time of Artaud's first theatrical experiments, Paris was playing host to the fledgling surrealist movement. Surrealism sought to give form to the inner realm of humanity rather than its outer casing (the province of realism), and this was achieved mainly through painting. You can see examples of surrealist art in the works of Salvador Dali and Max Ernst. Their philosophy was that if art was to reflect the reality of the world, it must embrace the unconscious and not be restricted to the realm of the conscious.

For Artaud, obsessed with his inner demons, surrealism was a school of thought with which he could identify and work. However, although presenting work of an experimental anti-naturalistic nature was no longer an outrageous concept, Artaud's efforts in the theatre still failed to find critical favour with many in Paris.

Meanwhile, the surrealist movement (particularly its leader, the painter André Breton) was increasingly moving towards a formal acceptance of communism. Artaud broke away on the grounds that it had simply swapped one set of restrictions for another. He believed that art should be free of political allegiance.

In partnership with Roger Vitrac and Robert Aron, Artaud founded the Théâtre Alfred Jarry in 1926. Subsequently, adherents of the surrealist movement thwarted Artaud's work at the theatre, particularly by protesting at one of his few critical successes, a production of the Swedish dramatist August Strindberg's *Dream Play*, which had received subsidies for its performance in Paris from wealthy expatriate Swedes.

The failure of the Théâtre Alfred Jarry was a further source of frustration to Artaud, particularly as personal failure only intensified his periods of depression and torment. However, he continued to write about his theoretical approach to theatre.

Alfred Jarry (1873–1907) and *Ubu Roi*

The playwright Alfred Jarry was a significant influence on Artaud. His most famous play, *Ubu Roi* (1896), had caused a storm when first performed in Paris in the year of Artaud's birth. The sight of the monstrously fat Ubu waddling onto the stage and emitting his first word '*Merde!*' ('shit') evoked howls of protest. *Ubu Roi* was an anarchic work, a crude parody of *Macbeth* featuring a vengeful, grotesque and murderous central character. Jarry's language was harsh and experimental, employing seemingly obscure rhythmic patterns and alliteration. Jarry's work stripped down the world of respectability and pomp and displayed Ubu in all his obscene vulgarity.

Balinese Theatre

Just as Stanislavski had a moment of revelation when he saw the Meiningen Players in Moscow in the 1880s, so too did Artaud when he saw the Balinese Theatre at the Colonial Exhibition in Paris in 1931. He was struck by the quality of the visible action and the non-verbal communication. In the Balinese Theatre he saw a fresh importance accorded to such features as facial expressions, mimetic devices and gesticulation, triggering in his mind the idea of a new language of theatre, where movement and gesture were of equal importance with words.

This emphasis on movement was extremely important to Artaud, who had found words to be a restrictive rather than a liberating force when attempting to describe or explain his feelings. He felt that movement conveyed the unconscious mind more successfully than words — a fundamental consideration for a surrealist. Seeing the Balinese Theatre confirmed Artaud's opinion that words were incapable of expressing certain thoughts and feelings and that a language of gestures or hieroglyphs with their visual impact was a far more potent and meaningful method of communication.

Antonin Artaud was inspired by the visual impact of the Balinese Theatre

Ralph Paprzycki/Alamy

Artaud's ideas

Over the next 4 years, inspired by the Balinese Theatre, Artaud formulated his ideas on theatre through a series of essays and articles:

- The actor should not just be an emitter of words, reduced to playing a mundane character. Myth and ritual rather than characterisation should lead theatre.
- An ensemble of actors using their bodies and chanting, singing and gesturing as well as using words is far more powerful in communicating with an audience.
- 'Reality' does not necessarily mean 'truth' — indeed, reality often obscures the truth. To get to the truth one has to expose humanity and show its inner being.
- The human soul should be laid bare on stage to show humanity's unconscious state, stripped of its sophistication and societal pretensions. The audience must recognise this and be affected by it.

Where Stanislavski wanted a theatre that drew the spectator in and Brecht wanted a theatre to motivate the spectator into action, Artaud wanted his spectator to be 'cured'. The cure was spiritual and not necessarily a pleasant or relaxing experience. Indeed, Artaud likened a trip to the theatre to a visit to the dentist.

Theatre and the plague

Artaud likened his conception of theatre to the plague. Plague can ravage a civilisation and attacks indiscriminately. Wealth or position cannot protect you, and catching it means that you are out of control.

For a society to suffer the plague is a visceral, painful experience, but its overall effect may, bizarrely, be one of cleansing, providing an opportunity to move forward in ways that are new and different. Artaud felt that a theatrical production should evoke the same extremes of response from an audience, leaving it breathless and shocked but ultimately healed and cleansed.

'No more masterpieces'

Artaud felt that the written text was the overriding and most significant element in traditional theatre. As a result, other theatrical elements were subjugated to the text and could only be partially used. Moreover, he felt that many of the plays hailed as masterpieces and great art were now redundant.

In his essay 'No more masterpieces' (from *The Theatre and Its Double*), Artaud explained that the great works of the past, although literary masterpieces, could not move, thrill or terrify an audience in performance as they may have done when they were first created. This was because modern man was no longer of the culture of the Greek tragedians or Shakespeare. In order to develop a new theatre for the twentieth century, Artaud considered it necessary to create fresh and modern ways to inspire and excite an audience, as the classics had done when they were first performed. Tragedy and epic themes of war, tyranny and cruelty would still be the subject matter of drama, but new forms of presentation were needed.

Artaud's new theatrical language would encompass the ancient and the modern in terms of artefacts and images but remain topical. The topicality of his theatre was not like that of Brecht, who wanted to communicate and evoke a response to a variety of political issues. Artaud was interested in creating a universal topicality of existence itself — of man's struggle with himself and his world. The new language of theatre that Artaud sought to identify promoted all aspects of the theatre on an equal level.

Voice

In his attempts to break theatre's subjugation to text and reveal a language somewhere between gesture and thought, Artaud claimed that 'theatre can still derive possibilities for extension from speech outside words, the development in space of its dissociatory, vibratory action on our sensibility'. In other words, Artaud believed that the actor should not rely solely on the meaning of words to communicate a message. The sound of words was also important, and the actor should use his or her voice like an instrument, in order to articulate the underlying emotions.

Using words like this, in an almost primordial manner, made considerable demands on the actor's breathing and vocal control. During Artaud's production of *The Cenci* (which is discussed on pages 149–51), he suffered considerably from loss of voice, such were the gruelling demands he made on it.

Sound effects

Sound was a hugely significant aspect of Artaud's new style of theatre. This sound should not be perceived as merely an accompaniment or an embellishment; it was part of the whole visceral theatrical experience and often required intricate and detailed orchestration.

A combination of instruments would be used in conjunction with the actors' voices to create the required disturbing sounds. There should be no confusion of this approach with the concept of 'musicals'. The sound effects Artaud experimented with were neither soothing nor realistic. They were — in common with many of Artaud's ideas for theatre — the kinds of sound we might associate with dreams and nightmares: distortions and sounds layered upon sounds.

Lighting

Artaud thought that lighting should be a fundamental part of the theatrical experience. Indeed, he was one of the first practitioners to demonstrate that lighting could create different moods and atmospheres. He explored the interplay of lighting effects, paying particular attention to colours, angles and intensity.

Lighting for Artaud was a theatrical force capable of evoking terror or passion in an audience. He was also aware that these experiments with lighting influenced performance too. A scene from a play feels different to actors performing it under natural light and under stage lights. The intensity, colour and direction of light are all factors that can influence performance.

Role of the audience

While we sometimes discuss the genre of 'total theatre' in relation to the works of Berkoff and other playwrights and directors who adopt a largely physical approach to production, it is a concept that has come about largely as a consequence of Artaud's theories. Quite apart from the concept of all the theatrical elements coming together to create a total and sensory experience (as opposed to an intellectual one with Brecht, or an emotional one with Stanislavski), Artaud wanted to establish the idea that in the theatre there was no barrier between audience and performer. This would be achieved by putting the audience in the centre of the performance on swivel chairs, so that the action could be experienced not just on a stage but at all the surrounding levels.

The audience should be immersed in the action, feeling what it is like to be caught in a world of sensations from which there is no escape. This experience was intended to stimulate the inner existence and spirit of the audience.

Use of set and costume

Artaud maintained that the theatre should not be a place of ornamentation or decoration but of spirituality, like a temple. Simple, symbolic sets should be used, with a suggestion of place rather than a realistic representation of it. The skills of the actors should be sufficient to convey context to the audience.

Costume and masks were also a fundamental component of Artaud's approach, as they were part of the beauty, colour and dream-like world of the theatre. Modern dress was not advocated, as it would fail to stimulate the audience's imagination. However, masks — comical, grotesque, beautiful, garish or terrifying — would enhance the sense of the surreal and the totality of the theatrical experience.

Artaud's failed experiments

In his lifetime, Artaud was afforded few opportunities to see his ideas put into practice. Although he submitted a variety of projects to the leading Parisian directors of the day, they were constantly rejected. His frequent bouts of illness had gained him the reputation of unreliability, and his mental anguish, though undoubtedly at the root of his genius, made him difficult to work with. His ideas were regarded as too extreme, and directors were reluctant to stage theatrical ventures which were intended to cause anguish and terror in an audience.

Although a number of drafted *mise en scènes* are still in existence, Artaud was only able to attempt one major production that utilised the theories he had spent 4 years formulating and writing up in the series of essays eventually published as *The Theatre and Its Double*. This production was *The Cenci*.

The 'theatre of cruelty': Artaud's 'The Cenci'

Artaud attempted to realise his ideas in 1935 with his own adaptation of Percy Bysshe Shelley's tragedy *The Cenci* (1819). *The Cenci* tells the story of Francesco Cenci, a historical figure who plotted the murder of his two sons and raped his daughter. In turn his daughter, surviving son and wife hired assassins to kill him, which they did by driving one nail into his eye and one into his throat. His wife and daughter were then brought to trial and, along with his son, were executed.

This violent story appealed to Artaud as a suitable vehicle for his newly identified 'theatre of cruelty', which was to provide a visceral experience for the audience. He described the action he envisaged in his own version of *The Cenci* as a 'devouring hearth' and he wanted the audience 'to be plunged into a bath of fire'. Here was a story of murder, incest and rape which lent itself to the special theatrical language Artaud had fashioned, with its emphasis on incantatory and rhythmic words, gestures, movements and imaginative uses of sound and light. It was supposed to be his greatest experiment and herald the dawn of a theatrical revolution. If the theatre establishment of Paris was not prepared to hire him or incorporate his ideas, he would commission the theatre and the actors and take the risk personally.

However, the play ran for only 17 performances and then closed. It was a financial and critical disaster.

TopFoto

Antonin Artaud (just left of centre stage) in a performance of *The Cenci* at the Théâtre des Folies-Wagram, Paris, in 1935

The Cenci in performance

It is difficult to imagine the nature and the effect of the original production from looking at the annotated script, but some idea can be gained from reading through it. Notable moments include the following:

- The sound of footsteps at the Cenci banquet was amplified in order to heighten the sense of violence and obsession as the guests, motivated by fear and greed, rushed towards the banquet.
- Later in the play, as the assassins approached Cenci, they did so using gestures to express their fear and their guilt. No words were used, since the impending horror of the moment rendered words inadequate. As the scene heightened in foreboding and violence, the word 'CEN–CI' was heard chanted using human voices and recorded sounds at varying and harshly contrasted pitches. The effect of this would have been a human, yet simultaneously dehumanised, sound — a discordant and violent assault on the audience's senses.
- During the banquet scene involving nobles and priests, the sound and effect of a great wind, like a 'cosmic breath', was used to indicate the idea of a force belonging to the 'world beyond' invading the real world. To enhance the

celestial nature of the moment, Artaud used recordings of the peal of the great bells of Amiens Cathedral. To increase the effect even further, he used what must have been one of the earliest examples of quadraphonic sound by placing speakers behind the seats in the four corners of the auditorium. The sound was so loud and oppressive that audience members were subjected to considerable discomfort by the cacophony. However, this was partly the effect that Artaud wanted: to attack the senses of his audience, to reach them beyond a purely intellectual or emotional level.

◆ The play focuses on the cosmic battle of good and evil, and Cenci's sense of his own evil and consequently his awareness of the existence of God. To become closer to the 'One', or the creator, Cenci feels he must commit yet more acts of unrelenting evil. In order to express this sense of spiritual confusion and chaos, the actors were required to breathe and speak in a rhythmic and forced manner. However, the effects of this vocal control (as explained in Artaud's essay 'An Affective Athleticism', first published in *The Theatre and Its Double*) caused the actors to put great strain on their voices, particularly Artaud, who started to lose his voice towards the end of the run.

As we have seen, the essence of Artaud's genius was also partly the origin of his downfall. His amazing gifts as a visionary were not matched by his practical skills as an organiser. Furthermore, the demands the production made on both him and his fellow actors meant that a run of more than 17 performances was probably a physical as well as a financial impossibility.

After *The Cenci*

The failure of *The Cenci* was a grievous disappointment to Artaud. He departed for Mexico, where he found some spiritual fulfilment away from the materialism of the Western world.

Many of Artaud's theatrical quests attempted to discover a form that explored the spirituality of the world as well as the sources of his own torment. The unspoilt, dramatic landscape of Central America and the rituals and religious ceremonies of its people now helped Artaud to find an excitement and sense of spiritual destiny that had eluded him so far. However, he continued to earn a living through writing articles and essays for a variety of artistic journals.

An expedition to Ireland in 1937 ended in disaster when he was arrested for breach of the peace outside a monastery and deported to France. On arrival, he was immediately committed to an asylum and remained in a variety of such institutions until 1946. By this time, although only 50 years old, Artaud was a frail old man. In the last 2 years of his life, Artaud returned to work and embarked upon a number of writing and broadcasting projects. However, he was by now suffering from cancer and died on 4 March 1948.

Summary

Although he was frustrated by failure in his lifetime, there is little doubt that many of Artaud's ideas have found currency in the work of modern practitioners. For example, a strong sense of rhythm and incantation is clear in the language patterns employed by Berkoff in *Metamorphosis* (see Chapter 6).

While it is difficult to prove precise levels of influence, both Artaud and Berkoff valued the sound and structure of language, perhaps considering these to be more important than the content. Both explored the sensory impact that language can make through dialogue, chorus work and amplifications.

Summary of Artaud's ideas

♦ Artaud's vision for theatre differs from Brecht's and Stanislavski's; he wanted to create a sensory assault on the audience.

♦ Artaud's work coincided with the era of the surrealists, and for a time he was a part of their movement. The rejection of the rules of realism and the scenic possibilities of a theatre inspired by dreams are points for comparison between the work of surreal artists and Artaud's vision for theatre.

♦ Artaud was significantly influenced by a visit to the Balinese Theatre in 1931. The emphasis on physical performance, movement, dance and gesture helped Artaud to clarify and identify his own theatrical ideas.

♦ Artaud rejected the reverence in which 'masterpieces' are held. For example, the impact of Greek tragedy has lessened because modern audiences no longer subscribe to the same belief system, nor are they afraid of the same things. Modern theatre must focus on the spiritual world of humanity so that its effects can be as profound as in the past.

♦ Artaud wanted to create a theatre which explored the inner spiritual truth of humanity, rather than just the outer trappings of realism.

♦ Artaud regarded all the individual theatrical elements as having equal status. There were particularly important implications for the use of sound and light.

♦ The function of the actor in the 'theatre of cruelty' was to be fundamentally different from that in the theatre of reality. Rather than just repeating words, the actor's whole body was to be used as an instrument of expression.

♦ Artaud promoted new breathing techniques which would vocally dehumanise some of the text as well as allow a more graphic method of expression.

♦ There should be no physical barrier between actor and audience. The audience should be in the midst of the action and, therefore, part of it.

♦ Artaud suffered from mental illness during much of his life. The torment that he felt, as well as his frustrations at failure, contributed to the deeply introspective and spiritual dimension he gave to his vision of theatre.

Group activity

The poem *Dulce et Decorum Est* by Wilfred Owen graphically depicts the death of a soldier during a gas attack in the trenches in the First World War. As a group, try to adapt the poem using some of Artaud's ideas. Bear the following points in mind:

- You should not necessarily adapt the poem so that it presents a logical sequence of events. Artaud was concerned to depict a visceral and violent world, where the audience was subjected to a sensory experience. The aim, therefore, is not to create a historically accurate adaptation so much as to realise the essence of the horror of the piece. Explore the sounds of the language as well as the content, and perhaps use repetition of the sounds to intensify the disturbing nature of the scene.

- Reflect on the ideas of Berkoff, who uses *Metamorphosis* as a means of externalising Gregor's state. Find the ways in which you can physically — as an ensemble — portray the graphic horror of the poem. Do not try to act it out as a story, but rather look for moments of striking physical imagery.

- Use lighting in a variety of ways to accompany the scene. Evaluate the difference it makes to you as an actor, as well as to an audience watching the scene.

Chapter 14

Applying Artaud's principles

Woyzeck by Georg Büchner

Eugène Ionesco (1909–94)

Eugène Ionesco was born in Slatina, Romania, the son of a French mother and Romanian father. He is considered one of the foremost playwrights of the 'theatre of the absurd', an innovative form of theatre designed to startle the members of an audience and shake them out of their comfortable, conventional conception of life. It revolves around a distrust of language as a means of communication, believing that language fails to express the essence of human experience.

Inspired by the repetitive and nonsensical phrases of his textbook while attempting to learn English, in 1948 Ionesco conceived the idea for his first play, *La Cantatrice Chauve* ('*The Bald Soprano*'), produced in 1950. It is composed mainly of the type of clichés found in a foreign-language phrasebook and a series of meaningless conversations between two couples.

The work of the absurdist playwright Eugène Ionesco contains ideas that may have been inspired by the theories of Artaud. In *The Lesson* (1951), for example, a professor stabs a pupil with an imaginary knife, chanting and screaming the word 'knife' as he does so. This is a play which shows the tyrannous power of words and language translated into a weapon of murder.

Perhaps one of the greatest exponents of the ideas of Artaud has been the director Peter Brook (see Chapter 15), who, with the American director Charles Marowitz, created a 'Theatre of Cruelty' season at the RSC in 1963. His subsequent production of Peter Weiss's *The Persecution and Assassination of Jean-Paul Marat as Performed by the Inmates of the Asylum of Charenton Under the Direction of the Marquis de Sade* (1963) — normally shortened to *Marat/Sade* — was a masterpiece of visceral and explicit theatre, assaulting the sensibilities of its audience in a variety of ways that could not fail to leave a sensory impact.

The 'in yer face' playwrights

The bold theatrical experiments of the 'in yer face' playwrights of the 1990s, such as Sarah Kane and Mark Ravenhill, demonstrate the force with which social issues and values can be explored in theatrical form. Even the title of Ravenhill's first play *Shopping and Fucking* (1996) was designed to create an impact on an audience. Sarah Kane's *Blasted* (1995) shows the violent impact of war — but in a hotel bedroom in Leeds. The journalists who watch and report from the safety of distance suddenly find the war and its plague-like, indiscriminate assault in their midst.

Critical reactions to these productions echo some of the responses to Artaud's work. Kane particularly received mixed reviews for *Blasted*. However, it remains a provocative work of tragic, violent theatre and should not simply be dismissed (as some were keen to do at the time) as gratuitous filth.

Sarah Kane's *Blasted* remains a provocative work of tragic, violent theatre. (The Barbican Theatre, London, November 2006)

Technical theatre: sound and light

While his philosophical and spiritual ideals are being realised by modern playwrights, Artaud's influence also extends to the use of technical elements of theatre by designers and directors. Sound and light are now a fundamental part of the theatre experience, rather than just a supporting feature. Again, the work of Berkoff is a useful example, as his stage directions give specific, detailed and complex instructions as to how both sound and lighting effects should work.

Another example might be Peter Schaffer's *Royal Hunt of the Sun* (1964), which charts the story of Pizzarro's conquest of the Inca empire led by Atahualpa (coincidentally, Artaud drafted but never produced the story of Cortez and the destruction of the Aztec civilisation of Montezuma). In *Royal Hunt of the Sun*, much of the action takes place in the South American jungle and mountains. The lighting required is ambitious in its technical scope, illuminating the actors' bodies to create for the audience the impact of the vast landscapes.

In this kind of total theatre, the aim is not to convince the members of an audience that what they are watching is real, but that a real sense of the physical and spiritual essence of the world is being depicted. The scenes involving the worship of Atahualpa and the incantation offered up by the Incas are strongly reminiscent of Artaud's ideas on rhythmic and choral speaking.

Georg Büchner (1813–37)

Georg Büchner was a German playwright who had completed only three plays by the time of his death in 1837 at the age of 23. He died before ever finishing *Woyzeck*, leaving behind four unpolished manuscripts and a series of notes, so it is impossible to possess a definitive version of the work. It has been pieced together posthumously by scholars, who have passionately scrutinised issues such as which scenes to include, the order of the scenes and the ending. It was not published until 1879 and even then the result was regarded as being somewhat unsatisfactory. It was only when photographic techniques had been developed to a sufficient level that Büchner's writing could be deciphered accurately. Consequently, the play did not reach the stage until 1913 and was subject to some argument as to its genre.

Woyzeck

Just as with Stanislavski and Brecht, there is no virtue in applying the ideas of Artaud as a rule book when interpreting plays, nor should the ideas of one theorist be explored to the exclusion of others. You should note that when Brecht and Artaud were writing essays and journal entries, they may well have rejected the ideas of others; in practice, however, they were clearly influenced by the principles of other theorists. Nonetheless, it is useful to consider how the theories of Artaud might be of interest to a director of the play *Woyzeck* by Georg Büchner.

The plot

The eponymous protagonist, Franz Woyzeck, a poor military barber stationed in a provincial German town, is the father of an illegitimate child by his mistress, Marie. In order to support his family, Woyzeck earns extra money by undertaking menial work for the Captain and participating in medical experiments conducted by the Doctor. As part of one of these experiments, Woyzeck is forced to eat only peas.

The constant diet of peas causes Woyzeck's physical and mental health to break down and he begins to experience a series of apocalyptic visions. Meanwhile, Marie turns her attentions to an arrogant but handsome Drum Major who, in an ambiguous scene taking place in Marie's bedroom, appears to rape her.

With his jealous suspicions growing, Woyzeck confronts the Drum Major. A fight breaks out, which the Drum Major easily wins. Finally, Woyzeck stabs Marie to death beside a pond. The fragment of script left by Büchner ends with Woyzeck disposing of the knife in the pond, although some scholars maintain that the original conception of the play involved a trial in the third act. However, most productions (including Werner Herzog's 1979 film) conclude with Woyzeck drowning while trying to clean the blood from his hands.

A 'theatre of cruelty' experience

In the intervening years between the writing of *Woyzeck* in the 1830s and its first performance over 70 years later, the schools of realism and expressionism emerged. Although Büchner predates both of these movements, one can detect certain ingredients in his work which are common to both. You should always bear in mind, however, that it is rarely the playwrights themselves who coin the names of the schools of thought into which they are sometimes all too neatly fitted.

The play is based loosely on the true story of Johann Christian Woyzeck, a former solider convicted for the murder of his mistress, despite the defence mounted at his trial to spare his life on grounds of diminished responsibility. Perhaps linked to these real-life influences, it certainly has elements of social realism. However, in exploring the central character's descent into paranoia and his subjection to eccentric and cruel experiments, it also offers a 'theatre of cruelty' experience of disturbing extremes of human behaviour and psychology. There are moments of graphic violence, sexuality and even defecation.

The play is structured into short, powerful scenes that are not necessarily placed in chronological order. It also has something of an 'epic' feel to it, particularly as some of the characters are quite stereotypical and named after their function, e.g. 'Doctor' or 'Drum Major'.

Without necessarily taking a political stance, the play explores the nature of humankind and the injustices it imposes on itself. Büchner had strong links with revolutionary movements in his youth, but by the time he was writing *Woyzeck*, at the end of his life, he had largely abandoned his political aspirations. However, his awareness of social injustice and the effects of poverty on human behaviour and relationships are clearly concerns explored in the play.

Managing the setting

The nature of *Woyzeck* is such that unless revolving scenery is available, it is practically impossible to set each scene in a naturalistic context. The set design, therefore, has to convey a conceptual interpretation. It would not be out of place to devise a surreal style of set, incorporating images and objects from the play — doctor's apparatus, military iconography or the knife which Woyzeck uses to kill Marie.

The use of surrealistic artwork — nightmarish, graphic, colourful and distorted — could provide a suitable backdrop for the action.

Graphic physicality

There are many scenes in the play when the action is dominated more by physicality than by dialogue. Early in the play, a scene takes place in the fairground when Marie first sees the Drum Major. The Showman is inviting people to 'roll up' and see his array of animals:

Showman: Roll up, ladies and gentlemen! Come and see a monkey walking upright like a man! He wears a coat and trousers and carries a sword.

Art improving on nature: our monkey's a soldier. — Not that that's much. Lowest form of animal life in fact. (I.3)

Later, the Showman introduces the horse, describing its virtues while it defecates on stage. The Showman comments that the lesson to be taken from this act is:

Man, be natural! (I.3)

The absurdity of this section is apparent, as well as its uncompromisingly graphic nature. Since it is extremely difficult to stage realistically, the opportunity for physical theatre work here could extend the notion of the play's surrealism.

Nightmare

For Artaud, sound and light were fundamental parts of the language of the theatre. They could certainly enhance the quality of many scenes in *Woyzeck*, helping to define the play's nightmarish quality. For example, the scene with the horse quoted above offers opportunities to create distorted and disturbing images.

Later in the play, Woyzeck is taunted by the Captain, who knows of Marie's sexual encounter with the Drum Major. The use of music and/or sound effects, accompanied by an intensifying light focused on his face, could help to suggest the disquieting intensity of Woyzeck's growing jealousy.

When Woyzeck sees the Drum Major and Marie dance in the peasants' scene, his sense of jealousy and frustration reaches fever pitch. The dance and the music could reflect not only the lustful reality of the Drum Major and Marie's relationship, but also the agonised state of Woyzeck's mind. The music could become louder and more hurried (almost like the *Danse Macabre* by Saint-Saëns), more sensual and more ritualistic, and Woyzeck's response to it could accordingly become increasingly enraged and emotional. Lighting too could focus on the couple in such a way as to reflect the distress Woyzeck is experiencing as he watches them. It could become more intense, perhaps tinged with red to portend the inevitable oncoming violence.

Photostage

When Woyzeck (Edward Hogg) sees Marie (Myriam Acharki) and the Drum Major (Tim Chipping) together, his jealousy reaches fever pitch. (Gate Theatre, London, November 2004)

Absurdity

The Doctor — who is dispassionately observing Woyzeck's changing behaviour — is a figure of cruel absurdity. The dress and make-up of this character (and other absurd characters, such as the Captain and the Drum Major) could be colourful and outlandish to enhance their surreal qualities. The Doctor's use of voice might accentuate his absurdity too. As he presents Woyzeck to his students, his speech is both pompous and deranged:

If we take one of those creatures in whom, gentlemen, capacity of the divine for self-affirmation most clearly manifests itself and we examine its relation to space, the earth and the planetary universe. If, gentlemen, I take [producing a cat] this cat, and throw it out of the window — what will be its instinctive behaviour relative to its centre of gravity?

— Woyzeck! — Woyzeck!!

(He runs back in as the **Doctor** throws the cat at him which he catches.)   (I.8)

Use of language

The Doctor exploits Woyzeck and equates him with the lowest forms of animal life. His lecture to the students gives him an opportunity to use his voice in an overbearing and self-regarding manner. The actor and director could experiment with vocal pitch and pace to enhance these qualities. For Artaud, the language of the Doctor would demonstrate his tyranny and lack of humanity. The vocal projection, therefore, must immediately and graphically reflect those traits, perhaps through a harsh, brittle-sounding oration. The physical sound of the words is more important than their precise content in revealing the Doctor's contempt for Woyzeck in this impersonal and cruel lecture.

After the peasants' dance scene, the crowd falls silent as Woyzeck screams out his agony:

Woyzeck: Turn, turn. Go on turning, dancing! — Why don't you blow the sun out God? Let everything fall over itself in lewdness. Flesh, filth, man, woman, human, animal. — They all do it in the open day, do it on the back of a hand like flies. Slut!! — She's hot, hot! (l.12)

Here again, the actor should concentrate on the visceral rage inherent in the language. The mood — realised through pace and volume — is more important than the content, which is bordering on the incoherent.

The almost savage rage with which these lines are spat out more than reflects Woyzeck's state of mind and exposes his psychological disposition to the audience. This should be a truly terrifying moment in the play. At this point, we know that something terrible and violent is going to happen.

Violence

The play, in places, is prone to strong violence. Following the dancing scene, Woyzeck seeks out the Drum Major. The Drum Major easily defeats him in the ensuing fight, which at one point contains the stage direction:

(Jumps on Woyzeck's back with his knees) (l.15)

The brutality of this scene should be disturbing for an audience. It might be played surrealistically or even choreographed as a violent dance sequence. As we have seen, Artaud appreciated the disciplined physical work of the Balinese Theatre, and the director here may consider executing a more stylised than literal version of the fight. However, the impact of the violence should not be compromised, and an audience should be shocked and frightened by this moment of appalling savagery rather than admiring of its artistry. The injustices being heaped on Woyzeck and his developing madness as a consequence should be experienced by the audience rather than just passively accepted.

The most violent scene of the play is preceded by an atmosphere of eerie calm, as Woyzeck and Marie walk in the woods. Marie is unaware of what is to happen, and this makes the moment of the stabbing all the more terrible and frightening. The use of lighting and music could add to the dramatic climax, perhaps creating a cacophony of sound as well as highlighting the ferocity of the repeated stabbing.

The scream that Marie emits should be harsh, lengthy and filled with pain and perhaps echoed by other members of the ensemble.

Cleansing and closure

As the end of the play arrives, Woyzeck drowns himself in the river, taking the body of Marie with him. There is a ritual element about this self-sacrifice, as well as an image of cleansing. As we have already discussed, Artaud extolled the potential of theatre to offer spiritual cleansing.

It would be difficult to achieve a realistic setting for this challenging scene. A more surreal approach, such as immersing the actors in a blue light, might be a striking way of overcoming the problem.

The last two scenes of the play are additions by playwright John Mackendrick, Büchner's translator. As the play was unfinished at the time of Büchner's death, there are a number of options for how to end the play, and indeed several other versions exist. Mackendrick's version fits well with Artaud's vision, using red lighting and maintaining a mystical, almost ritualised conclusion.

Mackendrick's penultimate scene shows the Doctor carrying out autopsies on both corpses, showing that even in death Woyzeck cannot escape exploitation. The Doctor is confused that in piercing Woyzeck's body he cannot find any blood. In the final scene, the mysterious figure of the blind grandmother looks on, as Woyzeck's friend, Andres, picks sticks and discovers a patch of blood. The blood increases until it is revealed as 'Woyzeck's gore'. Andres rushes away in fear as red light fills the stage and the grandmother laughs.

Summary

Some directors might wish to take Artaud's concept of the theatre of cruelty further in this play. To some extent, at least, we are still subjugating all other theatrical elements to the text, since the script remains unchanged.

Some would argue that the text should be substantially reduced and a greater use of gesture, movement and dance be introduced. However, there is then a tension between delivering the author's text with integrity and delivering the vision of Artaud. A dramaturge would argue that the author's intentions should not be compromised and that the text should be as faithfully rendered as possible. This is a point for debate. Bearing in mind that much of Büchner's unfinished script was posthumously assembled and completed from notes, some compromise is inevitable. On this basis, it should be possible to retain the integrity of the text while still using principles of theatre presentation consistent with Artaud's vision.

Discussion questions

1 Reflecting on the plays you are studying, which of Artaud's ideas might prove useful for a director preparing a production?
2 What plays have you seen where you think the director or actors may have used some of Artaud's ideas in their preparation?
3 Are there any styles of play where the ideas of Artaud might not be useful? Explain your answer.

Essay questions

1 Plan a rehearsal of a play you are working on. Show how you might introduce some of Artaud's ideas on sound, light or design to your cast, either through text or off-text work.
2 Do you believe it is possible to incorporate the ideas of Brecht, Stanislavski and Artaud into one production? How would this work and with what play(s)?

Chapter 15

Modern directors

It would be far too sweeping to suggest that all theatre directors over the last 100 years have been influenced by the theories of Stanislavski, Brecht and Artaud. While it is tempting to try to identify 'family trees' of influence from one leading theatrical exponent to another, it should be remembered that these three drama theorists were working in different social and cultural contexts. These contexts overlapped from time to time, when companies went on tour or when individuals visited and sampled other cultures.

The development of directorial practice has been a sophisticated process, yet these three practitioners in particular have helped to establish a discipline of directing and a theatrical world where the role of the director is pivotal.

Twentieth-century British theatre

Two great national theatre companies emerged in the UK during the twentieth century — the Royal Shakespeare Company (RSC) and the National Theatre (NT). Not only have they become associated with excellence in acting, they have also forged and nurtured talent in directing.

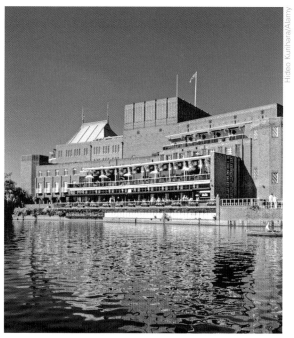

The Royal Shakespeare Theatre in Stratford-upon-Avon

Hideo Kurihara/Alamy

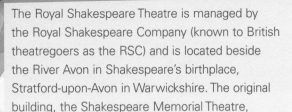

The Royal Shakespeare Theatre

The Royal Shakespeare Theatre is managed by the Royal Shakespeare Company (known to British theatregoers as the RSC) and is located beside the River Avon in Shakespeare's birthplace, Stratford-upon-Avon in Warwickshire. The original building, the Shakespeare Memorial Theatre, opened in 1879. This was destroyed by a fire in the 1920s and replaced in 1932 by a modern building designed by Elisabeth Scott. This building was named the Royal Shakespeare Theatre in 1961. The 1930s building is being redeveloped from 2007, with completion planned for 2010.

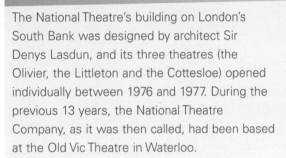

The National Theatre

The National Theatre's building on London's South Bank was designed by architect Sir Denys Lasdun, and its three theatres (the Olivier, the Littleton and the Cottesloe) opened individually between 1976 and 1977. During the previous 13 years, the National Theatre Company, as it was then called, had been based at the Old Vic Theatre in Waterloo.

The term 'Royal' was added to the National Theatre's name in 1988 to mark the twenty-fifth anniversary of the National Theatre Company's inauguration and the retirement of its board chairman Max Rayne. This change was opposed by the theatre's then director, Richard Eyre, as he feared that productions would be viewed as 'worthy' as a result. The addition was quietly dropped (but never rescinded) when Rayne retired.

Most British theatregoers refer to both the company and the venue as 'the National'.

Twentieth-century British directors

Peter Brook and Peter Hall both enjoyed the early days of their careers with the RSC before developing their talent in other arenas. Brook has spent the second half of his career mostly working in France, while Hall became the director of the National in the early 1970s before becoming a freelance director in 1988.

Trevor Nunn, Richard Eyre and Nicholas Hytner have all been artistic directors of either the RSC or the National (in the case of Trevor Nunn, both) and now have enviable international reputations as gifted directors.

Other great directing figures include George Devine, the founding director of the Royal Court Theatre, probably the most important theatre in the country for the development of new writing talent. William Gaskill and Max Stafford Clark were important successors to Devine at the Royal Court and are still active in the theatre.

Some — though not all — successful theatre directors develop their careers in the world of film, for example Stephen Daldry (*Billy Elliot*, 2000) and Sam Mendes (*American Beauty*, 1999 — for which he won an Oscar — and *Road to Perdition*, 2002).

Peter Brook (1925–)

The theatrical producer and director Peter Brook was born in Chiswick, west London. He was educated at Westminster School, Gresham's School, Holt, and Magdalen College, Oxford. An avant-garde, non-conformist and controversial figure, Brook engineers productions that utilise the whole stage, favouring bold, abstract and unembellished sets over realistic backdrops. His approach is notably physical, and he often requires actors to sing, play musical instruments and perform acrobatic feats.

Brook has been influenced by the pioneering theories of Bertolt Brecht, Russian director Vsevolod Meyerhold and Polish director Jerzy Grotowski, among others, in addition to the 'theatre of cruelty' of Antonin Artaud. In 1964, Peter Brook and Charles Marowitz undertook the 'Theatre of Cruelty' season at the Royal Shakespeare Company, exploring ways in which Artaud's ideas could be used to find new forms of expression and redefine performance methods.

Peter Hall (1930–)

Sir Peter Reginald Frederick Hall CBE is an English theatre and film director. He was born in Bury St Edmunds and attended the Perse School, Cambridge. He pursued his education at St Catharine's College, Cambridge, where he produced and acted in several productions. In 1953, the same year he graduated with his master's degree, he staged his first professional play at the Theatre Royal in Windsor.

Hall is best known for his work with the Royal Shakespeare Company, which he founded in 1960 at the age of 29. He served as artistic director there from that time until 1968. From 1973 to 1988 he was director of the National Theatre and was also a member of the Arts Council of Great Britain, ultimately resigning from both roles in protest over cuts in public funding. After leaving the National Theatre, he founded the Peter Hall Company. This new company worked around the world, appearing in more than 40 productions in London, New York, Europe and Australia. During this period, Hall also produced operas and directed films and television productions for the BBC.

Sir Peter Hall is best known for his work with the RSC, which he founded in 1960

Many directors are what may be termed 'jobbing directors', and just like most actors, their careers are unglamorous and poorly paid. A number of regional theatres have their own in-house theatre companies with their own artistic directors, for example Mark Babytch at the Octagon Theatre, Bolton or Ian Brown at the West Yorkshire Playhouse. Such individuals are not only responsible for the artistic repertoire of their companies but also — and often far more stressfully — their financial wellbeing.

George Devine (1910–66)

George Devine CBE was an eminent theatrical manager, director, teacher and actor in London. He also worked in the media of television and film.

While reading history at the University of Oxford, Devine developed a passion for theatre, and in 1932 he became president of the Oxford University Dramatic Society. After graduation, he moved to London and became an actor, appearing in a number of John Gielgud's productions. He co-founded the London Theatre Studio in 1936, and in 1939 he became a stage director with an adaptation of Charles Dickens' *Great Expectations* (1946).

During the Second World War, he was a member of the Royal Artillery, stationed in India and then Burma. Returning to London after the war, he was instrumental in setting up and running the Old Vic Theatre School and the Young Vic Company. However, severe disagreements with the Old Vic board of governors in 1948 led to his resignation.

By this time a renowned authority in stagecraft, Devine directed opera at Sadler's Wells Theatre and both directed and acted at the Royal Shakespeare Theatre in Stratford; he also directed at the Bristol Old Vic.

Tony Richardson shared Devine's ideas about transforming the English theatre. After Richardson cast Devine in a television adaptation of Anton Chekhov's *Curtain Down*, the two co-founded the English Stage Company.

Trevor Nunn (1940–)

Trevor Nunn was born in Ipswich, educated at Northgate Grammar School, Ipswich, and at Downing College, Cambridge. After graduation, he joined the Belgrade Theatre in Coventry as a trainee director, going on to become producer there. He has held the post of director at both the Royal Shakespeare Company and the National Theatre. At only 28 years of age, Nunn was the youngest ever director of the RSC. Nunn has directed acclaimed performances of almost all of the major plays of Shakespeare (and many of the minor ones), as well as classic texts by Ibsen, Shaw, Chekhov and Brecht. He has also worked with highly talented contemporary playwrights, including Robert Bolt and Tom Stoppard.

Richard Eyre (1943–)

Sir Richard Charles Hastings Eyre CBE is a renowned theatre, television and film director. He studied English at the University of Cambridge before becoming associate director, and then director of productions, at Edinburgh's Lyceum Theatre. He went on to serve as artistic director of the Nottingham Playhouse, and produced the BBC Television 'Play for Today' series.

Eyre's association with the National Theatre began in 1981, when he became an associate director. He subsequently became director, between 1987 and 1997.

Nicholas Hytner (1956–)

Nicholas Hytner is an award-winning producer and director. Born in Didsbury, Manchester, to a Jewish family, he attended Manchester Grammar School before reading English at Trinity Hall, Cambridge. While at university, he co-scripted and performed in a televised production of the 1977 Cambridge Footlights Revue and directed Brecht and Weill's *Rise and Fall of the City of Mahagonny*.

Following graduation, Hytner's first paid job was assisting productions at the English National Opera. He then worked as an associate director at Manchester's Royal Exchange Theatre between 1985 and 1989, and at the National Theatre in London between 1989 and 1997. He was appointed director of the National Theatre in 2003 and is renowned for choosing much more controversial pieces than his predecessors.

The three directors discussed on pages 167–75 are all still working. They come from diverse backgrounds and employ different methods of practice that have evolved over a period of time. Each has contributed significantly to the development and expansion of theatre, especially in terms of the audience it reaches and the imaginative techniques it employs.

It is not always appropriate to direct a play in the style of another director — certainly, this is impossible where directors devise their plays from scratch as well as directing them. However, it is useful to learn about existing directorial practices and philosophies, as their influence will always shape the work of young and up-and-coming directors.

Directorial constraints

The artistic aspirations of the vast majority of directors are subject to two controlling influences:

- financial constraints, in the context of a highly competitive profession
- audience trends (likes and dislikes)

For a regional theatre director to plan a programme of plays and events that does not pay due heed to audience tastes is to risk rapid financial ruin for the theatre company.

Declan Donnellan

Declan Donnellan was born in 1953 and grew up in London. He read English and law at university and was called to the Bar in 1978. However, he then became involved in the world of theatre and in 1981 he co-founded the Cheek by Jowl Theatre Company with the designer Nick Ormerod.

An actor's theatre

Interestingly, for one of the country's most renowned directors, Donnellan believes strongly in an actor's theatre. In a recent interview with Suzanne Worthington from the RSC (2005), he said:

> I think that the theatre is the actor's art first and last, more than it's about directing or even writing. My sort of theatre is. What I do is to try to get actors to work together as well as possible. I'm a coach of actors more than a teacher.

This approach, with the actor at the centre of the process, is perhaps reminiscent of Stanislavski's quest to generate an atmosphere conducive to creating truthful acting.

TopFoto

Declan Donnellan (left) is often referred to as an 'actor's director'

An actor's director

Being described as an 'actor's director' testifies to Donnellan's fascination with the process of acting, as does his book *The Actor and the Target* (2002), in which he dissects and analyses performance techniques in minute detail. Through his work with Cheek by Jowl, as well as undertakings with the RSC, the National and the Maly Drama Theatre in St Petersburg, he has earned an international reputation as a director of classic texts, both plays and operas. Despite not having a dance background, his curiosity has led him into the world of ballet, and recently he directed the Bolshoi's production of *Romeo and Juliet* (2004).

Improvisation and insight

What is distinctive about Donnellan's practice? Is he a natural successor to Stanislavski in his pursuit of truthful acting and his desire to create a theatre that is a vehicle for the 'actor's art'?

For someone interested in classic texts, there is little that can be said to be traditional about Donnellan's approach. He never starts with a read through, preferring initially to improvise around the main themes of the play, and claims always to be looking for fresh insights. Rather like Peter Brook, whom he cites as a major influence, Donnellan despises some of the conventional practices in British productions of Shakespeare.

Donnellan investigates classic texts in as thorough and rigorous a way as possible, using the ensemble of actors at the centre of the process. Indeed, his methods of casting are lengthy, often choosing to see actors three or four times before selecting them. He regards the function of a director as being 'someone who releases an actor's confidence in their ability to act'. Although highly disciplined as well as creative, Donnellan starts the rehearsal process with few preconceived ideas.

Matthew Macfadyen, one of the stars of the television series *Spooks*, has worked with Donnellan. He said in an interview for the *Daily Telegraph* (8 June 1998):

> The most striking thing is that when you enter rehearsals there's seemingly no plan about how to proceed. Both of them [Donnellan and Ormerod] are hysterical when they're in a rehearsal room and you have tremendous fun. So many directors have a preconceived idea of what they want, but we played lots of games and the process was as organic as possible.

Design

Donnellan may be an actor's director, but undoubtedly design is a vital part of his theatre. Designer Nick Ormerod is present throughout the rehearsal process, and his creative ideas emerge as the rehearsals progress. In part, this is to ensure that the design is responsive to the work of the actors, rather than the actors fitting their performances into a pre-planned set.

Style of directing

Donnellan usually directs classic texts and works from a completed script. His directorial style embraces the following ideas and beliefs:

* Actors must have learned their lines before rehearsals commence.
* Design is an important part of the theatrical process and the designer should attend all rehearsals.
* An actor's theatre is more important than a director's or a writer's theatre.
* There should be no preconceived ideas about a play before rehearsals commence.
* Painstaking care should be taken over casting, in order to create the right ensemble.
* A director to actors is like a coach to athletes.

Peter Cheeseman

Peter Cheeseman was born in 1932 and has earned a reputation as a director of theatre-in-the-round (where the audience is seated on all four sides around the auditorium). Cheeseman was artistic director of a regional theatre in Staffordshire for more than 30 years.

After working with theatrical pioneer Stephen Joseph in the 1950s, Cheeseman became artistic director of the Victoria Theatre (a theatre-in-the-round in Stoke-on-Trent) and later the New Victoria Theatre in Newcastle-under-Lyme. He retired from there in 1998 but carried on working as a freelance director.

Spatial relationships

Cheeseman refers to traditional proscenium-staged theatre as 'mono-directional'. Clearly, the influence of Stephen Joseph as a pioneer of theatre-in-the-round proved pivotal, not only to him but also to his colleague, the playwright Alan Ayckbourn, who stepped down as the artistic director of the Stephen Joseph Theatre in Scarborough in early 2008.

Not surprisingly, given his passion for theatre-in-the-round, Cheeseman is preoccupied with the spatial relationships in theatre, and during his early years he found the remoteness of the actor a continual source of frustration. As television began to gain a greater currency in the cultural life of Britain, much of the aloofness of acting and drama was overcome, as audiences could watch intimate drama in their living rooms.

Breaking down barriers

With the development of 'thrust' (or 'apron') stages, attempts were made to break down barriers with audiences. Cheeseman recalls the sense of freedom he felt when he first directed for theatre-in-the-round. In proscenium theatre, he saw the necessity to organise groups of actors and almost choreograph them. However, theatre-in-the-round affords all its audience members the same opportunities to view the play. It is likely that in an ensemble piece a member of the audience will have to watch an actor's back at some point; thus the old adage about never turning your back on an audience has to be broken. Cheeseman sees nothing definitively wrong with such a situation, since theatre-in-the-round is 'structured like life'.

Like Declan Donnellan, Cheeseman is concerned with integrity in theatre. He believes that theatre-in-the-round, in particular, exposes the actor to the audience's scrutiny and that therefore dishonest acting (or 'lying') will soon be discovered.

Documentary theatre

Although during his long career Cheeseman has directed many classic texts, including those by Shakespeare, Molière, Brecht and Ibsen, he has developed a reputation for creating original documentary theatre: dramatic productions based on real events.

Living and working in 'the Potteries' in Staffordshire (where most of the UK's china factories are found), he chose to create plays about his local community, using the reminiscences of members of that community as a basis for a script. The process of preparation for such plays has developed over the years. He has used tape recordings of local residents or even involved the original people themselves in improvising in front of actors, for instance for *Nice Girls* (1993), which was based on the story of three women who occupied Trentham Colliery.

When Cheeseman creates a piece of documentary theatre, he is adamant that the actor who plays a role is an 'advocate for that person' and that there is no pretence at being the person. The actor is required to address the members of the audience directly and tell them that he or she represents the person he or she is playing but is not that person. One could argue that this distancing of the role from the actor is a Brechtian technique. Certainly, the ambience generated by the theatre-in-the-round is similar to the 'boxing ring' atmosphere advocated by Brecht.

Cheeseman's work in revealing stories from the community is motivated by social conscience and the need to communicate a political message. Thus we are presented with stories of workers from particular industries or wives of redundant miners. Perhaps this message is not underpinned by a revolutionary aspiration, like Brecht's, but there is clearly a strong desire to tell uncomfortable truths about social deprivation and injustice.

The audience's representative

It is almost as if Cheeseman feels that he needs to be the audience's representative. Although he is interested in acting, perhaps the main contrast with Donnellan is that he is more absorbed with the *experience* for the audience. By spending most of his working life in a particular geographical region, he has developed a loyalty to the interests of that area and a sense of responsibility as to how theatre should represent the region. Rather like John Godber in Hull, by focusing on the community as a source of inspiration for new pieces of theatre he has been successful in attracting local people to the theatre who perhaps would not ordinarily attend.

Style of directing

Cheeseman's directorial style is outlined by the following observations:

* He is a strong advocate of theatre-in-the-round.
* He has a preoccupation with spatial relationships between actors, and between actors and the audience.
* He has directed classic texts, new writing and original documentary/community plays.
* He is motivated by social and political factors when creating documentary theatre.
* He believes that, as a director, he is the audience's representative.

Lloyd Newson

Lloyd Newson was born in Australia in 1957 and has worked in the UK since 1980. He trained in contemporary dance but also has qualifications in psychology. Since 1986 he has been the artistic director of the dance theatre group DV8 Physical Theatre.

Newson and his company have been responsible for some of the most innovative theatre pieces of the last 20 years. His interest in both dance and psychology has led him to develop a highly analytical approach to movement, which questions why we use certain movement patterns and how these patterns express relationships, cultures and traditions.

Physical theatre

Although Newson is credited with coining the term 'physical theatre' when he established DV8, it is a phrase he is now reluctant to use:

> When we formed the company in 1986 in Europe, nobody that I knew of called themselves a physical theatre company. Within 2 years there were schools in physical theatre in Britain. I thought, 'I have hit a term that is appropriate and a lot of people want to throw themselves into'. Then I got very upset seeing all these physical theatre companies emerging who for me weren't physically trained, and I thought that this has lowered the tone of this term, and I don't want to be associated with that term.

All of Newson's actors are rigorously dance trained and his work is unequivocally physically led.

Arguably, Newson's work allows for the use of a wider-ranging theatrical language than that found in traditional theatre. The frustration with a theatre subjugated to text, which led Artaud to develop his manifesto for new theatre practices, is echoed in the philosophy of Newson, who uses physical interpretation of ideas before the development of any text. However, Newson does not abandon the use of words, and where they are necessary he incorporates them. Much depends on the nature of the piece he is creating.

Improvisation

Although the storylines for his pieces are devised in advance, Newson uses improvisation extensively. The performers participate in the cultivation and development of story and style, and this gives them a greater ownership over the final result. Video cameras are constantly trained on the action during the rehearsals and there is a lengthy process of editing and selecting following the improvisations. A 3-hour rehearsal might only yield around 30 seconds of material that is retained and developed.

A performance of *Never Again* by DV8 in 1989

Controversial subject matter

Newson and DV8 are concerned with exploring prominent social issues and controversial subjects through their work; the results are often hard-hitting and with an unashamed edge. When *MSM* (1993) — a play about sexual encounters in male public toilets — reached London's West End, a lawyer was present at rehearsals to monitor levels of decency, following concern from the theatre management.

Is Newson's work designed to shock?

Newson's work with DV8 focuses on taboo subject matter to create engaging pieces of physical theatre. In his refusal to adapt his work to expectation, many of his pieces tend to shock. This is certainly the case at the beginning of *The Cost of*

Living (2003), when a dancer, David Toole, emerges from a box on stage and we realise he has no legs. However, this shock is a response that reflects the audience's perception, rather than anything intrinsically shocking: after all, why should seeing a man with no legs come on stage be a shocking experience? What does the shock say about the audience's prejudices and preconceptions?

The shock that we experience as members of an audience derives from an uncompromising approach to the dynamics of theatre that reflects and explores society's and humanity's extremes.

Devised work

Newson always creates new work, so he is concerned with devising as well as directing. Although he has been invited to direct various pieces, he finds little in plays or books that reflects how he sees the world. He is responsible for innovating not only the technicalities of the physical production but also the intricacies of the script. As such, he is as much an author as a director.

His actors are a crucial part of the creation process, rather than performers who are presented with a completed script or a preconceived piece of choreography. Newson is clear that everything that occurs on stage is the result of his decisions. He described his role in an interview with Jo Butterworth in 1998 as 'stimulator, facilitator, editor and constructor'. It is an interesting relationship with performers since, on the one hand, there is no misunderstanding that all physical and vocal action has been subjected to approval and creative shaping. However, he strives to find innovative and individual performers, without whom he says 'nothing'.

Other elements of production

Newson is interested in the stage environment and the relationship between 'architecture and the body'. In a style of theatre that is led by imagery and visual stimulation, this is unsurprising. Music and lighting also play an important role in his work. Lighting designer Jack Thompson has worked on a number of DV8 productions, and over the last 20 years, the company's pieces have always been performed to commissioned new scores.

Style of directing

Newson's directorial style is extremely dynamic:

- His work is movement led — but cannot be termed purely 'dance'.
- He is interested in the 'psychology of movement' and why people express themselves through the use of particular movement patterns.

- His work is often hard-hitting and controversial.
- Although there is a starting point and a theme, much of the work is created from improvisation.
- His work is always original.
- His work often contains text but is not text-led.
- Design and music are important features of his work.

Discussion questions

1 What plays have you seen that you thought were either weakly or strongly directed? Identify what specific aspects of the productions led you to believe that the director was either a positive or negative influence.

2 Reflecting on the directors discussed in this chapter, consider (a) What must a director do? (b) What should a director do? (c) What could a director do?

Essay question

Focusing on a production you have seen, analyse and evaluate the director's concept of the production. Give clear examples of directorial influence on the production.

Hints

- Directorial influence can be subtle and more focused on acting style than complex design ideas.
- In interviews and programmes directors may discuss their ideas for a production in some detail. However, it is for you as an informed member of the audience to decide whether they are successful or not.

Chapter 16

Devising

The etymology of 'playwright' comes from Old English, where 'wright' meant 'maker' or 'craftsman'. A playwright therefore 'makes' a play, rather than merely writing the script. The purpose of this chapter is to draw your attention to ways and means of devising pieces of theatre that do not necessarily involve sitting down and writing. There are also some suggestions for developing your own style of devising.

When you are devising a piece of theatre, it is important to be aware of some of the practices of professional devisors. Many theatre companies create their own work, as well as producing previously written compositions. Lloyd Newson and Peter Cheeseman (see Chapter 15) are preoccupied with innovating pieces to reflect their own theatrical ambitions, albeit using widely differing methods. They are not alone: Simon McBurney of Complicite, Mike Alfreds of Shared Experience and Emma Rice of Kneehigh Theatre Company often create work from scratch with their companies. Sometimes a writer is involved (for example, Polly Teale with Shared Experience) and sometimes the director is also the author. Although the majority of his work is in film, Mike Leigh is well known for his use of improvisation, constructing characters and providing dramatic contexts for them to meet and interact with each other.

The process of devising often takes more time than the rehearsal of scripted plays, since the devised play has to be created before it can be rehearsed. Furthermore, actors often create their own characters, which then have to be researched and developed.

There are no specific, proven methods of success, and devisors employ different approaches depending on their choice of subject matter. Whatever the method employed, however, the success of the devising process depends on thorough, detailed and organised work. It may or may not lead to a final script, and it may be created in such a way that it uses or explores a specific genre of theatre. The choices are vast — and that, of course, is one of the potential problems. Constraints often lead to innovation, whereas limitless freedom can produce something hackneyed, wandering and self-serving. Demonstrate this to yourself by sitting down with a group of people to devise a play. How easy was it to produce a compelling piece of theatre?

The 'ruling idea'

For the devising process to be effective, there has to be a firm foundation, a 'ruling idea' that will help to shape the piece and influence its final form. For example, in her book *Devising Theatre* (1994), Alison Oddey refers to the theatre company Age Exchange and its work in devising a piece of theatre to commemorate the fiftieth anniversary of the outbreak of the Second World War. The anniversary provided it with a clear ruling idea. Even though the company was not sure about the final form or indeed the content of the piece, it had a specific context which it wished to explore.

Stimulus

A specific historical event or context is often a useful stimulus for a piece of devised theatre. For example, a group of students chose to create a play about the Jarrow Hunger March — a march of unemployed men from Jarrow to London in 1936. Having made this decision early in the process, they never looked back. The group first explored the historical background to the march, and then investigated the most appropriate genres of theatre available to tell the story. The result was a moving, compelling and thorough piece of documentary theatre. Furthermore, it was a piece about which each person in the group cared deeply.

However, the stimulus does not have to be as specific as a historical event. Famous images (for instance paintings and photographs), popular quotations or well-known music may also be used to initiate the devising process.

Stimulus materials can be chosen almost at random and need not have an obvious connection to each other. When you sample the materials, you should not feel confined to choosing just one stimulus.

Responding to stimulus material

Watching or listening to stimulus material should evoke a sensory response as well as an intellectual response. If you find your material dull, you need to re-evaluate its suitability. Your teacher will, however, take care to present your stimulus material in an inspiring way. One helpful method is to create the atmosphere of an art gallery by placing the stimulus pictures around the available space using theatrical lighting; the materials are viewed in silence and notes taken. Alternatively, materials can be shown in a PowerPoint presentation. In either instance, music can be used to heighten the atmosphere.

Initially, it is important for you to experience and respond to the stimulus material as an individual. Much of the work of the subsequent task of devising will test your teamwork skills but you must also be able to contribute a strong personal response. You will always find this helpful, particularly if your group is dominated by a vocal or persuasive individual. Everyone's response to the stimulus material should be treated as equally important. This is the means by which each individual can connect with the material and begin to feel a sense of ownership of it.

Your final piece does not have to demonstrate a direct response to the stimulus. A stimulus should do precisely what the name implies: stimulate ideas that will help to create a piece of drama. A photograph of an emaciated man looking through the gaps in a barbed wire fence may provoke thoughts on physical entrapment and incarceration, which may in turn lead your group to reflect on entrapment in a relationship, a society or a religion. The group's final piece may not, therefore, show much that is traceable to the original stimulus. However, all the stages of your dramatic journey, from experiencing the initial stimulus to the completion of the final product, should form part of your analysis and evaluation of the work.

Theatre visits

Theatre visits are a vital stimulus for introducing you to various dramatic genres, so that you are able to make informed choices about the appropriate direction for your piece. It is crucial that you see as much high-quality theatre as possible before and during your devising process, in order to enrich your understanding of genre.

Developing work from the stimulus

Once all the members of the group have individually seen, heard and made notes about the stimulus, you are ready to interact with one another in order to share ideas. This interaction may be conducted in a variety of ways, depending on whether your teacher wants to form groups at this stage. You might be asked to compare notes and ideas as a whole class and to make a joint decision as to how best to create a devised piece from the stimulus.

Using an image or tableau

It is often useful to come up with an image or tableau that demonstrates or underpins some of the ideas the class or group has exchanged. There is no need to 'explain' your ideas in this context; rather the image should serve as an expression, release or even exploration of ideas. Remember that an image can only serve to express part of the idea or ideas discussed by your group. This is fine — there should be no pressure to produce something that somehow manages to encompass all the ideas expressed by group members. Such a feat would probably be impossible anyway. You are looking for a starting point, a simple physical statement. The image then forms the basis of the work, even if it is not retained later.

Developing the image into action

Much depends on the strengths and aspirations of your group as to whether you choose to develop work physically or vocally from the initial image. Either option is valid.

1   Using the image as a starting point, your group could create a piece of movement that continues to underpin the ideas you discussed. This process may help you to encompass a greater number of the ideas put forward by your group. If your group is anxious about movement or someone feels that he or she lacks the necessary skills, then you could create a series of images to connect with the first one and, by a process of rehearsal, find a way to link these images together seamlessly.

2   Each member of your group could create a monologue connecting him or her to the image. If the image is naturalistic, and composed of realistic characters, this is a reasonably simple exercise. Each participant or 'character' needs to create a short passage or speech (about 2 minutes) that comments on or makes an expression linked with the tableau he or she is a part of. For example, a group of students decided to create an image of a murderer in America (Timothy McVeigh — the Oklahoma bomber) eating his last meal on death row while his captors and family looked on. Each student chose a person present in the tableau and created a monologue expressing the feelings of his or her character at the time. Chillingly, the student who played McVeigh made an almost childlike speech about the relative merits of the brand of ice cream he was eating compared with other types.

In order to develop the image into action, each member of your group could create a monologue

Using the monologue approach described above is more problematic if your group creates a conceptual image and therefore offers no realistic characters (for example a surreal or supernatural image, or a machine). How can someone create a monologue for a dehumanised concept? Here you should remember that the notion of monologue can be interpreted freely. There is no reason why your speech should not contain a more expressionistic (perhaps Artaudian?) approach to language. Language may repeat itself or have a poetic, non-realistic style. Indeed, if the image itself is surreal, it is probably more appropriate if the language which accompanies it is similarly oblique. You have complete freedom as to the content, style and subject matter of your monologue.

In this exercise, it is important that all monologues are heard by each member of your group. Even if the individual monologues produced by members of the group seem utterly disconnected, this is no barrier to all of them being presented.

This work should be carried out individually rather than the group taking responsibility for the creation of each speech. It is essential at the early stages of preparation that each group member learns the significance of making an individual contribution to the material, rather than relying on other group members to do the work.

Developing the work into action

The work now needs to be developed into action. This can happen in a variety of ways, and much depends on the nature of the ideas you have created. You may find that more material needs to be created before you can launch into your devised piece; to achieve this you can revisit the stimulus material.

At this point, you should either discuss the monologues created by your group earlier, or adlib new monologues. These speeches may well provide ways to develop dialogue for your piece. Alternatively, your group may choose to focus on one particular monologue — either because of the strength of its content or its style — and develop it dramatically.

You now have a number of options for taking your piece forward: theme-based work, plot-led work, character-led work and genre-led work.

Theme-based work

As a result of ideas discussed before the construction of your chosen image, or as a consequence of the monologues, your group may decide that your devised piece of drama is going to be thematically led.

Finding a suitable theme

A theme is not defined by one word, for instance 'war' is not a theme. However, 'the effects of war on the civilian population' is a theme suitable for dramatic development. Similarly, 'homelessness' is not a theme, but 'the impact of home-lessness on the spirit of the individual' is. In other words, a theme gives direction and focus to a piece.

Try to avoid issues that have a 'soap opera' feel to them. One of the notice-able features of soap opera is that issues are often dealt with simplistically and in such a way as to imply that they may be overcome in a matter of weeks or even days. The friends and family of Vera Duckworth, for instance, appeared to recover quickly following her demise in *Coronation Street*. Do not be too influ-enced by the soap opera approach.

A theme-based devised piece need not depend on plot — indeed, such a piece may be relatively plotless. A successful piece called *This is how it ends* chose to focus on the idea of truth being the first casualty of war. War scenes from the First World War through to the war in Iraq and an imagined future nuclear conflagration were depicted. The through-line in this piece was the theme — not the storyline or its characters.

Should there be tragedy?

Despite the preconceptions of many students, theme-based material does not have to be 'heavy' or tragic. One A-level group devised a piece entitled *We stand for things*, which depicted the preoccupation of members of the public with trivia and showbiz gossip, even when their country was at war. Much of the group's work was comic — albeit in a satirical, bitter way.

Do not expect the audience for issue- or theme-based work to be moved when a character dies. By their nature, issue-based pieces are short, and the identification necessary to establish a naturalistic relationship between character and audience cannot take place.

Should there be shock?

Often, a group of students will say that they want to 'shock' their audience. Shocking an audience gratuitously is unnecessary and, more importantly, it is also dramatically pointless.

It is, of course, important that a group has a firm idea of how it wants its audi-ence to react, but the desire to 'shock' does not go far enough. Does your group want to achieve the Brechtian aim of stirring the members of an audience into action or instilling in them a desire to change the society they are in? In other words, does the piece of theatre have a political or social aim?

Alternatively, the nature of the 'shock' your group may wish to instil might be more closely identified with the work of Artaud. Again, however, the aim of 'shocking' an audience needs further clarification. Artaud's aim was to deliver a sensory experience that would enliven an audience.

Our society regularly witnesses the ravages of war via television broadcasts and the internet. We are increasingly difficult to shock. Do not be tempted to assume that just because a character dies, your piece of drama is shocking or thought provoking. You need to make sure that your work is focused and specific, and that the issue is clear.

Plot-led work

Most A-level devised pieces are either plotless or the plot is not the dominant feature. However, there are a number of exceptions. A few years ago, one group of students took the children's book *The Three Little Wolves and the Big Bad Pig* by Eugene Trivizas (which was one of the elements of their stimulus material) and decided to perform a straight adaptation of it. The plot is familiar, albeit an inversion of the traditional tale, and although there are clearly some social issues implicit in the piece, it is essentially plot led. In this case, the group's work, aimed at a young audience of upper primary children, was successful.

However, problems can arise in plot-led pieces, when every dramatic feature becomes enslaved to the plot. If you find yourself working on a group piece where the discussions are dominated by the issue of 'what could happen next', it is possible that your piece has become too plot driven. One group of students performed a piece that gave an account of one family's struggle during the miners' strike of 1984–85. Although it was sensitively performed and demonstrated a reasonable knowledge and understanding of the issues involved, the piece became very much plot driven. As a result, it sacrificed some of its theatrical potential in favour of storyline.

There is nothing wrong with a strong plotline. Remember simply that your piece is, by its nature, quite short, and it is therefore not advisable for the plot to dominate.

Character-led work

Your group may choose to create a piece based around the exploration of a number of key characters. The film director Mike Leigh works in this manner, and the results can be fulfilling and exciting.

You should take care to avoid overambitious character exploration, since the piece will probably last no longer than around 20–30 minutes. 'Hot seating' is always a good technique to explore characters for devised work — particularly if it is important to create a 'back story' for them — but you should always keep the questions focused on your drama. Do not gather information for its own sake.

Character-led pieces work best in smaller groups, so there is an opportunity to develop characters fully and for audiences to develop relationships with them. One A-level group created an intense piece about three sisters whose abusive father had recently died. The plot was not particularly strong but it did not need to be. The interaction of the characters with each other, and with the audience through monologues, ensured a moving and compelling piece. A less successful example was when a larger group attempted a story set in a psychiatric ward. The individual characters were insufficiently developed because of lack of performance time and so tended to drift towards stereotype.

Where characters are the most significant dramatic feature, it is important that you render them as compellingly as possible. If your characters are unconvincing, your audience will not care about their fates. As noted before, it is not a given fact that an audience will break down in tears when the central character kills him/herself, and this is even more the case where the character is a faulty creation in the first instance. Indeed, this kind of 'shock' denouement often serves to disappoint, and it can be embarrassing to watch if overacted or if there is insufficient development. Remember that in a 20-minute piece you are unlikely to be able to develop an audience–character relationship strongly enough to move the audience if that character dies.

Genre-led work

Having studied a particular play or practitioner, you may feel inspired to create a piece which is in the style of the source of influence. This is an entirely legitimate choice and often leads to dramatically articulate responses. Many students draw on the work of Artaud and the 'theatre of cruelty', perhaps excited by the anarchic possibilities and visceral dimensions that this genre opens up. Similarly, students are often inspired by 'in yer face' theatre and, in particular, the works of Sarah Kane.

Take care, however, that you do not struggle to fit your work into a particular genre. Remember that genre 'labels' are often coined by literary critics, rather than by the writers themselves. For example, when asked to define the term 'Pinteresque', the playwright Harold Pinter refused to do so, on the grounds that he had not created it. It is perfectly possible for a piece to contain elements of different genres — you could combine both physical and documentary, for example.

Genre may provide you with your initial inspiration and give guidance to the realisation of your ideas, but it should not be slavishly adhered to.

How to avoid common mistakes

In general, you should try to avoid clichés. This may involve approaching the following areas with great caution:

- Court cases. While often compelling in film or on television, they rarely work in devised pieces. The language used is often a hybrid between different cultures and courtroom practices. Consequently, it is possible to devise a piece that is a combination of *Judge Judy* and *LA Law*. The serious point here is that a piece requiring technical or specialist language has to be impeccably researched, otherwise the result is embarrassing. Court cases in live theatre are often fussy, limited and dull.
- Chat show, game show and — in particular — reality programmes used as metaphors. Occasionally, a group might be able to pull off something funny or convincing using these formats. All too often, however, the pieces emerge as contrived and missing their point. You have to be certain of why you are using these largely televisual formats and the dramatic impact you want them to create.
- Psychosis or mental illness. Again, these issues need to be researched carefully. Frequently, pieces concerning mental illness become 'mental home' dramas, involving deranged teenagers who have violently assaulted their families and hear voices in their heads. Such issues are potentially compelling, but the characters and situations are often reduced to stereotypes in practice. Without realising it, a group of dedicated and intelligent students might create a piece of drama which is offensive, because it focuses on the immediacy of dramatic effect at the expense of soundly researched facts. Drama can be, and at times should be, shocking and disturbing, but in creating the dramatic impact there should be no dilution of fact.

The importance of research

Research is essential in creating effective devised work and can take many forms. There are some basic rules of research that should be acknowledged and followed, and these are discussed on pages 185–86.

Using the internet

Entering a concept, practitioner, theme or genre into a search engine will not automatically provide you with the information you are seeking, nor is all the information on the internet correct. The online encyclopedia, Wikipedia, should be used only as the means by which more specialised research material can be found. Anyone can put anything on the internet, regardless of its accuracy, but a book has to be published and its contents have therefore been scrutinised.

In short, the internet is a useful tool to point you towards more detailed and scholarly research. Thereafter, it is advisable to refer to books, journals and other published materials.

Using interviews and observation

If you are researching a true event — perhaps an industrial dispute, an accident or series of important events — it may be possible to interview someone who was involved.

If your piece is about children, it is useful to talk to them, observe them and see them at play. The same principle is true if you are trying to portray older people. Often, our interpretations of older people owe more to comic, stereotyped creations from the television than to characterisations based on observations and understanding.

Dedicated playwrights often carry notebooks around with them in order to record snippets of conversation, which they might adapt and use later. Finding the voice of a character is often a difficult undertaking, and there is no substitute for listening to and observing real people.

If you are researching a true event, it may be possible to interview someone who was involved

Going to see innovative theatre

Watching and listening to high-quality theatre work is an invaluable part of understanding theatrical processes. You cannot create theatre if you have not seen it. Without attempting to apply some kind of hierarchy of productions, it is clear that some types of theatre will be of more use than others. Big West End musical productions may contain magnificent techniques, but the size, scale and spectacle of them will probably have little in common with the A-level devised piece. Try to see productions by companies that focus more on innovative styles of acting — there is really no substitute for watching the likes of Complicite, Kneehigh, Shared Experience, DV8, Cheek by Jowl and Out of Joint.

It can be argued that watching and, where possible, taking part in workshops with ground-breaking theatre companies is the most effective form of research. You will then be able to bring to your own devising work first-hand experience of their innovative approaches to theatre and their daring attitudes towards realisation.

Undertaking genre and practitioner research

Your research does not need to be confined to the subject matter of your piece. Researching a genre or an influential play or practitioner is equally valid. It may be that a workshop has had a particularly strong impact on you and your group, inspiring further research into the work of the practitioner and the creation of a piece in that specific style.

It is important to realise that for some styles and practitioners there is a great deal of material. Therefore, you should always keep a strong focus for your research. The subject of physical theatre, for instance, is enormous, but if you focus on French postwar physical theatre, or the work of a specific individual, the material you have to cover is more confined.

Research is not purely about finding something out. It is about finding something out that will benefit and inform the piece you are creating.

The role of technology

The increasing availability and accessibility of multimedia facilities (video, PowerPoint etc.) has had a huge impact on theatre production. Although it may not always be possible to build convoluted or detailed sets for devised pieces — particularly if there are many pieces being created and shown one after another — it should be possible to generate images relevant to the presentation, which might enhance it.

Use technology with discretion, however. Bear in mind that while the use of technology can enhance your piece, it should not overwhelm the drama. It is worth reflecting on the philosophies of Brecht and Artaud and their approaches to the use of scientific, theatrical elements. Many devised pieces are created using their ideas, even though theatre technology is now much more sophisticated than when they were working more than half a century ago.

Design

When devising a piece, the full theatrical impact needs to be taken into consideration, as well as the acting and the content of the script. Often, the devising process is an opportunity for group members who may not favour acting as a specialism to exercise their skills in design — be it set, costume, lighting or sound. Remember, however, that a deliberately economic approach to design is just as valid. Clearly there are situations where, because of time or resource constraints, technical elements have be kept to a minimum, but often a 'forced simplicity' inspires highly imaginative ideas about staging and interpretation. Necessity, at times, is the mother of invention.

Your group needs to discuss its approach to technical features and make decisions appropriate to the genre and purpose of your piece, as well as to considerations of time and budget.

The role of the script

It may be possible to improvise your piece and never arrive at a final script. This is particularly true for pieces that are more movement-orientated or even choreographed. If dance is a strength within the group, a piece of theatre that is predominantly led by the creation of physical images, shapes and movement patterns is entirely legitimate. However, if the piece is driven more by the spoken word, a final script is more desirable, particularly if the language used is stylised or poetic. For example, it is difficult to improvise in the dialogue of a different era. If your piece is set in the past, inappropriate modern expressions can jar with an audience and damage the integrity of the piece you are creating.

Scripts can also be used as stimulus material (a speech from a play, for example), or the monologues described on page 179 under 'Developing the image into action' may be used to move the piece along but not form part of the final production. In other words, your script can be as much a working tool as a part of the finished article.

It is important, however, that as the script develops, so too does the piece. All too often, groups work hard at creating excellent scripts, only to leave too little time to realise them effectively. The rehearsal process must be evenly balanced between the creation of material and its preparation for performance. It is essential that there is some kind of finished document if a technician is to provide effects on the right cue.

Summary

Devising can and should be an exciting area of practical theatre to explore, providing a vehicle for your most innovative and creative ideas. However, in order to achieve your potential as a devisor, you must ensure that the process is coherent and well organised.

Your group must work effectively as a team, allocating specific tasks to individuals and providing an opportunity for feedback. It is also important to respect the ideas of others, even if you do not agree with them.

Ensure your group does not allow discussions to take up too much rehearsal time. As you create your piece, you need to rehearse it simultaneously, otherwise there may be too little time at the end of the devising process. Rehearsing ideas is a practical method of discussion, and is often about learning through getting things wrong. To see if an idea works, get it on its feet. Try a number of different methods of exploring ideas practically before deciding whether they are going to work or not.

If you are undertaking work on a serious issue or theme, the research must be thorough and detailed. Devised pieces fail to make an impact if they seem stereotyped, vague or ill informed. Even if your piece is led more by style than content, research may still be necessary in order to determine the effectiveness and relevance of that style. It may be useful to examine the styles of well-known theatre practitioners.

Technology can enhance the quality of your work, through lighting, sound, multimedia etc. However, do not allow it to dominate the work. You are not making a film, even if film is used as a part of the overall practical presentation.

Section C

The world of the audience

Many plays written in the distant past have continued to be performed throughout the years and still feature on the modern stage. However, the expectations of the audiences are likely to have changed significantly. For example, for members of an audience in ancient Greece, the theatre was inextricably linked with religious festival, while the audience attending a Restoration comedy would have expected to be entertained at a fashionable event in a fashionable venue.

Audience expectation and experience can be described in terms of:

- the nature and intended message of the play
- political, social and cultural allusions in the play
- the physical nature of the theatre in which the play takes place
- the use (or non-use) of technical theatre equipment
- the audience's size and behaviour

In preparing for the final unit of your A-level examination, you need to focus on three eras of theatrical history.

- 525 BC–AD 65
- 1564–1720
- 1828–1914

Chapters 17, 18 and 19 supply a flavour of the historical and cultural context of each of these periods. Just like any art form, theatre is in a constant state of change, evolving and developing over time. Therefore, it is difficult to identify periods that can be defined in specific theatrical terms. However, it is possible to identify the performing conditions of an era and therefore the likely experiences for the actors and the audiences.

In each of these chapters there are notable areas of omission; the main focus is on Greek tragedy in the first time period, Shakespeare and Restoration comedy in the second and melodrama in the third. The rise of naturalism — perhaps the most important development in theatre during the nineteenth century — was examined in Chapter 4. Furthermore, in Chapters 18 and 19 the text concentrates largely on developments in British theatre. Look at Chapters 9 and 10 on Stanislavski's work for reference to developments in nineteenth-century European theatre. What follows is not exhaustive or definitive. However, you should gain a sound understanding of some of the important developments in theatre over these periods, and a sense of how those developments represented the world beyond the theatre.

Historical audience

As part of your A-level course you are required to consider the impact of a play on its audience when it was first performed, as well as its impact on a modern audience. It is almost inevitable that the response of a twenty-first-century audience to a production of *King Lear* will be quite different from that of an audience in 1604, for instance:

- It is highly unlikely that an audience in Shakespeare's time would have prior knowledge of the play's content, and many members of the audience might well see a performance of the play only once in their lives.
- *King Lear* was written and performed at a time of great change in the English monarchy. In 1603, King James VI of Scotland became King James I of England and Ireland, succeeding the last tudor monarch Elizabeth I and uniting the kingdom of Great Britain. The theme of a kingdom united or divided would have been resonant for Shakespeare's contemporary audiences.

There is a good possibility that members of a modern audience have seen other performances of *King Lear* or read the text, or at the very least they are probably familiar with the plot. The united or divided theme may not now be as meaningful or socially pertinent as its wider themes, which are less rooted in specific historical circumstances and include the tyranny of fathers and the nature of love and loyalty. The level of impact these themes have on an audience depends on the treatment of the play by the director, designer and actors.

When you watch any play from a different era, you need to remember that it has been interpreted for a modern audience. Even if a play by Shakespeare is staged in the Globe Theatre and costumed in Elizabethan fashions, it is performed in the context of twenty-first-century Britain with the intention of reaching a twenty-first-century audience. It cannot, therefore, be described as 'an Elizabethan production'. There may be features — perhaps many features — which are common to both the original staging conditions of the play and the way it has been staged now, but this does not make it anything other than a modern-day production. This distinction is a common area of confusion in written work, and you should therefore take great care when writing about a production in terms of its era.

Modern audience

Chapter 20 examines how you, as a modern audience member, might respond to a piece of theatre. However, you are not simply any audience member. As a student of drama, your responses will be and should be influenced by what you have studied or performed.

The examiner will expect you to evaluate and make sense of your experiences. Your initial response to a play may be spontaneous and emotional, but ultimately you need to explain this response in intellectual and academic terms. It is important, therefore, that you respond intelligently to a piece of theatre by analysing what you see.

Chapter 17

Ancient Greek and Roman theatre

While there is some evidence to suggest that forms of dramatic representation were a part of early Egyptian religious festivals, it was only in the fifth century BC that theatre started to emerge in the form in which we recognise it today.

The beginning and end dates of this era are significant: 525 BC marks the birth of the first great Greek playwright, Aeschylus (see page 23), and AD 65 saw the death (suicide ordered by the Emperor Nero) of the renowned Roman dramatist and tragedian Seneca. Both were luminaries of the period, each representing equally wealthy and advanced civilisations. However, these civilisations differed markedly from each other in their respect for drama.

Greek drama

Greek drama stems from an Athenian religious festival dedicated to the god Dionysus and known as the Dionysia. This was not a sombre ritual. Dionysus was the god of wine and the celebrations were designed to lead to a state of 'ecstasis', from which we derive the word 'ecstasy'. In his book *All the World's a Stage* (1984), Ronald Harwood suggests that in this context we might interpret 'ecstasy' as meaning anything from 'being taken out of yourself' to 'a profound alteration of personality'. Harwood further asserts that the nature of the worship of Dionysus was 'dangerous and arousing' and involved complete surrender to the experience. It is therefore significant that the participants of this festival should have evolved into the audiences of the first great Greek plays.

The nature of this Dionysian experience is important when we consider the potential impact of a play on an audience. There is a sense of surrendering to the forces of a piece of theatre — the members of an audience allow themselves to believe in and to feel the elements of another world. From the beginnings of 'ecstasis', the audience member is not just a bystander or acquiescent repeater of religious chant but a participant in a process of emotional and sensory intensity.

Around 530 BC, the Dionysian festival developed into a competition of dramatic performances, music, singing and dancing. The first winner was reputedly a man called Thespis (from whom we derive the term 'thespian', meaning actor). Although Thespis himself may just be a legend, the role of the actor had begun to emerge.

Dionysus with a group of actors holding masks

The emergence of playwrights

By the middle of the fifth century BC, the Dionysian competition had transformed itself into a showcase of playwrights' work. Of all the entrants, the playwright Aeschylus was the most successful. His *Oresteia* trilogy of tragedies has survived as the most famous of his works. They tell the story of the aftermath of the Trojan War, the murder of the Greek king (Agamemnon) by his wife and her lover and the ensuing revenge of his son and daughter.

The other three great playwrights of this era were Sophocles (see page 23), Euripides and Aristophanes, the famous writer of comedies.

Euripides (*c.* 480–406 BC)

Euripides was born in approximately 480 BC, and was the last of the three great tragedians. He first competed in the Dionysia, the famous Athenian dramatic festival, in 455 BC, the year after the death of Aeschylus. However, he did not claim his first victory until 441 BC, and in his lifetime won only four victories at the Dionysia. Some scholars attribute this lack of success to the anti-war stance and consequent criticism of the state reflected in his work. This can be seen particularly in *Hecuba*, *Andromache* and, above all, *The Trojan Women*. His anti-establishment reputation often made him the target of satire by writers of comedy, particularly Aristophanes.

Euripides wrote some 90 plays, and by chance there are more than twice as many of them extant than plays by either Aeschylus or Sophocles. He is often referred to as a 'realist': in his *Poetics*, Aristotle quotes Sophocles as saying that he (Sophocles) presented men 'as they ought to be', while Euripides presented them 'as they are'.

Surviving tragedies

- *Alcestis* (438 BC)
- *Medea* (431 BC)
- *Heracleidae* (*c.* 430 BC)
- *Hippolytus* (428 BC)
- *Andromache* (*c.* 425 BC)
- *Hecuba* (*c.* 424 BC)
- *The Suppliants* (*c.* 423 BC)
- *Electra* (*c.* 420 BC)
- *Heracles* (*c.* 416 BC)
- *The Trojan Women* (415 BC)
- *Iphigenia in Tauris* (*c.* 414 BC)
- *Ion* (*c.* 414 BC)
- *Helen* (412 BC)
- *Phoenician Women* (*c.* 410 BC)
- *Orestes* (408 BC)
- *Iphigenia at Aulis* (410 BC)

A statue of Euripides holding the mask of tragedy

TopFoto

As the era of the great playwrights developed throughout the fifth century BC, the role of the dramatic performer became more prominent and the competitions of the Dionysia were extended to actors too.

Audience experience and expectations

The Dionysia was the largest Athenian gathering of the year, and its audience has been variously estimated at between 10,000 and 20,000. It is likely that slaves and women in Athens were ineligible to attend, but we know that visiting foreigners and dignitaries were made welcome to what was, essentially, an Athenian cultural showcase.

When considering the impact of a play of this era for a modern audience, it is helpful to know the preoccupations and concerns of the society in which the play was created. Although we are discussing an era from thousands of years ago, there are nonetheless parallels to be drawn between the socially salient issues of then and now. For instance, the role of religion in society, how it affects our behaviour and its relationship with the law are issues with contemporary relevance. The significance of the nature of leadership — particularly in a time of conflict — is also apposite in modern society.

The presentation of themes and situations

Greek tragedies, as we have seen in the example of *Oedipus Rex* (see pages 22–23), explored themes and situations that would have provoked anxiety and distress in the Athenian citizen. They regularly included:

Aristophanes (c. 450–386 BC)

Aristophanes' plays are the only surviving complete examples of Old Attic Comedy, although extensive fragments of the work of his rough contemporaries Cratinus and Eupolis are still extant. He is famous for writing comedies for the two Athenian dramatic festivals: the City Dionysia and the Lenaia. He wrote 40 plays, only 11 of which survive complete. While his earlier plays are bawdy and outrageous, his later plays (including *The Frogs*) have been described as 'Middle Comedies'. These plays are less plot-driven, more politically focused and have a lesser reliance on the chorus.

Aristophanes' *Lysistrata*, *The Birds* and *The Frogs* are still often performed. A new version of *Lysistrata* called *Lisa's Sex Strike*, produced by Northern Broadsides, toured parts of the UK in 2007.

Surviving plays
- *The Acharnians* (425 BC)
- *The Knights* (424 BC)
- *The Clouds* (original 423 BC, uncompleted revised version from 419–416 BC survives)
- *The Wasps* (422 BC)
- *Peace* (first version 421 BC)
- *The Birds* (414 BC)
- *Lysistrata* (411 BC)
- *Thesmophoriazusae* ('*The Women Celebrating the Thesmophoria*', first version *c.* 411 BC)
- *The Frogs* (405 BC)
- *Ecclesiazusae* ('*The Assemblywomen*', *c.* 392 BC)
- *Plutus* ('*Wealth*', second version 388 BC)

- unspeakable acts of cruelty, for example the killing of the infant Astyaniax by the Greeks in *The Trojan Women* (Euripides, 415 BC) for no other reason than that he might constitute some kind of figurehead
- acts of tyranny, for example Creon's imprisonment of Antigone in *Antigone* (Sophocles *c.* 442 BC) because she wants to bury her brother
- acts of vanity, for example Oedipus's belief in *Oedipus Rex* that he alone can solve the curse of Thebes, even though he is the cause of it

The most successful Greek tragedies explore the extreme depths of human suffering, and you may well wonder whether the Athenian audiences simply enjoyed being made miserable. There is, of course, more to it than that. It has been suggested that the audience was supposed to experience the catharsis of fear and pity, which was thought to be both instructive and healthy. This emotional purification is identified by Aristotle in the *Poetics* as an important dramatic ingredient. The plays may also serve a didactic function, showing the consequences of wrongful behaviour such as arrogance and excessive pride.

In the fifth century BC, Greece was a place of learning and almost frantic development. The pace of political and social change was extreme, with the old tribes and kings of ancient Greece giving way to a new form of democracy. Harwood (1984) quotes the Athenian statesman, Pericles thus:

> Our constitution is called a democracy because power is in the hands not of a minority but of the whole people. When it is a question of settling private disputes, everyone is equal before the law; when it is a question of putting one person before another in positions of public responsibility, what counts is not membership of a particular class, but the actual ability a man possesses.

Possessing as they did a relatively advanced view of the way an individual can and should learn and take responsibility for the events in society, Greek citizens therefore made an intelligent, questioning and sensitive audience, although we should not draw too many comparisons with modern-day Western society. The Mediterranean in the fifth century was a slave-owning, polytheistic and andro-centric culture, which largely ignored women apart from their roles as mothers and home makers.

As this emerging society questioned itself, drama was used to stage these questions, although answers were not always found or indeed sought. The great plays of this era explore:

- the human condition
- the consequences for ordinary citizens of the actions of their rulers
- the ways in which humanity responds to the edicts of the gods

In most ancient plays, there is a conflict or potential conflict between religious belief and human behaviour. Both Oedipus and Creon ignore the spiritual advice of Tiresias and suffer the consequences in Sophocles's Theban Plays. Orestes and Electra murder their mother and stepfather in revenge for the fate of their father, Agamemnon. They believe they have righted a terrible wrong, but they have done so without the permission of the gods. Orestes is therefore banished and is tormented by female spirits known as the Eumenides — or 'the Furies' — who manifest themselves as a swarm of insects invisible to all but him and who constantly blight his physical life and play tricks on his mind.

The Theban Plays

Written by the Greek dramatist Sophocles in the fifth century BC, the three Theban Plays follow the tragic downfall of the mythical King Oedipus of Thebes and his descendants. As a young man, Oedipus heard a rumour that he was adopted and asked the Delphic Oracle about his true parentage. The Oracle instead advised that he was destined to 'Mate with your own mother, and shed with your own hands the blood of your own sire'. Not understanding this cryptic response, and distressed at the thought of killing his own father, he travelled to Thebes. During his journey, he met a man at a crossroads and they argued about which wagon had the right of way. Oedipus's pride led him to kill the man, ignorant of the fact that he was actually King Laius, his biological father, therefore fulfilling part of the Oracle's prophecy. Oedipus then went on to free the kingdom of Thebes from the Sphinx's curse by solving a riddle, the reward for which was kingship and the hand of the queen, Jocasta. She was his biological mother, although both parties were ignorant of this.

The first play in the trilogy, *Oedipus Rex*, begins years after Oedipus is given the throne of Thebes. The citizens of Thebes ask Oedipus for salvation from a terrible plague. He declares his intention to find the cause of the affliction, not realising that it has been sent by the gods in response to Laius's murder. However, his quest leads him to the realisation that he has fulfilled the prediction of the Delphic Oracle in killing his father and marrying his mother, and therefore the curse can only be lifted with his banishment. The play ends with Oedipus entrusting his children to Creon, his mother's brother, and declaring his intent to live in exile. In *Oedipus at Colonus*, Oedipus reaches the end of his life but accepts that he is only partly responsible for his crimes as he committed them in ignorance. His daughters Antigone and Ismene return to Thebes. In *Antigone*, the eponymous heroine is arrested and condemned for conferring on her dead brother Polynices the honour of a burial, in contravention of King Creon's decree. Antigone's cousin and fiancé, Haemon (who is also Creon's son), supports her actions. Creon emasculates his son for being influenced by a woman, and decides to let Antigone starve to death in a sealed cave. Faced with a terrible prophecy from the blind seer Tiresias, Creon comes to the conclusion that Polynices must be buried and Antigone must not be killed. Haemon goes to rescue Antigone, but she has already committed suicide, and Creon finds Haemon leaning over her body. Haemon threatens Creon, before stabbing himself and taking his own life. Creon's wife, Eurydice, also kills herself in grief over the death of her son. It is only after these tramautic events that Creon is able to confront his appalling lack of judgement. The tragic curse visited on the city of Thebes thus runs its course.

Many ancient Greek tragedies question the values of society and the role of religion — they are not dramatic constructs that automatically support the status quo. *The Trojan Women*, for instance, is an anti-war play and would have been recognisable to its audience as more of a statement about the recent behaviour of the Greek armies than a simple historical tale about events of long ago.

The notion of 'fate'

It is perhaps difficult for a modern audience to grasp one of the most important features of ancient drama to a contemporary Greek audience: the notion of 'fate'. The tragic hero in Greek plays often appears locked into an inescapable destiny. Oedipus's fate is pre-ordained in the lamentable predictions of both Tiresias and the Delphic Oracle, and the more he tries to escape from it the more assuredly he races towards it. In a modern secular society like that in the West — where religion is not the dominant force — most people believe, at least to a degree, in the notion of free will. Consequently, the concept of the power of fate might find few sympathisers in a modern audience. However, Oliver Taplin argues in the *Oxford Illustrated History of Theatre* (ed. J. R. Brown) that:

> It is not true, however, that Greek tragedy is dominated by 'Fate' or that the characters are merely helpless victims of 'Destiny'. On the contrary, many of the plays tangle with issues of free will and responsibility and of human attempts to make the best of life despite ignorance.

On close examination, there is clearly some truth in Taplin's theory. In one of Euripides' last plays, *Iphigenia at Aulis* (written in 410 BC), Agamemnon is waiting with the Greek navy at Aulis, ready to advance to Troy in order to rescue his brother's wife Helen from Trojan prince Paris. However, they are unable to set sail due to a strange lack of wind. The seer Calchas reveals that the cause of the meteorological phenomenon is the goddess Artemis, because Agamemnon has offended her. Calchas informs the general that in order to placate the goddess, he must sacrifice his eldest daughter, Iphigenia. Agamemnon must choose between his daughter's life and his brother's honour. Ultimately, despite the agonies of such a decision, he tricks his wife into bringing his daughter to Aulis on the pretext of marrying her to Greek warrior Achilles. As Iphigenia approaches the altar she is grabbed by soldiers and her throat is cut.

By this action, Agamemnon sets in motion the wheels of his own downfall. Clytemnestra, his wife and Iphigenia's mother, plots her revenge and slays Agamemnon on his return from Troy. This in turn leads to the further revenge of Agamemnon's surviving children Orestes and Electra, who murder their mother. It would be naïve to suggest that these actions — while observed, judged and influenced by the higher authority of the gods — do not involve free will and individual responsibility.

At the opening of Euripides' *Trojan Women*, the gods Poseidon and Athena discuss the fate of Troy and its inhabitants. Although they supported opposing sides during the war (Poseidon, the Trojans, Athena, the Greeks), both are outraged at the behaviour of the Greeks in raping Cassandra in the temple of Dionysus. They therefore agree to visit a storm on the Greek fleet as it sails home, and the ensuing events of the play are placed in this dramatically ironic context. The audience is aware that many of the Greeks — who appear complacent and triumphal in their victory — will not survive the journey back to their homeland. However, we should not feel that human intervention is irrelevant to the fates of some of these characters. For example, Helen's fate is to be decided by her husband, Menelaus. Hecuba implores him to execute her before she has a chance to return to Greece. However, Menelaus weakens and allows her to travel back to Greece with him so that she can be executed by her countrymen in revenge for the loss of life she has caused. On the return journey, however, Menelaus allows Helen to work her charms on him and she is spared the execution. So, although fate is an important feature in Greek drama it would be a mistake, as Taplin suggests, to assume that its characters are purely at the mercy of the gods.

Gender politics

Although the audience and the actors of this era would have been exclusively men, many of the plays were preoccupied with gender politics. Medea's terrible revenge for her husband's infidelity and Helen's openly flagrant rejection of her marital duties in order to pursue a more exciting and fulfilling life in Troy with her lover, Paris, would have challenged the social sensibilities of the Athenian audience. Women characters often took the leading or the title role in Greek tragedy (and in Greek comedy, e.g. *Lysistrata* written by Aristophanes in 411 BC) and, although involving the upper echelons of Greek society and the conflict

Lysistrata

Classical Greek comedies were frequently bawdy, dependent on overt physical humour, wordplay and sexually explicit language. *Lysistrata*, written by Aristophanes in 411 BC, is one of the most sexually focused comedies of its time, due to its subject matter. In simple terms, the plot depicts Athenian women who decide to orchestrate a sex strike and barricade the Acropolis, in order to force their husbands to vote for peace with Sparta and end the Peloponnesian War. To make this action more effective, Lysistrata enlists the support of women in Sparta, Boetia and Corinth. At first, the women are aghast at Lysistrata's suggestion of sexual abstinence. Finally, however, they swear an oath of allegiance by drinking wine from a shield. This was comical to its contemporary audience, because Greek men believed women had no self-restraint, shown by their fondness for wine as well as for sex.

There is also a comic reversal of societal norms. At a time when women did not have the vote and men had ample opportunities to whet their sexual appetites elsewhere, the success of Lysistrata's actions is pure fantasy. The comedy manipulated gender roles to appeal to contemporary humour: besides women acting like men (having political influence), there were men acting like women in that all the actors were male. It is likely that Aristophanes' contemporaries would not have seen the idea of women having power over men as a real possibility, but as a comic idea.

between gods and rulers, plots often concern domestic issues of familial strife: infidelity, rebellious children and generational misunderstandings.

A performance of Aristophanes' *Lysistrata* at Battersea Arts Centre in 1999

Performance conventions

Many Greek plays were written to be performed in trilogies, with only short intervals, so contemporary audiences would have been engaged in an intense 6-hour experience with few scene changes and little of what we might understand as comic relief. The audience was required to concentrate on an unchanging theatrical landscape, dominated by lengthy speeches and complex explanations of plot. Mostly, these plays deal with the aftermath of events, and much of the action takes place offstage, to be reported onstage. For example, the *Oresteian* trilogy starts at the end of the Trojan War and the Theban Plays start long after Oedipus has killed his father and married his mother.

Staging a modern production

The *in medias res* approach, together with lengthy monologues, high poetry, paucity of onstage action and continuous presence of the chorus, runs counter to the dictates of modern entertainment, making Greek drama demanding for modern audiences to watch. If a director is considering presenting one of these plays, he or she will need to transplant and refigure the drama into a modern theatrical experience. One approach would be to break up the structure of the long speeches and use a more physically-based method of staging. At the end of *Oedipus Rex*, the attendant bursts out of the palace and reports the suicide of Jocasta and the self-blinding of Oedipus. Such a moment may require physical action and accompaniment to make a lasting impression on the audience.

There are many examples of modern production of Greek tragedies. Two in recent years were Nottingham Playhouse's adaptation of *Antigone* entitled *The Burial at Thebes* (Seamus Heaney, 2005) and Liz Lochhead's version of *The Thebans*, presented at Edinburgh Fringe in 2003. Interestingly, both these productions used simple technology and little in the way of modernised costume to suggest any conscious updating. In finding the appropriate mode of performance, attempts were made to create a physically-led ensemble piece and to present precise choral speaking. There was no attempt to force either play into some form of modern metaphor. Directors creating modern revivals of old plays, particularly Greek tragedies, would do well to follow such an example.

In attempting to make a play accessible to a modern audience, many directors may choose to use modern dress, give the actors contemporary weapons or use a set reminiscent of a present-day modern suburb. In fact, the demands made on a director of a modern production of a Greek play are far more subtle. To make the drama accessible, it is more important to identify theatrical devices and performance disciplines to engage the imaginations of present-day theatregoers. The same principle is true for the revival of any play, regardless of the era from which it comes.

Physical environment

Having identified some of the major themes of Greek tragedy, we need to consider the likely experience for audiences and performers in the physical environment of the ancient theatre. The size of the surviving theatres (particularly at Epidaurus, one of the oldest surviving theatre sites in Greece) gives us some idea of the scale of the performances.

The Greek amphitheatre was a huge, open-air construction that took advantage of sloping hillsides for semi-circular terraced seating (known as the *theatron*, literally 'seeing place'). The seating was not segregated, as was the style of

Ruins of an amphitheatre in Delphi, Greece

Elizabethan and later Georgian and Victorian theatres, and there was no division of 'circle', 'stalls' or 'upper gallery'. While this arrangement reflected the democratic ideals of the society, this did not mean that all social strands were represented there (unlike the theatre of Shakespeare). As we have noted before, women and slaves — a significant proportion of the population — were probably not included in the ancient idea of democracy.

The *orchestra* and the *skene*

The audience would look down on the circular stage, originally called the *orchestra*. Beyond this was a backdrop or scenic wall called a *skene*, which was effectively the changing area for the actors. The action of the plays would therefore take place on the *orchestra* in front of the *skene*. The death of a character was always heard '*ob skene*' ('behind the *skene*'), as it was deemed inappropriate to show a killing before the audience. The word 'obscene' derives from this.

It would be all too easy to assume that the theatres of ancient Greece were crude or rudimentary. However, it should be recalled that thousands of people could be seated in these auditoria and, without the aid of any artificial amplification system, plays of 6 hours in length would be performed. Mathematics played an important role in the construction of these theatres, in order to create acoustics such that the actors' voices could be heard throughout the immense structures. This was a society that clearly wanted to listen. Nonetheless it should not be assumed that the audiences would tolerate inaudible or substandard performances. Ronald Harwood claims that:

> If authors or actors failed to please at the City Dionysia, the populace expressed rowdy disapproval. The audience had no inhibitions about pelting the performers with picnic leftovers, and dried fruit, pomegranates and tomatoes would rain down on the Thespians, accompanied by loud hissing and booing, hostile hand clapping and the sound of thousands of pairs of heels drumming against the backs of the wooden seats.

Although this account is entirely conjectural, it brings alive for us a society for whom the celebrations of the Dionysia and the playwrighting festival were far too important to tolerate inadequate material or performance.

Greek actors

Greek performers were professionals paid by the state. Theirs was initially a respected profession — partly because of the hallowed status of the religious festival in which they were key participants. As the acting profession moved further away from the influence of religion, however, society's respect for the actor lessened.

To gain attention in the huge theatre space, the actor would wear high-soled shoes or boots (called *cothurni)* to elevate him to a commanding height — often over 7 feet tall. He wore padding and his costume was colour coded; for example, purple denoted royalty and black indicated mourning.

The actor would also wear a mask with exaggerated features — partly because he was expected to play many different roles, but also (it is supposed) because the internal shape of the mask assisted the actor in making himself heard in such a vast auditorium.

The main requirement of the actor in Greek theatre — apart from audibility — was versatility. There were often a large number of characters in plays of considerable length and complexity. However, if you examine the plays of Aeschylus and Sophocles, it is rare that there are ever more than two or three individual performers on stage at any one time. One actor would therefore be required to play many roles, often changing gender. The immediacy of change afforded by a mask allowed the audience's attention to remain focused.

Roman drama

Just as Greece was famous for its tragedies, Rome was famous for its comedies. Terence and Plautus are perhaps the most famous of its comic writers. The Roman playwright Seneca — less successful in his lifetime — wrote tragedies that have remained popular.

Emulating Greek culture was important to Rome, as it sought to establish its identity as a cultural, political and military centre. However, the social role of theatre in Greek culture did not translate to Roman culture: the mass entertainments staged in huge venues such as the Colisseum were conceived more as large-scale crowd pleasers than analytical pieces of drama. The large theatrical arenas in Rome tended to be used for gladiatorial contests, circuses and other spectacles.

Plautus was renowned for his comic satires, lampooning elements of the society in which he lived and subverting expectations, with lowly characters often being the most resourceful, wily and influential. His plays were representative of what was popular in an entertainment-seeking culture. They were later a source of influence on the French farceur Molière.

Terence (195–159 BC)

The Roman playwright Publius Terentius Afer, better known as Terence, was probably a native of Carthage and was brought to Rome as the slave of Terentius Lucanus, a Roman senator. His master ensured he was educated and later freed him, impressed by his abilities. Terence adapted Greek plays from the late phases of Attic comedy.

Although during his lifetime he was less popular than Plautus — the major Roman comic playwright of the previous generation — he is generally regarded as having a more subtle and original style to his craft.

All six plays written by Terence are extant:

- *Adelphoe* ('*The Brothers*')
- *Andria* ('*The Girl from Andros*')
- *Eunuchus*
- *Heauton Timorumenos* ('*The Self-Tormentor*')
- *Hecyra* ('*The Mother-in-Law*')
- *Phormio*

Plautus (251–184 BC)

Although little is known about the life of Titus Maccius Plautus, it is supposed that he was originally an actor or clown, a training that informed his comic writing. Unlike Seneca or Terence, he was extremely popular in his own day. His plays are more farcical than those of Terence, characterised by trickery, mistaken identity and disguises. His play *Menaechmi* was the inspiration for Shakespeare's *Comedy of Errors*.

Plautus's comedies were often based directly on the works of the Greek playwrights, reworking the material to appeal to Roman audiences.

Surviving plays

- *Addictus*
- *Amphitryon*
- *Asinaria*
- *Aulularia*
- *Bacchides*
- *Captivi*
- *Casina*
- *Curculio*
- *Epidicus*
- *Menaechmi*
- *Mercator*
- *Miles Gloriosus*
- *Mostellaria*
- *Persa*
- *Poenulus*
- *Pseudolus*
- *Rudens*
- *Saturio*
- *Stichus*
- *Trinummus*

Seneca (4 BC–AD 65)

As well as being a dramatist, Lucius Annaeus Seneca was also a Stoic philosopher and statesman. For a time, he was tutor to the Emperor Nero. Works attributed to him include 124 letters dealing with moral issues, 12 philosophical essays, 9 tragedies, a satire and a meteorological essay. His works generally reflect his philosophical leanings and contain traditional Stoic themes, such as living in accordance with nature and fulfilling duty to the state in order to enjoy a contented existence, and how human suffering should be accepted and has a beneficial impact on the soul.

It is a matter of debate whether Seneca's plays were ever written to be performed, and there are a number of instances where characters fall into silence but it remains unclear whether they have left the stage. The violence in his work would have been regarded as unstageable at the time, unless a more stylised manner of presentation was assumed. It is thought that the extreme brutality of Seneca's plays served to influence the writers of revenge tragedy in the Elizabethan and Jacobean eras.

Plautus's most famous comedy is *Pseudolus* (191 BC), from which Stephen Sondheim created his brilliant and often performed musical *A Funny Thing Happened on the Way to the Forum* (1962).

In *The Oxford Illustrated History of Theatre* (ed. J. R. Brown, 2001), David Wiles states that Seneca's tragedies should be seen as a reaction against Roman drama rather than representative of it. In his epistles, Seneca seemed to take a particularly dim view of gladiatorial contests and the spectacle that accompanied them:

> Unhappy as I am, how have I deserved that I must look on such a scene as this? Do not, my Lucilius, attend the games, I pray you. Either you will be corrupted by the multitude, or, if you show disgust, be hated by them. So stay away.

The intellectual tragedy developed by Seneca was largely confined to readings and private performances.

Roman actors

Unlike Greek actors, whose profession evolved from participation in a religious festival, Roman actors had no social standing; they were often slaves and rarely rose above such status. However, it was not impossible to achieve fame in the Roman theatre. Roscius (131–62 BC) was perhaps the most renowned Roman actor. While Greek actors showed their prowess in tragedy, Roman actors were most readily associated with comedy. In later comedies — particularly bawdy mimes and pantomimes — women were allowed to act.

Summary of the era

- Greek theatre emerged from an Athenian religious festival dedicated to the god Dionysus and known as the Dionysia. Around 530 BC, the festival developed into a competition of dramatic performances, music, singing and dancing. By the middle of the fifth century BC, it had transformed into a showcase of playwrights' works.
- The three most successful tragedians of this era were Aeschylus, Sophocles and Euripides, while Aristophanes was widely regarded as the most accomplished writer of comedies. Greek tragedy was originally defined by Aristotle, although it developed according to the playwrights' intentions.
- Greek theatre productions were well attended, although women and slaves were usually excluded.
- Plays were often performed in trilogies, demanding the attention of an audience for up to 6 hours. There were up to 20,000 spectators, 2 or 3 main actors and a chorus of around 16 members.

- All the actors were male.
- It has been suggested that Greek audiences were supposed to experience cartharsis — the purgation of fear and pity.
- Greek theatre often explored the relationships between the gods and man. At the centre of tragedies was the tragic hero — an honourable protagonist with a fatal flaw, which eventually would lead to his demise.
- The important social and religious role of Greek theatre did not translate to Roman culture. The most successful type of theatre in Rome was comedy, with Terence and Plautus the most skilful writers. Seneca was a tragedian, but his work is unusual.
- Many Roman actors were slaves. In contrast, Greek actors had high status.

Discussion questions

1 What features of Greek or Roman theatre were evident in a production you have seen recently?

2 Can you think of any plays written in the last 50 years that use Greek or Roman ideas for staging or the presentation of dialogue?

   Hint: refer to earlier chapters, particularly the work of Berkoff.

3 What is the value of staging a play in today's theatre that was written thousands of years ago? Think of specific examples from either Greek or Roman times.

Essay question

Comment on the production values of an Ancient Greek or Roman play that you have recently seen in performance. Identify how those production values contributed to the success of the play now.

Hint

Think about the strongest parts of the production. Why is it that the play can still make an impact on you and/or the audience so many centuries after its first performance?

Chapter 18

British theatre: Elizabethan and Restoration

The term 'Elizabethan theatre' covers the plays written and performed in England during the reign of Queen Elizabeth I (1558–1603). It is distinguished from Jacobean theatre (belonging to the period 1603–25, when King James VI of Scotland reigned as James I of England) and Caroline theatre (associated with King Charles I, 1625 until the closure of the theatres in 1642). All these are sub-classifications of English Renaissance theatre.

English Renaissance theatre derived from a number of medieval theatre traditions, such as mystery plays and morality plays. The Italian *commedia dell'arte* was also significant in the shaping of public theatre.

The 70-year period from Elizabethan times in the 1580s to the end of the Jacobean period with the execution of Charles I in 1649 saw some of the most significant works of English literature ever written.

Elizabethan theatre

The most famous and influential playwright of all time, William Shakespeare, was born in 1564, and his name is inextricably linked with the era of Elizabethan theatre.

Another successful playwright of his generation was Christopher Marlowe, who many contemporaries considered to be Shakespeare's superior. He was highly talented, and his works included *Tamburlaine the Great* (1587), *The Jew of Malta* (1589), *Edward II* (1592) and *Doctor Faustus* (1592 — see Chapter 7). However, Marlowe's career was cut short when he died in a tavern fight in Deptford at the age of 29.

Thomas Kyd was also highly renowned at this time, and it is arguable whether he too would have been held in the same esteem as Shakespeare if he had lived longer — he died at the age of 35. Kyd's *The Spanish Tragedy* was a hugely popular play of its time.

Thomas Kyd (1558–94)

Thomas Kyd probably began his career as a playwright around 1583 and produced his most significant work, *The Spanish Tragedy*, some time between this date and 1589. This play did much to shape the tragedies of the later Elizabethan and Jacobean periods. It is the earliest example in English of the 'revenge play', which was later developed and refined by such dramatists as Shakespeare, George Chapman and John Webster. Inspired by the tragedies of Seneca, it had a violent and exciting plot, which proved popular with audiences. In its day, *The Spanish Tragedy* was even more popular than Shakespeare's plays. It was subject to revivals after Kyd's death, and Samuel Pepys reported seeing the play during the Restoration era in 1668. Much of Kyd's work has been lost; perhaps most intriguingly, he is believed to have written an earlier version of *Hamlet*, which was used as stimulus by Shakespeare.

Kyd was implicated in an accusation of atheism, and although he was released, he died in some disgrace.

Thomas Dekker (1572–1632)

Most of Thomas Dekker's plays were written in collaboration with other writers, including John Day, John Webster, John Ford and Philip Massinger. About 20 of these plays survive, the most famous and highly regarded being *The Shoemaker's Holiday* (1599), a city comedy concerning the daily lives of ordinary London citizens. It tells the story of how a humble shoemaker, by virtue of industry and good luck, rises to become Lord Mayor of London.

In 1603, Dekker began to write prose pamphlets, *The Gull's Hornbook* (1609) being the best known. While these have little merit as literature, they provide an intriguing insight into the more sordid side of London life in the early seventeenth century. During this time, he continued his dramatic work, but most frequently as a collaborator. He wrote nothing in the period 1613–19, and it is suggested he spent these years in prison. Dekker reappeared again on the literary scene in 1620. In his later dramatic works, he collaborated on a number of projects, most notably *The Witch of Edmonton* (1621) with John Ford.

While the works of Shakespeare, Marlowe and Kyd are still performed today, it is unfortunate that the works of other playwrights have not endured. The plays of Thomas Dekker, John Ford and Philip Massinger, for example, are rarely performed in the modern theatre.

John Ford (1586–1632)

John Ford is considered by some to be the last of the great Elizabethan playwrights, although his playwrighting career took place exclusively in the Jacobean period.

From 1621 to 1625, he collaborated with Thomas Dekker, John Webster and Samuel Rowley — all accomplished dramatists. From 1625 until the end of his literary career he worked alone, writing about a dozen plays (some of which are lost). He is best known for his successful play *'Tis Pity She's a Whore*, a tragedy based around the themes of incest, adultery and murder. Perhaps rather harshly, Phyllis Hartnoll refers to Ford's other works as 'effeminate' and contributing to the 'emasculation of the English stage' before the closure of theatres in 1642. However, his humane approach to the themes of *'Tis Pity*, and the dramatic intensity of this piece alone, make him a noteworthy playwright.

Philip Massinger (1583–16...)

Most of Philip Massinger's plays were written in collaboration with John Fletcher, one of the most popular dramatists of the Jacobean period who probably worked with Shakespeare on *Henry VIII*. For a time after Fletcher's death, Massinger was the chief playwright for a company of actors known as The King's Men. His most famous play was *A New Way to Pay Old Debts*, with its central character of Sir Giles Overreach being a favourite role for a number of famous actors over the years, including Edmund Kean and Donald Wolfit.

Theatre construction

During the sixteenth century, London grew enormously as a trading centre, and between 1520 and 1600 the population quadrupled from 50,000 to 200,000. During the latter part of the Tudor dynasty, land rents increased and wages fell in real terms, polarising the rich and the poor. In some respects, the theatre architecture that emerged in the sixteenth century reflected the new urban culture of London.

In 1567, John Brayne built the Red Lion Theatre, one of the first Elizabethan playhouses. An era of new theatrebuilding in London followed over the next 30 years, with the erection of the Theatre in 1576 (again built by Brayne, in collaboration with James Burbage), the Curtain in 1577, the Rose in 1587 (built by Philip Henshawe), the Swan (*c.* 1594) and the Globe in 1599.

Elizabethan theatres were built in a similar style to Graeco-Roman amphitheatres, although on a smaller scale. They often maintained the circular shape, with a central stage and tiered gallery seating. They were remarkably effective arenas for performance, creating an intimate atmosphere while housing between

2,000 and 3,000 audience members. Perhaps the remains of Roman theatres in Britain provided the inspiration for this theatre design, or maybe the theatres were a natural progression from the earlier inn yards, many of which had tiers of galleries on all sides.

Intimate theatre: the Blackfriars Theatre

Blackfriars Theatre was the name given to two separate theatres in the Blackfriars district of London during the Renaissance, built on the site of a dissolved thirteenth-century Dominican monastery. The first theatre (c. 1576) was small, and admission was expensive; these factors limited attendance to a select group of affluent gentry and nobles.

The second Blackfriars was built in 1596 at the behest of James Burbage, manager of theatrical company the Lord Chamberlain's Men (which became known as The King's Men in 1603, when King James ascended the throne and became the company's patron). This playhouse was among the first to rely on scenery and artificial lighting, and it featured music between acts, a practice not common in public theatres at that time.

In 1609, The King's Men began using the theatre as a winter venue, performing at the Globe during the summer.

Inn yard theatres

Before the building of theatres in the late sixteenth century, plays were often performed in the courtyards of inns. The architecture of Elizabethan theatres owed much to these origins, with their balconies and central open space for performance. Some of the inn yards were converted into permanent theatres and existed alongside the larger, more established playhouses. Even high-profile companies used inn yards — the Queen's Men performed at both the Bell Inn and the Bel Savage Inn.

Theatre design

Although the modern Globe Theatre is not an exact replica of its original incarnation, with many of its features based on guesswork, and others governed by fire regulations and the need to accommodate a modern audience, the design can, to an extent, provide us with useful information about the conditions for an Elizabethan or Jacobean audience. If we supplement this with a study of the famous picture of the Swan Theatre, copied from a drawing made by Johann de Witt in 1596, we can start to establish some ideas about how Elizabethan theatres functioned.

The stage

The stage area of an Elizabethan theatre was covered by a canopy and supported by columns. The wall at the back of the stage would have had a number of openings — probably three — with a prominent entrance for royal or high-ranking characters in the middle. The structure at the back of the stage (the equivalent of the *skene* in Greek theatre) was known as the 'tiring house' and was where costumes and props were stored and where actors dressed themselves before a performance. The ceiling of the stage was often referred to as 'the heavens' and sometimes decorated with stars.

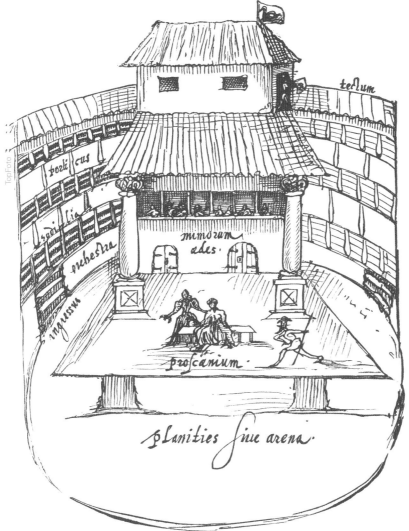

Johannes de Witt's sketch of the interior of the Swan Theatre, 1596

The seating

The stage was surrounded by three tiered galleries of seating, while the area in front of the stage would house the 'groundlings' — poorer audience members who would pay an entrance fee of one penny. Richer patrons would sit in the covered galleries, paying as much as half a crown each for their seats. It is supposed that nobles sat on the stage, nearer to the actors. It seems, therefore, that audience composition was representative of London society.

Although the early theatres had part of the stage covered, they were still reliant on good weather and natural light if the audience was to enjoy the performance to the full. Indoor theatres did exist, however; the boys' company of St Paul's performed in a private theatre — seating only about 200 — within the precincts of St Paul's Cathedral.

Theatre companies

Towards the end of the sixteenth century, two major theatre companies emerged in London: the Lord Chamberlain's Men and the Admiral's Men. The former company was housed initially in the Theatre and later in the Globe, while the Admiral's Men performed in the Rose. Shakespeare joined the Lord Chamberlain's Men as both an actor and a playwright. Often actors in the company also part-owned it — underwriting the costs but sharing in the profits.

As the number of theatres increased, so the competition between them intensified, and the need to find a playwright with the ability to write a successful drama was essential. In *The Oxford Illustrated History of Theatre* (ed. J. R. Brown, 2001), Peter Thomson suggests that the number of players needed to perform in a play during the late sixteenth century rose from around 12 to 16 people. This would indicate that some doubling of roles was commonplace.

Classic Image/Alamy

Edward Alleyn was arguably the greatest actor in Elizabethan England

Elizabethan actors

In the Elizabethan era, a number of leading actors emerged. Edward Alleyn (1566–1626) was arguably the greatest actor in Elizabethan England, rivalled only by Richard Burbage. He dominated the English theatre during the 1590s with his performances of Marlowe's great roles. A number of Marlowe's plays (such as *Doctor Faustus*, *Tamburlaine* and *The Jew of Malta*) have a strong principal character who is central to most of the action and appears in nearly every scene: see the discussion in Chapter 7 on the plot of *Doctor Faustus*.

Although Shakespeare's plays often have a singular leading character, this is not always the case, for example *Twelfth Night*. Furthermore, some plays have a main protagonist and a number of other pivotal characters, such as *Julius Caesar*, in which Caesar, Brutus, Cassius and Antony are all, arguably, leading roles. This feature is connected with the ethos of the theatre company and the ways in which the group of actors would have grown and matured in their work together.

Richard Burbage (1568–1619), who vied with Edward Alleyn for the accolade of greatest actor of his generation, played many of the Shakespearian title roles — particularly the tragic heroes.

Will Kemp was a popular comedian, and many of the comic interludes in Shakespeare's plays (such as Lancelot Gobbo in *The Merchant of Venice* and the Porter in *Macbeth*) were written for him.

Costume

Costume was important for the Elizabethan actor, although it always consisted of contemporary dress, irrespective of the period of history being evoked. However, accessories would be added to the outfit according to a character's racial or national stereotype, for example a breastplate for a Roman soldier.

The Elizabethan era was dominated by class structure, with strict laws dictating which materials and types of clothes could be worn by members of each social stratum — laws that actors were allowed to break onstage. Consequently, the importance of a character would be instantly recognisable to an Elizabethan audience. Since all the audience members were relatively close to the stage, such recognition was achieved without the extra padding, masks or high heels resorted to by the ancient Greek actor.

Sets

Unlike modern theatres, where seating is limited to the front view, Elizabethan playhouses were open to the public eye from all sides, and scenery could not be changed easily as there was no curtain to drop. Setting would therefore have been simple, and basic pieces of scenery, props or furniture would have been the only way to suggest the backdrop of the action to the audience. As a result, the actors often had to convey such information verbally, and there are many examples in plays of this era of speech being used to suggest location. Take the following example from *Macbeth*:

First witch: Where the place?
Second witch: Upon the heath.   (I.1.6–7)

Elizabethan audience

The popularity of the theatre in the Elizabethan era should not be underestimated. As a pastime, it would have been comparable to attending a football match nowadays. Ronald Harwood asserts that in a population of around 160,000 (in 1590), about 20,000 people would visit the theatre every week, and that 'since it was not the same twenty thousand every week, much more than one in eight must have been regular theatregoers'. It is little wonder that with a rapidly rising population and such an appetite for theatre, an abundance of great works emerged at this time.

Contemporary audiences were generally less educated than in Greek (though perhaps not Roman) times. It was left to the skill of the playwright, as well as to the actors, to ensure that all sections of the audience were entertained. Shakespeare knew his audience well, and his plays appealed on a number of levels. Although he did not often pander to his audience so directly, much of the

Porter's speech in *Macbeth* II.3.1–30, for instance, is dedicated to a series of 'in jokes' and name drops connected with the gunpowder plot.

Shakespeare's work offers many insights into his audience's preoccupations. The opening of both *Hamlet* and *Macbeth* would have been terrifying for a contemporary audience, featuring supernatural figures in an era when spirits and witches were believed in almost universally; both had to be guarded against. Witchcraft was a capital offence, and James I had written a book about it. A play that opened with a scene featuring witches would therefore have appealed both to the fears of the general population and the particular preoccupations of its monarch.

The same may be said of *Hamlet* (with its ghost of a murdered king), or *King Lear* (with its upsetting of the natural order of king and subject and its subsequent violence), or indeed the history plays, whose issues and implications, as much as their action, were of active concern to their Elizabethan and Jacobean audiences.

Although Greek audiences may have been generally more intellectually able, Elizabethan audiences were nonetheless willing to sit through long plays requiring good listening skills. A 5-act structure pravailed, which made plays 3 to 4 hours in length (longer than the single Greek plays, but not as long as the trilogies).

Being scholars of Greek literature and theory, as were all educated men of the time, many Elizabethan playwrights used principles of writing similar to the Greeks. The unities of time, action and place identified by Aristotle (see Chapter 4) are adhered to in some plays such as *The Tempest* but radically subverted in others like *The Winter's Tale*. In the latter, the personified character of 'Time' enters to advise the audience that the plot is moving forwards in time by 16 years and the location is moving to Bohemia.

Performing rights

Playwrights (or the publishers and agents of a play who represent a playwright) generally reserve the right to receive royalties (usually a sum of money) any time their play is performed in public. The performing rights laws last until 70 years after a playwright's death. Thus it is that while Brecht died more than 50 years ago, his work is still 'under licence' and permission must be sought and fees must be paid before it can be performed to an audience.

 *Modern audience*

Sixteenth- and seventeenth-century texts often constitute a significant part of the repertoire of modern theatre companies. From a pragmatic point of view, an artistic director knows that there will be a certain audience clientele for a production of *King Lear*, *Hamlet* or *Romeo and Juliet*. There is, furthermore, the attraction of not having to pay performing rights, although the number of cast members required may be off-putting in terms of the expense or size of venue. However, the structure of Shakespeare's plays, and those of his contemporaries, allow for a considerable amount of doubling of roles, and a relatively small company is therefore able to execute a successful performance.

The issue of context

Productions of plays from the Elizabethan era have been placed successfully into other historical contexts. A production of *The Taming of the Shrew* presented by the RSC in 1978 starred Jonathan Price as Christopher Sly. In his first scene, a seemingly drunken Price arrived on stage and started to tear apart the set: colonnades and scenery were sent flying as anxious stage managers, wearing headphones, appeared on stage attempting to apprehend him. Of course, the members of the audience were completely fooled (those who had not read the reviews), and some attempted to stop him themselves. What followed was one of the most celebrated modern-dress productions of a Shakespearean play, with Price re-entering as Petruchio on a motorbike.

Some may argue that devices such as these cheapen the impact of the play, but there is no doubt that they engage the audience. There are other examples of famous productions set in updated or unorthodox settings, which underpin a director's desire to challenge or provoke an audience in a particular way. The West Yorkshire Playhouse's 2007 production of John Webster's *The Duchess of Malfi*, featuring Imogen Stubbs in the title role, portrayed 1950s postwar Italy: a state of corruption, hypocrisy, sleaze and cronyism. Such themes are apparent in the text and were presumably clear to Jacobean audiences, but setting them in a recognisable twentieth-century context, using contemporary fashions and iconography, gives them particular resonance for a modern audience.

The issue of relevance

How can a modern, largely secular audience be stirred by the sight of Hamlet's father's ghost or the appearance of witches, or feel strongly over the folly of dividing up a kingdom? Do we hang on to the work of Shakespeare and his contemporaries just because academics insist we should? Even setting the plays in modern contexts might seem a waste of time. Can we honestly say that Bogdanov's depiction of fascist, anti-Semitic 1930s Italy in *The Merchant of Venice* is as powerful a piece of theatre as Arthur Miller's *Playing for Time*, telling the story of the women's orchestra in the death camp of Auschwitz? Surely, if we need to find contemporary or updated settings for old plays to make them appeal to a modern audience, wouldn't it be better simply to create new plays?

One problem with this argument is the implication that the only thing dramatically effective about a play is its relevance to an audience, and that there is a vital requirement to make old stories pertinent to a new audience. The word 'relevant' carries many assumptions. What is relevant for some members of the audience may not be for others, and since when was 'relevance' the only valid dramatic attribute? We do not need to feel that the voice of Pavarotti or the ballet of Fonteyn and Nureyev is relevant to our lives in order to find them entertaining or significant performances.

An audience can be moved, thrilled and uplifted by works that may mean nothing to them in terms of personal identification but that still communicate with them, in perhaps new and surprising ways, on a deeply emotional or intellectual level.

The issue of language

Many people view the language of Shakespeare and his contemporaries as an obstacle to understanding and, therefore, appreciating their works. What should be acknowledged, of course, is that if you change the language of Shakespeare it ceases to be Shakespeare — it becomes, well, *West Side Story* for example. It becomes an *adaptation* of Shakespeare. While *West Side Story* (Bernstein and Sondheim, 1957) is a work of great merit, its creation does not eliminate the need for productions of *Romeo and Juliet* or make such productions any less important. Shakespeare's use of language provides an actor with the opportunity to perform in verse, which conveys meaning through structure as well as content. While aspects of Shakespeare's language may seem unfamiliar or confusing, the structure of the verse, if understood and faithfully executed by the actor, can enhance and illuminate a dramatic performance.

Aural versus visual

A director in the twenty-first century must recognise that modern society is stimulated as much by the visual as by the aural elements of performance. Modern audiences go to see as well as hear a play; an Elizabethan audience would, in essence, have gone to hear a play. A director must decide whether to try to challenge this and develop the play in such a way as to make the audience listen more carefully to the spoken word or to deliver a production which simultaneously engages visual and aural senses. Certainly, the Elizabethan era of theatre must be valued for its ability to stimulate interest in the enormously expressive power of language.

The development of masque

It would be a mistake to think that Elizabethan theatre was devoid of dramatic spectacle, despite the focus on the spoken word. Shakespeare begins *Henry V* (1599) with the chorus exclaiming in despair:

O, for a muse of fire, that would ascend
The brightest heaven of invention,
A kingdom for a stage, princes to act
And monarchs to behold the swelling scene!   (Prologue 1–4)

Shakespeare, it would seem, longed for more facilities at his disposal to express the reality of the battles of the time. We can see from this play (and others — consider the ostentatiousness of *Doctor Faustus*) that spectacle was an important consideration for a playwright, and still is for any modern interpretation of the plays.

A form of entertainment known as the 'court masque' was gaining in popularity towards the end of Shakespeare's career. Due to its elaborate stage design and flamboyant costumes, it was expensive to produce and therefore to watch, but became enormously popular at the time among those who could afford it. It was made famous, in particular, by Ben Jonson.

Masques were especially presented to the king and his court, usually for a state occasion. Records show that for the investiture of Prince Henry as Prince of Wales in 1609, Jonson wrote a lavish court masque with extravagant sets and costumes designed by Inigo Jones. While sets were a simple affair in the traditional theatre of the Elizabethan and Jacobean playwrights, the sets for court masques were spectacular by the standards of their day. In 1605, *The Masque of Blackness* used adventurous scenic ideas. It opened with a tempestuous seascape, simulated by flowing and billowing clothes. It also used a turntable known as a *machina versitalis* to create a system of revolving flats with scenes painted on both sides, making scene changes virtually instantaneous.

An elaborate costume designed by Inigo Jones for Ben Jonson's *Masque of Blackness*, 1605

Ben Jonson (1572–1637)

Ben Jonson was a fiery-tempered playwright of the same era as Shakespeare, fiercely intelligent and belligerent; he narrowly avoided the gallows when he killed a man in a quarrel. He was a controversial character, whose work often led to trouble with the authorities. His early play *The Land of Dogs* (1597) and later *Eastwood Ho!* (1605) both led to terms of imprisonment for sedition.

Although his plays *Volpone* (*c.* 1605), *The Alchemist* (*c.* 1610) and *Bartholomew Fair* (*c.* 1614) are still popular today, at the time Jonson was most famous for his court masques. In all, he wrote eight of these with designer Inigo Jones. *Oberon The Fairy Prince* (1611) featured the young Prince Henry — the eldest son of James I.

It is perhaps interesting that Shakespeare chose to retire in 1611, at a time when the masque was gaining popularity. In some respects, despite the contribution of the great Ben Jonson, the masque was the antithesis of Shakespeare's theatre, relying on its lavish settings for effect and being an exclusive entertainment for the monarch and his court.

Restoration theatre

Theatres were closed down in 1642 with the onset of the civil war, and many were demolished in the ensuing period. This marks the end of the Jacobean era. Oliver Cromwell's Puritan regime (1649–59) forbade the public performance of plays, and it was only with the restoration of the son of Charles I to the throne of England as King Charles II in 1661 that theatre was once again legalised and given new life. When theatre returned, it was vastly different from what had gone before.

The theatre of the Restoration era (1660 to around 1700) in large measure mirrored the personality of King Charles II (1630–85). While he was an undeniably charismatic ruler, he was also something of a libertine and a womaniser. The theatre he had seen while in exile in France had made him want to intervene personally in the establishment of the new theatrical order but, in order to protect his interests and security as a monarch, he decided that performances could only be permitted under licence. He issued licences to two men, Thomas Killigrew and William Davenant. At Lincoln's Inn Fields Theatre, Davenant's company was known as the Duke's Players, and Killigrew's as the King's Players.

The arrival of the proscenium arch

Charles II wanted to watch plays accompanied by his court. The old theatre structures (those that were left standing) were therefore felt to be unsuitable. Initially, the royal indoor tennis courts were used as an auditorium. To Killigrew, Davenant and Charles II, these rectangular spaces were a familiar shape for the setting of theatrical productions. Tennis courts were ubiquitous in European cities during the time that all three spent on the continent away from the civil strife.

Eventually, both companies were housed in the original versions of two famous theatres in London: Killigrew's in Drury Lane and Davenant's in Covent Garden (originally Bridges Street Theatre Royal). The tennis-court principle prevailed in the structure of the new buildings, with one side of the 'court' being given over to the performance area and the other to the audience.

The proximity of the auditorium to the back of the stalls was never great, even though the new theatres had audience capacities of over 800 people, with stage dimensions of 51 by 30 feet at Bridges Street and 66 by 31 feet at Drury Lane. The stage had a new proscenium-arch arrangement, with doors built into it that gave the actors immediate access to the apron area of the stage. The arena was therefore considerably smaller than that offered by the Elizabethan theatres, and more intimate.

In this era, all areas of the auditorium would be lit by candles in wall brackets and chandeliers. The separation by light of the auditorium and stage area was only brought about in David Garrick's time, 100 years later.

Emerging playwrights

A number of successful playwrights emerged during the Restoration era, among them William Wycherley, Aphra Behn and William Congreve.

William Wycherley (1640–1716)

William Wycherley was one of the earliest writers of Restoration comedy. His plays — particularly *The Country Wife* — were among the bawdiest in an essentially bawdy era. Although David Garrick adapted (and sanitised) the play into *The Country Girl* in 1766, the play was not performed after the Restoration era in its original form until 1924 because of its explicit sexual content. Recently it has been revived at the Haymarket Theatre in London, starring David Haig and Toby Stephens. Wycherley retired from writing plays in 1680 but spent some years in poverty and debtors' prison.

Aphra Behn (1640–89)

Aphra Behn has the distinction of being the first woman who reputedly earned her living from writing, although she was by no means the only woman playwright of the Restoration era. A staunch supporter of the restoration of the monarchy, she worked at the court for several years. After a career as a spy led to the debtor's prison in the mid-1660s, she took up writing. *The Rover* (1677) is her most famous and successful play, although she was a prolific writer of both drama and poetry.

Aphra Behn was the first professional woman playwright

William Congreve (1670–1729)

William Congreve is often regarded as a master of language and one of the greatest exponents of 'comedy of manners'. His two most famous works are *Love for Love* (1695) and *The Way of the World* (1700). The latter has an extremely complex plot and was not as well received as his earlier work, although many now believe it to be his best play, and the characters of Mirabell and Millament to be two of the finest of the Restoration era.

Unfortunately, Congreve's career ended almost as soon as it began. After composing five plays, he retired from writing at the age of 30, as public tastes turned against the highbrow, bawdy theatre in which he specialised.

Tragedy was no longer such a popular genre, although the work of John Dryden (1631–1700) stands out as the most significant of the time.

The importance of wit

William Wycherley's *The Country Wife* (1675) was a highly successful comedy in its day, although it was banned from the mid-eighteenth century to the early 1920s. As an unashamed, sexually explicit comedy, its banning had less to do with the skill and craft of the play than with the growing prurience of the times, as the seventeenth century gave way to the eighteenth.

Wycherley's hero is Horner, an unabashed womaniser who pretends to be a eunuch so that other men leave their wives in his care while they go off philandering. Of course in their absence he seduces the women, cuckolding and making fools of the men. However, Horner, despite his amorality, is the 'hero' of the piece. At the end of the play, he is unrepentant and likely to continue in his habits.

In the Restoration society, wit was a virtue. It was almost as if it did not matter how one behaved, as long as one was comical while doing it. Horner proves this. He is witty and uses frequent asides to confide his motives to the audience.

One of the central strands of the plot is Horner's pursuit and seduction of Margery Pinchwife, the eponymous country wife. The 'virtuous' character, Mr Pinchwife, is portrayed as a bad-tempered, controlling bully. His rural background and parochial humourless attitudes would undoubtedly have been seen as an attack on the Puritan mindset that the court of Charles II had abolished. Consequently, the apparently virtuous character in the play is in fact the figure of ridicule, while the lecher is the hero.

The use of language and setting

The hallmark of Congreve's plays is the complexity of his language — not so much in the unfamiliarity of specific words but in the intricate and potentially tongue-tripping structure. Take the following example from Act III scene 5 of *The Way of the World*:

Lady Wishfort: But are thou sure Sir Rowland will not fail to come? Or will he not fail when he does come? Will he be importunate, Foible, and push? For if he should not be importunate, I shall never break decorums. I shall die with confusion, if I am forced to advance… No, I hope Sir Rowland is better bred than to put a lady to the necessity of breaking her forms…

The language is elaborate and mannered, requiring careful and precise articulation. The rhythms are not regular, in contrast with much of Shakespeare's verse, and are therefore more difficult to express. The movement also requires a specific mannerly execution.

Because Restoration plays are reflective of the behaviours and attitudes of their own society, it is difficult to set them in a different historical context, unlike many of the plays of Shakespeare and his contemporaries. While the Elizabethan playwrights made use of a wide variety of settings in European cities and countries, the Restoration playwrights largely used settings in and around London, Bath and other environments known to the fashionable members of the audience.

The emerging role of women

Restoration theatre offered women an unprecedented public presence and identity, especially in its inclusion of women on the stage for the first time. Women had been involved in the earlier masques, although often it was the members of the audience who were allowed to become participants.

It was an express command from King Charles II himself that led to the appearance of 'actresses'. His experiences in France and his somewhat libertine attitude to sex motivated his desire to see women on stage. Many of the plays of the Restoration era included scenes where women dressed as men (known as 'britches scenes').

Although the advent of 'the actress' was a radical and important development in theatre, it was not necessarily a move towards feminism. The theatre in Restoration times was a place to be seen as well as to see, and the audience members happily (and noisily) continued their courtship during the play. Making the stage a domain for 'actresses' as well as actors, and the fact that Restoration theatre tended to highlight the sexual excesses of society, provided potency to such courtship, as well as an arena of a little more equality.

There were no female characters of the stature of Shakespeare's Cleopatra or nobility of Webster's Duchess of Malfi, but in some instances they were shown as the intellectual superior of their suitors.

Aphra Behn's play *The Rover* (1677) was notable in having two women as central characters. One of them, Helena, questions the traditional passive role of women during courtship, and during the first scene openly mocks her sister (Florinda) for her attitudes to love. Her views on relationships are perceived to be so subversive that, at the outset of the play, her brother is seeking to incarcerate her in a convent. However, Helena's attitudes are vindicated later in the play when she saves her sister from rape.

Modern audience

Plays of the Restoration era are still performed today. However, in many of these there are topical references to places or to people that would have been amusing to a contemporary audience, and the comic value of these references is likely to be lost on a twenty-first-century audience. The concern of the director must therefore be to heighten the entertaining aspects of the drama, rather than being preoccupied with making the play strictly relevant for the modern day.

At any rate, the lively comedy of manners and overt sexual nature of plays such as *The Country Wife* afford them modern topicality, and the constant asides, disguises and deceptions that permeate Restoration drama are still a source of great amusement to audiences today. However, it is essential that the director focuses more on ensuring that his or her actors gain a sense of the demands of the language and movement of a piece, rather than overplaying the humorous elements.

A 2007 revival of
The Country Wife
at the Theatre
Royal, London

Summary of the era

- The period from the latter half of the sixteenth century to the early part of the seventeenth century is considered a golden age for British theatre. The rapid increase in population and the establishment of London as a major trading centre gave rise to the prolific development of theatres, which in turn necessitated the skills of high-quality playwrights and actors. The dramatic output of this era is often referred to as 'Renaissance theatre', of which Elizabethan, Jacobean and Caroline theatre are sub-classifications.

- Theatregoing was a popular pastime during this period. At least 1 in 8 citizens regularly attended performances.

- The two major theatre companies were the Admiral's Men and the Lord Chamberlain's Men (the latter being renamed The King's Men following the accession to the throne of James I). Shakespeare worked for the Lord Chamberlain's Men as an actor and playwright, and the group performed at the Globe Theatre. The Admiral's Men were associated with Christopher Marlowe and performed at the Rose Theatre.

- Members of all social classes attended the theatre, with the 'groundlings' standing in front of the stage and the nobility sometimes sitting on the stage itself for optimum viewing. However, royal command performances took place in palaces.

- Masques were developed as a form of court entertainment, performed indoors and exclusively for royalty and honoured guests. Such performances became particularly popular during the reign of James I. Ben Jonson was renowned as the most prolific writer of masques, although he was also a successful and important playwright of the era. Inigo Jones was the principal stage designer of masques and responsible for innovative set designs such as revolving flats.
- Theatres were closed down in 1642 at the onset of the civil war, with many demolished at the start of the Puritan era in 1649. They were reopened under licence by Charles II, when he was restored to the throne in 1661.
- Restoration comedies were often preoccupied with themes of love and sexual infidelity. In terms of its characters, wit was considered more admirable than moral virtue.
- Theatres were built following the model of Charles II's tennis court: one side of the net was the stage, the other side the auditorium.
- By royal decree, women appeared on stage for the first time in Restoration drama. As well as actresses, the first female playwrights also emerged, most notably Aphra Behn.

Discussion questions

1 Select any play by Shakespeare or one of his contemporaries. As a director, what features of the play would you try to focus on in a production which aimed to bring young people into the audience?
2 Why was the type of bawdy comedy written by Wycherley and Behn so popular during the Restoration?

Essay questions

1 What theatrical devices (either dramatic/acting devices or technical devices) moved theatre forward from the Jacobean/Caroline era into the Restoration era?
2 If you were to stage a production of a Restoration play, what dramatic features used in an original production would still be useful in a modern interpretation?
3 Compare and contrast the challenges for an actor performing in the Elizabethan era with an actor performing in the Restoration era. Choose two roles from two different plays to illustrate your response.

Chapter 19

British theatre: melodrama and music hall

This chapter focuses on specific elements of nineteenth-century British theatre. In studying this era, it is vital to reflect on the innovations in naturalistic theatre that took place later in the century. While the forces of melodrama and music hall may not be regarded as being as significant a movement as naturalism, their popularity should not be underestimated. Indeed, as melodrama developed during the course of the nineteenth century, there was a sense of it evolving into naturalism, rather than simply being swept away by it.

Melodrama

Melodrama originated in the mid-eighteenth century from both France and Germany. The term is a fusion of the Greek words *melos* ('song') and *drame* ('drama'), and it is so-called because of the genre's use of music at climactic moments. The Victorian melodrama featured a limited number of stock characters, engaged in a sensational plot that generally concerned themes of love and murder.

Melodrama dominated nineteenth-century theatre, even up to the advent of plays emanating from the naturalistic movement of the late 1870s, such as those by Strindberg. The year 1828, which saw the birth of future naturalistic playwright Henrik Ibsen, also saw the first performance of a classic melodrama *Fifteen Years of a Drunkard's Life* by Douglas Jerrold (1803–57). Jerrold was a prolific writer of melodramas, comedies and nautical dramas (as a boy he had served as a midshipman in the Royal Navy), and he wrote around 60 plays in all.

Nineteenth-century melodrama tended to feature a limited number of stock characters with clear motives and obvious patterns of behaviour

An enormous number of plays written in the nineteenth century are now largely forgotten or no longer performed. This is perhaps no surprise; melodrama is often perceived as an unsophisticated genre in the twenty-first century. In *The Concise Oxford Companion to the Theatre* (1972), Phyllis Hartnoll describes some of the major elements of melodrama:

> …the noble outlaw, the wronged maiden, the cold-blooded villain, working out their destinies against a background of ruined castles, haunted houses, and spectacular mountain scenery.

Nineteenth-century melodrama tended to feature a limited number of stock characters with clear motives and obvious patterns of behaviour. This enabled an audience to recognise a character almost instantly and establish an appropriate relationship. In *Maria Martin* (*c.* 1840), one of the most famous melodramas of the time, which was based on a true story, the murderer William Corder addresses the audience as he prepares to do the dastardly deed:

> How dreadful the suspense each moment brings! Would it were over. There's not a soul abroad — everything favours my design. This knocking at the heart doth augur fear. 'Tis a faint, foolish fear that must not be. Suspicious self will sleep, ay, sleep for ever. Yet, 'twixt thought and action, how harrowed is the brain with wild conjecture. The burning fever round my temples gives to this livid cheek a pallid hue.
>
> (I.5)

While the language here is elaborate and highly descriptive, it is also utterly guileless. There is a sense of 'this is who I am, this is what I'm going to do and this is what I feel about it'. Ironically, therefore, despite the language being structurally quite complex, there is a simplicity about its explanatory qualities. The audience thus becomes a confidante for this character, albeit presumably an unsympathetic one: the character relates not only his motives but also how he feels about them. Such a relationship almost invites comment, and audiences of the time would not have hesitated to vocalise their feelings and concerns.

Good versus evil

Nineteenth-century melodrama was almost the obverse of Restoration comedy. The Victorian era (1819–1901) was a time of restrained manners and public virtue, personified by the attitude and behaviour of Queen Victoria. The licentious attitudes of the court of King Charles II were long since past. Melodrama, in its evocation of good triumphing against evil, reflects this preoccupation with morality and decorum.

Perhaps the success of melodrama during the nineteenth century also owed something to the constant influx of people from rural areas to the towns and cities: here, unlike in the provinces, the potential audience for theatre was continually expanding. In a world of instability and change brought about by the Industrial Revolution — a theme sometimes reflected in the more serious melodramas — the anticipated stock characters and recognisable polarised virtues of good and evil presented a world of greater certainties than the real one. Furthermore, melodrama could offer something of an escape for the audience.

Melodrama also fed into a rising tide of patriotism. Britain was victorious against the French at Waterloo in 1815 and during the rest of the nineteenth century sought to widen the boundaries of the British empire. Often this expansion — despite the undoubted commercial benefits — was conducted in the name of Christianity. Melodramatic plays such as *Black-eyed Susan* (1829), again by Douglas Jerrold, reflected the values of empire in its story of a heroic sailor fighting for his reputation and his life against the allegation of striking a superior officer.

We should perhaps not be too dismissive of the subject matter of melodrama. In *The Golden Age of Melodrama* (1974), Michael Kilgarriff refers to its 'phoniness' and 'prejudices', which may have some truth but is not universally the case. Some melodramas depicted scenes of appalling deprivation and unacceptable working conditions, such as J. T. Haines's *The Factory Boy* (1840), in which the villain is an exploitative and bullying mill owner. In some respects, such works portended the arrival of the harsher and more interrogative plays of naturalism — plays such as Ibsen's *An Enemy of The People* (1882), which ruthlessly exposed political intrigue and corruption, or Strindberg's *Miss Julie* (1888), which examined the iniquities of class structure and the agonies of presuming to reach beyond it.

The emergence of star actor and actor-manager

While the playwright was the most prominent figure in Elizabethan drama, the most eminent figures of drama in the early and mid-nineteenth century were the actor and actor-manager. Two actors predominated above all others during this period: Edmund Kean (1787–1833) and Henry Irving (1838–1905).

Acting as a star spectacle

After some years as a strolling player, Edmund Kean shot to fame as Shylock in *The Merchant of Venice* in 1814. According to Michael Booth in *The Oxford Illustrated History of Theatre* (ed. J. R. Brown), Kean was a:

> …romantic actor of a romantic age. His physical intensity, his abrupt transitions of mood, his violent (though carefully controlled) expressions of emotion, and his famous point making were drawn as much from melodrama as from current tragic theory and practice.

Kean was an actor of fiery temperament and demeanour. In an atmosphere resembling a prizefighter contest, he would see off competition in particular roles. In 1817 a young American actor, Junius Brutus Booth, 'took on' Kean in a production of *Othello* at Drury Lane, with Booth in the title role and Kean playing Iago — one of his favourite roles. Apparently, the contest was so one-sided that Booth was persuaded to leave the country as well as the stage. Kean died from alcohol-related illness in 1833 in his mid-forties, when he should have been at the height of his ability and fame.

What kind of atmosphere can have led to a Shakespearian play resembling a gladiatorial contest? It would appear that in this era, the actor had taken on 'star' quality, rendering an audience less interested in the content of the playwright's work than in the dramatic fireworks employed by their 'star' in its expression. There is no doubt that members of the Victorian audience — usually representing the lower end of the social spectrum — would respond to this acting competition in a similar fashion to a round of cock fighting or bear baiting, roaring their approval for their chosen star.

Acting as a business

Another figure of great stature dominated the theatrical industry towards the end of the nineteenth century, although he too made his initial impact in the genre of melodrama. Henry Irving, like Kean, shot to fame in a single performance, a production of Leopold Lewis's *The Bells* in 1871. As Mathias, the conscience-stricken mayor who, many years previously, had committed a murder in order to obtain his fortune, Irving was able to terrify, move and thrill his audience.

In *The Bells*, Mathias makes a visit to the local fair where a mesmerist makes him relive the night when, 15 years previously, he murdered a wealthy Jew for his gold. Irving was able to portray a role of considerable complexity; although Mathias has committed a murder, he is not an unsympathetic character. It was a role Irving would play periodically for the rest of his life, although he was perhaps most famous for his Shakespearean performances, especially in the Lyceum Theatre on the Strand.

Irving was also an actor-manager. He took financial responsibility for his productions, employed the other actors and bore the financial loss when a fire at his theatre caused extensive damage.

Up until the end of the nineteenth century, there had not been enough of a potential audience to sustain a long run of a play in the provinces, so the bill would change frequently. It is said that Irving played 428 roles in the first 3 years of his professional career. Clearly, there would have been little or no time for rehearsing these plays before performance. This was indicative of an era where the economic needs of theatres and their managements dictated a punishing schedule.

Though he became the first actor ever to be knighted, Irving died in relative poverty, still working years after he should have retired.

Henry Irving as Mathias in *The Bells*, the Lyceum Theatre, 1871

Theatre design

Nineteenth-century theatre seating was clearly segregated into comfort and price levels. Consequently there were stalls, circles, boxes and galleries arranged at different heights around an elaborate proscenium stage. Each area of the auditorium had its own exits to the outside world and its own refreshments area. In other words, the social separation was strict and reflected the class distinctions of the time.

It is perhaps worthy of note that modern theatres rarely have circles, galleries and boxes. The auditorium in many new theatres (for instance, the West Yorkshire Playhouse, opened in 1990) is similar to the arena found in Greek theatres.

Theatre sets

Nineteenth-century theatre sets were often pictorial in style — elaborate, decorative and designed to convey a sense of almost super-realism. A good example of this is the use of Ford Maddox Brown's paintings for a setting of *King Lear*; these were first created in the 1840s and were still being used by Irving for his production of the play at the Lyceum in 1893. The level of detail is extraordinary, with the emphasis placed on aesthetic richness rather than dramatic feasibility or adaptability between scenes.

Music hall

A new form of popular entertainment called 'music hall' emerged in the second half of the nineteenth century, around the same time that the naturalistic play appeared. The success of music hall led to the creation of a large number of variety theatres in the late nineteenth and early twentieth centuries.

Music hall was enormously popular with the lower strata of society; its immediacy and energy was an important part of the entertainer's relationship with his or her audience. A music hall comedian might perform in several different halls on the same evening, putting on three or four shows in each hall. For each show, a number of performers would entertain a large and rowdy audience, introduced by a chairman armed with a gavel to attempt to keep order. Music hall stars of the time included Dan Leno, Vesta Tilley, Marie Lloyd and George Robey.

Details from a programme for the Oxford Music Hall, London, in 1893; the bill included Marie Lloyd and Dan Leno

The range of acts was vast, including mesmerists, contortionists and dancers, but mainly this was the era of the comic song. Some of the songs — and their singers — became famous, and a song or an act might become synonymous with its performer.

Undoubtedly, this form of raw entertainment was the forerunner to stand-up comedy as we know it. In the early twentieth century, music hall began its evolution into revue and musical comedy.

Shakespeare in the nineteenth century

Given Shakespeare's initial popularity, it is not an unreasonable assumption that Shakespeare must always have been popular with audiences. However, for much of the eighteenth and nineteenth centuries, the full texts of his plays were not often performed.

As was mentioned on page 31, the poet laureate in the late seventeenth century, Nahum Tate, wrote alternative versions of some of Shakespeare's tragedies (for example *King Lear* with a happy ending). David Garrick, an actor and actor-manager from the eighteenth century (1717–79), also wrote a variety of alternative Shakespeare plays and, indeed, a cleaned up (and therefore pointless) version of Wycherley's *The Country Wife*.

Irving, on the other hand, worked hard to rehabilitate the full canon of Shakespeare's plays into popular nineteenth-century culture. That he was prepared to take this risk speaks well of his courage; that he largely succeeded speaks well of his talent. In touring plays to the provinces to the extent that he did, he attempted to ensure that all sections of society and all areas of the country were able to gain access to the literary classics.

Summary

- The most popular genre of theatre in the nineteenth century was melodrama. The term derives from the Greek words *melos* ('song') and *drame* ('drama').
- The language of melodrama was often elaborate, although the sentiment or thought processes expressed were usually simplistic or blatant.
- Melodrama usually involved a simplified moral universe, with good and evil embodied in a limited number of stock characters involved in perilous situations.
- The nineteenth century was particularly notable for its performers. The two most prominent actors of the time were Edmund Kean (1787–1833) and Henry Irving (1838–1905).

- The popularity of the theatre was enhanced by the movement of population from the country into the towns.
- The seating in theatre auditoria was carefully arranged around a proscenium stage, with the audience segregated according to class. Stage settings were detailed and pictorial.
- Some melodramas began to reflect the social conditions of the time, particularly as the naturalistic genre of the late nineteenth century began to emerge.
- The popular entertainment of music hall emerged in the second half of the nineteenth century. It was the forerunner of modern-day stand-up comedy, and was developed into musical comedy and revue on the outbreak of the First World War in 1914.

Discussion questions

1 What were the attractions of melodramatic theatre to a contemporary audience?

2 Choose a melodrama which you think a modern audience might still enjoy. Identify specific techniques you would employ as a director to make the play accessible for its audience.

Essay question

'Melodrama is a redundant force in modern theatre. Audiences today are too sophisticated to respond to such obvious plotlines and stereotyped characters.' Use specific examples of melodramas to explain how far you agree or disagree with this statement.

Chapter 20

Responding to the play

In this chapter we will discuss the crucial questions you need to ask in order to form a coherent and meaningful response to the theatre you watch. The questions are generic and therefore appropriate to any theatrical experience in any theatre.

What are your expectations of the visit?

It is almost inconceivable that you will not have expectations prior to a theatre visit. The state of mind and attitude with which you approach the production you are about to see will affect your response to it. It is therefore important to be honest about your preconceptions. If you are familiar with the play you are about to see, what do you anticipate about the performance? Did you enjoy reading the play in class or was it a disappointment? Perhaps you have seen the play on video or DVD, or a film adaptation. If so, how has this experience informed you? Are you approaching the prospect of seeing the play positively or negatively?

If the piece is by a writer of whom you have heard or whose work you have seen, it is likely you will be influenced by that knowledge. Perhaps it is a new play by a famous theatre company, such as Kneehigh or Shared Experience, and you have seen, or heard about, its previous work. You may have heard about one of the actors in the play.

It is unusual for an audience member to approach a play completely objectively. This is a factor you need to take into consideration when assessing the merits of a production.

What sort of place is the venue?

A theatre building can enhance or diminish the experience of watching a dramatic performance. Some pieces of theatre are created for specific venues. For example, John Godber writes plays exclusively for the Hull Truck Theatre — an intimate, virtually studio-sized space. Alan Ayckbourn, writing for the Stephen Joseph Theatre, knows that a cast has to perform to an audience seated on all four sides of a large auditorium.

Most plays, however, need to be adaptable to a variety of different spaces and audience seating arrangements, especially if they are written for a touring company. An intimate, intense piece of theatre, perhaps featuring a small cast, will inevitably work better in a smaller space. This will enable an audience to see the actors at close quarters, and the actors themselves will not need to project their voices above conversation level to be heard. In contrast, a Shakespearean play may be performed in a much larger venue (the Courtyard Theatre in Stratford-upon-Avon or the National Theatre, for example) in order to accommodate a sizable cast or to stage elaborate scenes. Even in these cases, there are intimate or intense moments to convey (for example, Hamlet's soliloquies or the balcony scene in *Romeo and Juliet*).

You must bear in mind that most theatres were built for entirely different genres of work than those shown today. It is important to be aware of the different types of theatre design and their particular merits.

The large proscenium arch theatres that dominate London's West End were, in most cases, built in the era of melodrama and music hall. Such theatres sometimes have an orchestra pit separating the stage area from the

Richmond Theatre has a proscenium arch and orchestra pit

TopFoto

auditorium. The seating is usually arranged in stalls and a circle, and sometimes an upper circle or gallery. While many of these theatres have undergone radical improvements in line with technological developments, it is something of a luxury when a play finds itself staged in an ideal venue.

More modern theatres often make use of a thrust stage, where the stage space extends into the middle of the auditorium. This is reminiscent of the ancient Greek theatre design: an arena stage rather than a raised stage, with seating rising up around it. You can see an example of this design in the Sheffield Crucible; its stage is the floor area with tiered seating around it. The West Yorkshire Playhouse is of a similar design.

Where are you sitting in the theatre?

Some theatres are so large as to afford entirely different perspectives on the action for different members of the audience, depending on the location of their seats. For example, being seated in the upper circle of a theatre places an audience member a long way away from, and a long way above, the action. At such a distance, it may be difficult to absorb the instensity and emotion of a play. This is not the fault of the actors, directors or designers. Consequently, it is critical to objectify the perspective you have on a play, considering carefully the effects of your seating position.

What information do you have about the production?

It is unlikely that you will go to see a play without having some information about it beforehand. Quite apart from the press releases that herald a major production, the theatre itself will usually provide a good deal of information through publicity material and its website. Much depends on the nature of the production — whether a premiere or a revival — but any professional theatre will want to generate as much interest and curiosity as possible about its current and forthcoming productions.

Programmes and education packs

As students often make up a significant proportion of an audience, a production will usually be accompanied by a detailed programme or a well-researched education pack. This may contain interviews with key members of the production team (for example, the director and designer) and commentary from the actors, as well as academic essays on the play and its themes written by a learned associate of the theatre or a specialist in the playwright or dramatic genre being presented.

It is important to use as much of this information as possible. Watching a play with knowledge of the director's concept or the designer's ruling idea enables you to identify the production team's philosophy in action. You can see a director's or designer's ideas unfold before you and make decisions about how successfully they are communicated, how fully they are realised and how they serve the play.

Reviews

Often, reviews of previous productions can alert you to the potential problems or most challenging moments of a play. For example, if you are going to see a production of *Hamlet*, most reviewers agree that the title role is one of the most challenging any actor can face. However, it is important not to be too influenced or diverted by a review, no matter how cleverly it is written. It is often the case that a production will receive a variety of reviews. It is best to approach your theatre visit with an open mind.

What kind of acting is called for?

Whatever the genre and subject matter of a play, the acting is likely to be the most dominant aspect of any production. That said, it is important to understand the relationship between acting and directing. An actor's interpretation of a role may combine his or her perceptions with the director's vision for how the role fits within the overall philosophy of the production.

In a traditional theatrical production, the quality of the acting probably affects an audience's enjoyment of a piece more than any other factor, especially where the play is a revival of a classic. Poor acting in a musical or in opera is not as problematic, since the quality of singing and choreography may more than compensate.

Recognising the elements of acting

In order to judge an actor's performance effectively, you need to identify the elements of acting being presented. Depending on the genre or history of a play, specific demands are made on actors in terms of physical representation and vocal dexterity. For example, the complexity of language in a Restoration comedy requires adept verbal skills to reflect the intricate semantics and elaborate structures. Such a piece may also require comic timing and physical agility. These would not be so important for a production of Shakespeare's *Othello*, where it is crucial that the actors convey the sense of tragedy in the verse and impress on the audience the eponymous character's inevitable journey into jealousy, rage and madness.

Appraising the effectiveness of acting

In a long and complex play, an actor's performance may have particular high points. If you are watching a production of *Strife* (1909) by John Galsworthy, the actor playing the part of Roberts — the leader of the strike — faces many challenges. In playing a charismatic political leader, he must show Roberts's great powers of oratory when he persuades the workers to stay out on strike, and yet in the same scene he must show an emotional vulnerability when the news is brought to him that his wife has died of starvation and cold as a result of the poverty forced on her by the strike. In such a production, an actor is required to explore an intense emotional depth to the character while simultaneously showing the technical skills of oratory and projection. As the role of Roberts is central, if the performance falls short of what is required, the entire production will falter.

Writing about an actor's performance

Distinguishing between character and actor choices

When making judgements about an actor's performance, you must distinguish between the choices made by the actor in his or her interpretation and the choices made by the character. Thus, the actor playing Romeo does not choose to kiss Juliet, the character of Romeo does, as governed by the script. How that kiss is approached, however, is decided by the actor. If you were writing a review, you should not state:

> Romeo showed his nervousness about his feelings for Juliet in the way he hesitated before kissing her.

This is inaccurate. Instead, you must appraise the actor's performance:

> [Name of actor] showed Romeo's nervousness about his feelings for Juliet in the way he approached the kiss. He created a sense of anticipation by hesitating before kissing her.

Not making the important distinction between the separate entities of actor and character is a common mistake, leading to confused descriptions of actors' performances.

Analysing your response

To describe a performance merely as 'good' or 'convincing' is not sufficient. You must gauge the demands a role makes on an actor and appraise the theatrical choices the actor makes in meeting those demands. Your initial response to a performance might be emotional and spontaneous. The skill required of you is to analyse what it is about the performance that is making you respond in the way you do.

What has the design contributed to the play?

The designer's role is an integral part of the production. In Chapter 15, we discussed how Declan Donnellan works closely from the outset of a production with his designer Nick Ormerod. However, it is more usual for the set to have been designed before rehearsals start.

You must be able to assess the impact of design on a production, and it is possible to make some initial judgements about this even before the play begins. The pre-show education pack or programme may well include an interview with the designer. The more information you can glean before the performance about how the philosophy of the design has been realised, the more you can appreciate the production.

The design will affect how a play's themes are assimilated and understood by an audience. For example, Ian Brown's 2002 production of *Hamlet*, starring Christopher Eccleston, was set in the royal castle at Elsinore, where the walls were huge and the entrances — concealed within the walls — were small, almost like cupboard doors. The costumes were plain and clearly twentieth century (possibly 1930s and reminiscent of Nazi uniforms). The design — clear and dominating from the outset of the play — promoted a sense of foreboding and greyness, a world of darkness and secrets. All this was inherent before a word had been spoken.

It is impossible to reduce a work of such enormity as *Hamlet* to a discussion of a few themes, but in choosing a simple, clear but impressive design idea, certain themes such as the abuse of power, a secretive state, and the monotonous yet intimidating atmosphere of court life were particularly emphasised.

In some productions, the design is the most memorable aspect for some audience members. If you ask people who have been to see *Phantom of the Opera* what the most memorable moment was, many of them will mention the scene when the chandelier seems to come crashing into the audience. Audiences of *Miss Saigon* rarely forget to mention the helicopter, and more recently there has been *Chitty Chitty Bang Bang* and the flying car. These observations are an indication of how far the designer's art can influence the enjoyment of the production.

TopFoto

Sometimes the design of a play is the most memorable aspect, for example the helicopter arriving in *Miss Saigon*

Damien Cruden's production of *Macbeth* at York Theatre Royal in 2005 (which he designed himself), with its actors dressed in colour-coded kimonos and its use of sand on the stage, successfully evoked the ideas and images of Japanese kabuki theatre. The ritual nature of the murders was emphasised, and the mystical properties of the witches (cleverly realised as puppets) appeared to play on the superstitions and psychosis of the central character.

Writing about the design

After a performance, it is important to recall and record the particulars of the design, but these observations should only be made within the context of appreciation and understanding of the whole production; there is no need to list every minute detail. Sometimes a design feature can enhance — or indeed diminish — a moment in the production, so you should always ensure that your observations are analytical as well as descriptive.

If you are reasonably skilled in drawing, you could sketch memorable elements of the set that are important to your analysis. However, you must always ensure that you refer to your sketch in your essay.

Finally, it is always important, but especially so in the area of design, to use appropriate and accurate vocabulary. Examples of design vocabulary include:

- **apron staging** — the stage extends forwards in front of the proscenium arch
- **auditorium** — the area in a theatre where the audience is located in order to hear and watch a performance
- **cyclorama** — a large curtain or wall, often concave, positioned at the back of the stage area
- **'end on' staging** — similar audience layout to a proscenium theatre, but without the arch; the audience is positioned in rows facing the stage
- **off stage** — anywhere the actors cannot be seen by the audience
- **on stage** — anywhere the actors can be seen by the audience
- **promenade staging** — the audience moves and the actors perform among them on a variety of stages
- **proscenium staging** — the audience is positioned in front of the stage, and the stage can be looked upon like a picture frame; the 'frame' itself is called the proscenium arch
- **stage directions** (e.g. 'down stage right', DSR) — directions in the script about how the playwright intends actions or arrangements to be carried out
- **theatre-in-the-round/arena staging** — the audience is seated all around the stage on four sides

- **thrust staging** — the audience is on three sides of the stage, as if the stage has been 'thrust' forward; this can be similar to a catwalk or more like an extended apron stage

- **traverse staging** — the audience members are seated on either side of the stage, facing each other

- **wings** — the unseen backstage area on either side of the stage of a proscenium theatre

What impact has the director had on the play?

A director is responsible for making decisions about artistic concepts, interpretation of text and staging, often working closely with the playwright, actors and creative team. As the primary visionary, he or she is the person most responsible for the overall impact of the production on the audience.

Sometimes — as in the case of Cruden's *Macbeth* — it is clear what the director's vision and input have been. Particular moments of staging or interaction between actors can be unmistakably the work of a specific director.

It is more challenging to discern the impact of a director on a production that has been staged very simply. For example, Kathy Burke's production of Joe Penhall's award-winning play *Blue/Orange* at the Sheffield Crucible in 2004 seemed — and indeed in many ways was — a straightforward production. However, the focus on the development of character and dialogue rather than on technical paraphernalia does not suggest a lack of directorial input. The production of *Blue/Orange* was highly successful and polished. The play is set in an office in the psychiatric wing of a modern hospital and never moves location. It centres around two doctors discussing the fate of a patient, who is also present for much of the action. As they interact with each other and the patient, the dialogue is intense and detailed, with clinical terminology and medical references. The shaping and pace of the dialogue, together with the blocking or movement around the stage, are vital to the play's success. There may be no demand for special effects or even special moments of choreography, but to achieve overall coherence and hold an audience's attention requires strong direction. There is no doubt that Burke's production received that level of attention and was highly acclaimed as a consequence.

When watching a production, try to discern the balance between the actors' achievements and the director's. This is not always obvious, but the pacing of dialogue and the intensity achieved between actors is usually a combination of their work and the director's.

How is lighting used?

Technical developments in theatre lighting have been significant in recent years. While you do not need to be an expert on lighting systems, you should be aware of how lighting impacts on an audience.

Like set design, lighting design can greatly influence the audience's enjoyment of a production. At its most basic, it illuminates the action or creates the effects of night or day or warmth or cold, but it can also serve to emphasise ambiance and emotion. The lighting design in Ian Brown's production of *Hamlet* at the West Yorkshire Playhouse in 2002 worked extremely well with the set. Light was focused on the great walls to reveal the small doorways as the action progressed, keeping most of the set in shadow and near-darkness. This lighting design augmented the sense of secrecy and paranoia that defined elements of the production.

In *The Wonderful World of Dissocia* by Anthony Neilson, staged at York Theatre Royal in 2007, the bright lights of the hospital room in the second half of the play — in contrast to the vibrant colours in the first half — made it almost painful to watch. However, that contrast was crucial in reflecting the state of mind of the central character as she moved from the colourful and lurid world of her fantasies into the harsh clinical world of her recovery. In other words, the lighting effects could not be judged as moments in themselves (apart from the perspective of technical merit); they were intrinsically relative to each other and to the experiences of the central character.

Writing about the lighting

While you should make mention of the relevant technical information, it is more important to make sense of how technical features influence the overall impact of the play on the audience.

When you are writing about lighting, it is essential to use correct terminology for the equipment. Examples of lighting terminology include:

- **floodlight** — a lantern that gives a wide-spreading, unfocused beam of light
- **follow spot** — a type of profile spotlight used to follow a performer around the stage in a beam of light of exactly the right size
- **fresnel** — a spotlight that employs a Fresnel lens (a lens with concentric ridged rings) to wash light over an area of the stage; the lens produces a wide, soft-edged beam of light, which is commonly used for back light and top light

- **gel** — a filter placed over the front of a lantern to change the colour of the light

- **gobo** — a piece of metal or glass, which fits into the gate of a profile spotlight and projects a pattern onto the set

- **par can** — a type of lantern that projects a near parallel beam of light

- **profile** — a type of spotlight that produces a narrow, hard-edged beam of light

- **spot** — a type of lantern whose beam is focused through a lens or series of lenses to make it more controllable

Who is the audience?

When you make assertions about the impact of a play on an audience, you must give some attention to who that audience is.

When John Godber took over the directorship of the Hull Truck Theatre in 1984, he wrote a play which he knew would attract an audience: *Up 'n' Under*. The play is about Rugby League, and Hull, at the time, had two world-class Rugby League teams. The play proved to be enormously popular, receiving in its audiences people who had seldom, if ever, been to the theatre before. Godber has long been credited with creating the kind of material that encourages otherwise reluctant members of the public to come to the theatre.

Similarly, in 2003 the playwright Mick Martin wrote a play called *Once Upon A Time in Wigan* — about the history of the northern soul scene at the Wigan Casino. Again, people came to see the play not because they were traditional theatre lovers but because they themselves had been involved in the all-night events at the Wigan Casino and other northern venues and therefore were interested in its subject.

Every production has a target audience. In arriving at repertoire for the season, an artistic director has to argue the value of each production and its relevance to a stipulated target audience. It could be that the target audience is you: students. It could be people from older age groups or interest groups, or it could be less definite than that. It is, however, an important consideration, because the impact of a piece of theatre on a group of school students will invariably be different to its impact on a group of pensioners. While it is unlikely that the audience will be exclusively one group or the other (unless of course it is a performance in a group-specific venue, such as a school) it may well be dominated by one group.

Summary

Responding to a piece of theatre requires:

- recognition of previous theatregoing experiences, or experiences as a drama and theatre student, that may be relevant to the event
- accessing as much information about the production as possible from a variety of sources
- acknowledgement that the theatre environment will affect the experience of a production
- awareness of the director's intentions in staging the play and identification of the target audience
- analysis of technical contributions to the production

Discussion question

Assess the productions you have seen recently. What were the distinguishing features which made them memorable? You should take into account all areas of the production.

Essay question

Choose a play written in a different era that you have seen recently. (a) Explain how the impact of the director and/or designer enhanced your appreciation of the play. (b) Identify the principal themes of the play and how this interpretation helped express them to you.

Bibliography and references

Artaud, A. (trans. Corti, V.) (1993) *The Theatre and Its Double*, Calder.

Benedetti, J. (1982) *Stanislavski: An Introduction*, Methuen.

Benedetti, J. (1988) *Stanislavski: A Biography*, Methuen.

Berkoff, S. (1981) *Two Theatre Adaptations from Franz Kafka*, Amber Lane Press.

Brecht, B. (1949). 'A Short Organum for the Theatre' in J. Willett (trans.)
    Brecht on Theatre: The Development of an Aesthetic, Methuen, 1964.

Brown, J. R. (ed.) (2001) *The Oxford Illustrated History of Theatre*, OUP.

Donnellan, D. (2002) *The Actor and the Target*, Nick Hern Books.

Hartnoll, P. (ed.) (1972) *The Concise Oxford Companion to the Theatre*, OUP.

Harwood, R. (1984) *All The World's a Stage*, Martin Secker and Warburg Ltd.

Kilgarriff, M. (ed.) (1974) *The Golden Age of Melodrama*, Wolfe Publishing.

Knapp, B. L. (1969) *Antonin Artaud: Man of Vision*, Swallow Press.

Miller A. (ed. Clurman, H.) (1971) *The Portable Arthur Miller*, Viking Press.

Miller, A. (1984) *'Salesman' in Beijing*, Methuen.

Miller, A. (1987) *Timebends: A Life*, Methuen.

Oddey, A. (1994) *Devising Theatre: a Practical and Theoretical Handbook*,
    Routledge.

Stanislavski, C. (ed. and trans. Hapgood, E.) (1963) *An Actor's Handbook*,
    Theatre Arts Books.

Stanislavski, C. (1980) *An Actor Prepares*, Methuen.

Stanislavski, C. (trans. Hapgood, E.) (1980) *My Life in Art*, Methuen.

Unwin, S. (2004) *So You Want to be a Theatre Director?* Nick Hern Books.

Walton, J. M. (1980) *Greek Theatre Practice*, Methuen.

Willett, J. (1977) *The Theatre of Bertolt Brecht*, Methuen.

Index

Bold page numbers indicate definitions of key terms